STRATEGY RULES

STRATEGY RULES

FIVE TIMELESS LESSONS FROM
BILL GATES, ANDY GROVE,
AND STEVE JOBS

DAVID B. YOFFIE and
MICHAEL A. CUSUMANO

HARPER
BUSINESS

An Imprint of HarperCollins*Publishers*

HarperCollins books may be purchased for educational, business, or sales promotional use. For information, please e-mail the Special Markets Department at SPsales@harpercollins.com.

FIRST EDITION

Designed by William Ruoto

Photograph on page xvi © Sonia Moskowitz/Globe Photos

Library of Congress Cataloging-in-Publication Data has been applied for.

ISBN: 978-0-06-237395-3

15 16 17 18 19   OV/RRD   10 9 8 7 6 5 4 3 2 1

David would like to dedicate this book to Andy Grove—mentor, critic, friend, and leader who inspired me to never give up and always try harder.

Michael would like to dedicate this book to both Xiaohua and Pico, who keep me focused on the future.

CONTENTS

PREFACE

We have been teaching strategy at Harvard and the Massachusetts Institute of Technology for almost thirty years. Over the past three decades, the field of strategy has made enormous progress in delivering rigorous, analytical frameworks, usually rooted in academic disciplines such as microeconomics, game theory, and sociology. While we provide students with numerous tools, we rarely talk about how great strategists think, learn, and put ideas together with actions. There is a deep hole in our understanding about what makes a truly great strategist. Academics frequently study companies and their leaders, but they rarely study in depth the individuals themselves, along with the decisions that define their careers and the organizations they build.

When we began this project, we made several important assumptions. One was that managers and entrepreneurs could learn a great deal from Bill Gates, Andy Grove, and Steve Jobs, despite their uniqueness and larger-than-life personalities. There was never any question in our minds that these three individuals were not your typical CEOs or entrepreneurs in terms of personal abilities or achievements. They were titans of industry, to say the least. At the same time, we concluded that their approaches could help managers and entrepreneurs think more systematically about strategy, as well as execution, because they tackled key problems in similar ways.

A second assumption was that, even though all three of our subjects were from the world of high technology, their experience can give us great insight into the role and importance of strategy and execution for many types of businesses. One of the reasons we have spent so much of our careers studying high-tech firms is that the pace of change puts an enormous premium on formulating the right strategy at the right time, as well as attending to the details of execution. In addition, quickly evolving technologies are becoming embedded in every business today. Rapid changes in social media, cloud computing, mobile devices, and even wearable technology will impact most firms over the next few decades. Understanding how strategy develops in the high-tech world has become part of everyday business life.

A third assumption is that strategy and execution are inextricably linked. When we are teaching, students often ask, "What's more important, strategy or execution?" After a brief pause, we usually respond with another question: "What would you rather have—a great strategy that is poorly executed or a bad strategy that is executed perfectly?" The answer, of course, is neither. There is no value in a great strategy that you can't execute or great execution that leads you in the wrong direction. Skillful CEOs must set the organization on the right path and then lead their organizations to deliver results. As Bill Gates once said, "A bad strategy will fail no matter how good your information is and lame execution will stymie a good strategy. If you do enough things poorly, you will go out of business."[1]

Finally, we believe that becoming a great strategist is not innate. Most successful executives *learn* over time how to think more strategically and how to execute more effectively, at the tactical and organizational levels. We return to this theme in the book's concluding chapter. In the meantime, we will show that Bill Gates, Andy Grove, and Steve Jobs were not born as great strategists: Jobs almost bankrupted the company during his first stint with Apple; Grove's first publication on how to run a business, *High Output Management*, was the quintessential guide to being an operations-oriented middle manager; and Gates's knowledge of management and business strategy when he dropped out of Harvard was hardly impressive. It was their ability to learn—about strategy, execution, and new domains within their own businesses—that made them such effective leaders over such long periods of time. We assume that other senior managers and entrepreneurs, if they put their minds to it, can learn these skills as well.

In many ways, the research on this book started in the mid-1980s, when we began studying, writing about, or working in the software, computer, and semiconductor industries. We have incorporated interviews conducted at the three companies dating back to 1987. In total, we have relied on some one hundred of our own interviews in different years, as well as on other books, articles, and cases we and others have written. We also spent approximately a year meeting a few times per month to compare ideas on our three subjects and lay out the structure of the book before we started writing. The current framework of five main "rules" and skill sets that we thought the three CEOs shared emerged in the first few days of our discussions, reinforcing our belief that Gates, Grove, and Jobs shared much in common with regard to how they approached strategic challenges.

While we have already thanked many of the individuals who have helped us in our research over the past two decades, we would like to express here our appreciation to the executives who gave us their time and perspectives during the fall of 2013, when we undertook the most current research. First and foremost, we want to thank Andy Grove. Andy met with us several times between September 2013 and July 2014. He read and commented on parts of the manuscript, as well as answered numerous emails. Besides Grove, we approached Bill Gates who, in late fall 2013, apologized for not being available.

Our interview strategy, with two exceptions, was to talk with executives who had worked closely with Gates, Grove, and Jobs, but no longer worked for their respective companies. We did not want to put anyone in an awkward position. The exceptions were Renée James, who worked for five years as Grove's technical assistant and was Intel's new president at the time of our meeting, and Joel Podolny, Apple's head of human resources, who worked with David at Harvard Business School before going to Yale and then Apple. In addition to meeting with Grove, James, and Podolny, we did twelve additional interviews in the fall of 2013: we wish to thank Fred Anderson, Dennis Carter, Tom Dunlap, Carl Everett, Pat Gelsinger, Frank Gill, Ron Johnson, Paul Maritz, Jon Rubinstein, Russ Siegelman, Avie Tevanian, and Les Vadasz.

We have also benefited greatly from numerous readers of the manuscript and others who provided written feedback on our seminars. These include our agent, James Levine; the publisher, Hollis Heimbouch; and Juan Alcacer, Deborah Ancona, Ankur Chavda, Scott Cook, Donna Dubinsky, Kathy Eisenhardt, Andreas Goeldi, Mel Horwitch, Reed Hundt, Renée James, Carol Kauffman, Karim Lakhani, Doug Melamed, Sanjiv Mirchandani, Tim Ott, Joel Podolny, Alec Ramsay, Steven Sinofsky, Brad Smith, Michael Scott-Morton, Ben Slivka, Richard Tedlow, and Eric Van den Stein. We also thank participants in seminars at Stanford Engineering's Department of Management Science and Engineering, London Business School, Imperial College Business School, Oxford's Saïd Business School, the Harvard Business School Strategy Conference and HBS Strategy Seminar, and the MIT Sloan Seminar in Technological Innovation, Entrepreneurship, and Strategy.

A few individuals were indispensable: Eric Baldwin was David's research associate, who dug into every aspect of the research, looking for new examples, insights, references, and perspectives to help us with every chapter in the book. We are deeply indebted to our editor, Mary Kwak, who pushed us to clarify our thinking, and played a crucial role in making the book more readable for a broader audience. David's assistant, Cathyjean Gustafson, was incredibly supportive at every stage of the process.

Of course, our wives, Terry Yoffie and Xiaohua Yang, read multiple drafts of the manuscript and were our biggest critics, our finest guides, and our biggest cheerleaders.

STRATEGY RULES

The Making of a Master Strategist

In early March 1998, Bill Gates, Andy Grove, and Steve Jobs, the CEOs of Microsoft, Intel, and Apple, posed together at a party in New York City celebrating the seventy-fifth anniversary of *Time* magazine. This had never happened before and would never happen again. The resulting photograph is the only one ever taken of the three together when they were all running their respective companies. Most astonishing were the tuxedos! For one night, Jobs had shed his black mock turtleneck and jeans, Grove his leather jacket, and Gates his habitual sweater and slacks.

In the center of the picture, Grove is beaming. Only weeks earlier, *Time* had named him Man of the Year, the crowning achievement of an illustrious career. Intel was enjoying the best results in its history, dominating the microprocessor business and leading the world in semiconductor revenues and profits. At the top of his game, Grove had just announced that he was retiring as CEO and stepping up to chairman, a position he held until 2005.

On the right, Gates has a more circumspect smile. As head of Microsoft, he had crushed every obstacle in his path, including Intel's foray into software, Apple's challenge to the desktop PC, and, most recently, Netscape's effort to leverage the Internet and unseat

Microsoft as the world's most powerful software company. But Gates's success had brought unwelcome attention. Just two months later, the U.S. Department of Justice, plus twenty states and the District of Columbia, would file a battery of lawsuits charging that Microsoft illegally used its market power to thwart competition. In 2000, Gates would end his twenty-five-year run as CEO. He remained as chairman of the board until 2014, when he again stepped aside to become an advisor to new CEO Satya Nadella.

On the left, Jobs displays his trademark smirk, looking as usual like the only one in on a secret. He had returned as Apple's interim CEO eight months earlier, refusing to make the title permanent until he was absolutely certain that Apple would survive. More pragmatic than the Steve Jobs of old, he had made peace with his old adversaries, Gates and Grove, but was no less maniacal than before about controlling product design and the user experience. Two months after this party, Jobs would introduce the world to the gumdrop-shaped, candy-colored iMac that began the company's turnaround. He would later champion the iPod and iTunes, and then the iPhone and iPad, positioning Apple to become the most valuable company in the world.

MASTERING THE RULES OF STRATEGY

We can only speculate what Gates, Grove, and Jobs were thinking when this picture was taken. But when it comes to the most important ideas and actions that brought them to this moment in their careers, we don't need to guess; we *know*. It has been our good fortune to have studied and worked with these three leaders and their companies for more than twenty-five years. David Yoffie has been a member of Intel's board of directors since 1989, and worked closely with Grove during his eleven-year tenure as CEO and seven years as chairman. He has also met and interviewed Gates, Jobs, and other industry leaders on multiple occasions as part of his research on high-tech strategy at Harvard Business School. Over the same period, Michael Cusumano has immersed himself in the strategy and operations of Microsoft. As a leading expert on the software business at the MIT Sloan School of Management, he has written extensively on the industry and conducted in-depth interviews with Gates and Grove, as well as many executives and engineers at Microsoft, Intel, and Apple. Together, in 1998, we wrote a bestselling study of Microsoft's epic battle with Netscape, *Competing on Internet Time*. As much as anyone, we can tell you what these three leaders were thinking as they made the decisions that drove Microsoft, Intel, and Apple to such great heights—and occasional lows.

Equally important, we have observed Gates, Grove, and Jobs side by side. This allows us to identify commonalities in their approaches to strategy, execution, and entrepreneurship that are often obscured by differences in personality and style. Surely, there is no shortage of case studies, articles, and books analyzing each of their companies. All three CEOs have been the subjects of full-length biographies, ranging from 650-page doorstoppers to illustrated paperbacks for kids. Inevitably, these treatments play up what is unique about each story—Grove's escape from communist Hungary and academic training, Gates's privileged upbringing and early immersion in software, or Jobs's humble childhood and later obsession with elegance in design. Hidden behind these differences, however, lies a common framework for company leadership.

This shared approach to the essentials of strategy and execution did not appear all at once or at the same time for all three men; it evolved over their careers, through abundant trial and error. The five rules we have identified to describe this framework are the heart of this book:

1. Look Forward, Reason Back
2. Make Big Bets, Without Betting the Company

3. Build Platforms *and* Ecosystems—Not Just Products
4. Exploit Leverage *and* Power—Play Judo *and* Sumo
5. Shape the Organization Around Your Personal Anchor

By applying these rules to their companies, Gates, Grove, and Jobs produced some of the best results ever seen. Financial performance captures only a small part of their complex stories, but it is an obvious indication of their success. For example, look at operating profits (Table 1). Bill Gates was Microsoft's CEO from 1975 to 2000. Over that span, the company's annual profit grew from practically zero to $11 billion. Andy Grove became Intel's CEO in 1987. The prior year, Intel had lost $135 million. In 1997, Grove's last full year on the job, Intel earned nearly $10 billion. In 1997, the year Steve Jobs returned to Apple, the company lost more than $400 million; in 2011, the year he resigned due to illness, Apple earned almost $34 billion.

Market share numbers tell a similar story. Intel's share of the microprocessor segment grew from less than 40 percent to more than 80 percent during Grove's tenure.[1] Under Gates, Microsoft took over 95 percent of the market for PC operating systems. By the end of Jobs's second time at Apple, the company had won 20 percent of the smartphone market, 60 percent of the market for MP3 players (the iPod) and digital media (iTunes), and as much as 70 percent of the tablet market (iPad).[2] In addition, Jobs took pride in the fact that Apple sold 90 percent of all personal computers priced over $1,000.[3]

Perhaps most striking, Apple was the most valuable company in the world when Jobs stepped down. Microsoft held the same distinction at the end of Gates's run as CEO. Intel was just a step behind, gaining the number-one spot in the world within twenty-seven months of Grove's move from the CEO's office to the chairman's suite (metaphorically speaking, that is—Grove actually continued to work from a cubicle, like every other Intel employee).

Profits and Peak Market Capitalization

	Operating Profits at Start of CEO Tenure	Operating Profits at End of CEO Tenure	Peak Market Capitalization	Approximate Market Capitalization (late 2014)
Gates (25 years) (Microsoft)		$11 billion	$612 billion (12/27/99)	$410 billion
Grove (11 years) (Intel)	($135 million)	$10 billion	$501 billion (08/31/00)	$165 billion
Jobs (14 years) (Apple)	($403 million)	$34 billion	$668 billion (11/14/14)	$688 billion

Gates, Grove, and Jobs owed part of their success to the explosion of activity launched by the invention of the personal computer, the advent of the Internet, and the widespread adoption of digital mobile devices. They were undoubtedly in the right place at the right time. However, many well-positioned businesses run by talented and hardworking individuals failed or fell behind during this very same period and in the same markets. Gates, Grove, and Jobs stand out because they achieved and maintained dominance in their industries, even as seismic shifts altered the landscape around them. In the process, they had a lasting impact on their companies, their sector, and their era.

Microsoft, Intel, and Apple have all faced major changes in their businesses since Gates, Grove, and Jobs were CEOs. Nonetheless, the financial performance of these three firms has been stronger than most people realize. Intel's sales more than doubled, from $25 billion to $53 billion in the sixteen years after Grove stepped down. Microsoft's revenues more than tripled, from $23 billion to $79 billion, in the thirteen years following Gates's resignation. Even Apple's annual sales grew nearly 60 percent in the two years following Jobs's departure, from $108 billion to $171 billion. All three companies also continued to generate enviable levels of operating income—in calendar 2013, $12.3 billion for Intel, $27.6 billion for Microsoft, and $48.5 billion for Apple.

These impressive numbers demonstrate that a great strategic position, combined with breakthrough products or dominant industry platforms, can generate huge economic benefits for long periods of time. Yet in recent years, the financial performance, market value, and public perceptions of Microsoft, Intel, and even Apple have fallen short of the high standards established earlier in their history. We no longer see growth rates double or triple the industry average, or truly revolutionary products. This is not entirely surprising. The CEOs who followed Gates, Grove, and Jobs were in a sense victims of their predecessors' success. Rather than nimble upstarts in rapidly growing businesses, they inherited large, maturing "behemoths" that faced significant disruptions in their markets, as well as hungry competitors on all sides. All three firms are challenged by the emergence of new technologies and business models, ranging from software as a service and cloud computing to "free" ad-supported software and services, social media, and explosive growth in relatively inexpensive smartphones and tablets.

While Gates, Grove, and Jobs built strong organizations and cultures that persisted, the leadership teams who followed our three CEOs bear ultimate responsibility for their companies' performance. The immediate successor CEOs at Microsoft and Intel—Steve Ballmer, Craig Barrett, and Paul Otellini—were capable stewards of the existing franchises. Yet they failed to match the strategic clarity and disciplined execution that became second nature for Gates and

Grove. As for Apple, it is unclear how the company will fare without Jobs at the helm. Although replacing any leader of his stature is perhaps an impossible task, in the three years following Jobs's departure in 2011, there were no major breakthrough products comparable to the iPod, iPhone, or iPad. The Apple iWatch may be an exception but, as we argue later in this book, there are good reasons to be skeptical about its long-run impact as an industry-wide platform. Overall, Apple, Intel, and Microsoft remain important and powerful firms. All three companies have relatively new CEOs, who we hope will drive their companies to new heights in the future. Their common strategic problem is that Microsoft, Intel, and Apple are no longer alone in leading the high-tech world.

Today, the spotlight is trained instead on a new generation of companies and CEO-entrepreneurs: people like Google's Larry Page (deeply trained in science and engineering, like Grove), Facebook's Mark Zuckerberg (a "hacker" and Harvard dropout, like Gates), and Amazon's Jeff Bezos (a compulsively consumer-oriented nonconformist, like Jobs), as well as Huateng "Pony" Ma of Tencent (founder of China's biggest Internet company). As we discuss later in this book, these CEOs are following in the footsteps of Gates, Grove, and Jobs. We can see their reliance on similar strategic principles in Page's prescient vision of the cloud, Zuckerberg's bold moves to build the Facebook Platform, Bezos's passion for creating platforms as well as delivering an unsurpassed consumer experience, and Ma's drive to "embrace and extend" the best Internet messaging and networking technologies.

It is not surprising that this later generation of high-tech entrepreneurs is building on the foundations Gates, Grove, and Jobs established. Like their famous predecessors, they operate in fast-paced "platform" industries defined by exponential growth potential and often unpredictable change. But beyond the technology sector, we believe that leaders in a wide range of industries can also benefit from studying these three CEOs. Dynamic industries such as computer software, semiconductors, consumer electronics, and digital media are the fruit flies of the business world.[4] Since change is so rapid and life cycles so short, we have many chances to observe why some companies succeed and others fail or stumble. By understanding how Microsoft, Intel, Apple, and other high-tech companies have managed their evolution, senior executives and entrepreneurs in other industries can learn how to better manage change in their own markets.

The word "learn" is essential here. After observing Gates, Grove, and Jobs—for more than two decades—it is clear to us that mastery of strategy is not an innate skill. Most great CEOs *learn how to become* better strategic thinkers and organization leaders. For example, early in his career, Grove believed that his managers in the trenches, those closest to the customer, should determine corporate strategy. He later realized that strategy required a top-down as well as a bottom-up approach. Gates was caught flat-footed by the rise of the Internet and nearly lost the browser wars to Netscape. But after being prodded by a few young and relatively inexperienced employees, he adapted quickly enough to save the company from potential disaster. Jobs almost bankrupted Apple during his first stint with the company before learning that simply designing great products was not enough. Eventually, Jobs realized that Apple had to form broader industry partnerships and work with competitors—notably Bill Gates and Microsoft—in order to survive and eventually thrive.

To be sure, high-technology markets have unique characteristics. That is a big part of what Gates, Grove, and Jobs had to learn. Technology-driven businesses usually revolve around industry-wide "platforms" rather than stand-alone products. Platforms such as a Windows PC or an iPhone are foundational products or technologies that succeed or fail depending on how many users they attract as well as how many third-party firms build "complementary" products and services. Rising numbers of users and complementors can generate powerful feedback loops known as "network effects" or "network externalities." These network effects can cause value to increase exponentially as more consumers and complementors adopt the platform. In addition, since platform markets can rapidly "tip" to a single big winner, even the most dominant firms risk constant disruption of the status quo. Such dynamics require high-tech managers to make extremely complex decisions quickly and with very little certainty about the future. There can be great rewards if they are right and devastating consequences if they are wrong.

Few people could have imagined (besides Steve Jobs) that a new cell phone called the iPhone would turn industry giants (Nokia and BlackBerry) into virtually irrelevant players within just a few short years. Or that a tiny start-up in Seattle (Microsoft) would upend its biggest customer and the world's largest, most valuable company at the time (IBM). Or that a small, nearly bankrupt semiconductor memory company (Intel), which needed a bailout from IBM, would go on to beat the Japanese, the Koreans, and the Europeans and become the world leader in a new critical technology—microprocessors—within a decade.

Gates, Grove, and Jobs were among the earliest CEOs and entrepreneurs to figure out how to compete in platform markets. They were keen students of strategy and organization, as well as history, and they dedicated themselves to learning about new technologies, new business models, and new industries. They shared a commitment to reflecting on their triumphs as well as their mistakes. This dedication to learning is a big part of what made them effective leaders for such long periods of time.

THE THREE CEOS

When we began this book, we thought of it as a conversation with Gates, Grove, and Jobs about what it takes to become a master strategist. We learned a great deal from dissecting and revisiting the rules that, in our view, they all seemed to follow. Through that process, we found that their personal histories and interests played a powerful role in shaping their approaches to strategy and organization building as well as entrepreneurship. Therefore, a good place to start this book is with a brief recap of their backgrounds and the businesses they ran, beginning with the most senior of the three.

Andy Grove and Intel

Andy Grove was born in Hungary in 1936. A child survivor of the Holocaust, he grew up behind the Iron Curtain and fled Soviet oppression during the failed revolution of 1956. Eventually, he immigrated to the United States. After working his way through the City College of New York, where he earned a degree in chemical engineering, Grove went on to complete a Ph.D. in the same field at the University of California, Berkeley. He began his career at Fairchild Semiconductor in 1963, leaving to help start Intel in 1968—a time when the adolescent Gates and Jobs were just beginning to experiment with computers.

Intel initially focused on designing and manufacturing memory chips for mainframe computers. The company went public in 1971 on the strength of its memory business. That same year it invented a new product—the microprocessor—that would later make it a global powerhouse. The microprocessor is also called a central processing unit, or CPU. Its function is to carry out computational tasks for computer systems or other programmable electronic devices, such as digital watches. In 1980, Intel won a contract with IBM to supply the microprocessor for its first personal computer, which was introduced the following year. As the personal computer market took off in the early 1980s, Intel's x86 line of microprocessors became the standard for the PC industry.

At the time, Intel still saw itself as primarily a memory products company. By 1985, however, aggressive Japanese manufacturers, combined with a slowdown in the market, had turned memories into a money-losing commodity. After getting a cash infusion from IBM to keep the company alive, CEO Gordon Moore and COO Andy Grove made the difficult decision to formally exit the biggest memory segment, called DRAMs, and focus on microprocessors. When Grove became CEO in 1987, he completed the transition out of DRAMs and cemented Intel's new identity as the world's leading supplier of microprocessors for personal computers. By 1992, Intel had become the largest semiconductor company in the world. Six years later, when Grove stepped down as CEO, Intel chips powered some 80 percent of the PCs sold. The company also became a powerhouse in data centers, eventually providing CPUs for roughly 90 percent of the world's servers. Along the way, Intel Inside became a household name. Intel transformed itself from a manufacturer of components known mostly to industry insiders into a technology leader with one of the most valuable brand names in the world.[5]

Bill Gates and Microsoft

Born in 1955, nearly two decades after Grove, Bill Gates got off to a very different start in life. He grew up in Seattle the privileged child of a well-connected lawyer and a prominent civic volunteer. In the late 1960s, while in middle school, Gates discovered computers and quickly became fascinated by programming. In high school, he wrote a software program that administrators used for student scheduling and even formed a small company with an older classmate, Paul Allen, to record traffic data. Gates enrolled at Harvard in 1973, but, after two years, he dropped out to start Microsoft with Allen in 1975.

Microsoft started off small. Gates and Allen initially adapted the BASIC programming language for the Altair 8800, an inexpensive minicomputer kit for hobbyists that ran on an early Intel CPU.

Their big break came in 1980, when IBM, which was racing to get its first PC to market, approached Gates to supply an operating system—the software that works with the microprocessor to handle routine but essential computing functions. Lacking a suitable operating system of its own, Microsoft purchased one from a local company, rebranded it as DOS, and licensed it to IBM on a nonexclusive basis.[6] Once the IBM PC became widely adopted, Microsoft achieved industry dominance by selling DOS to IBM's competitors. DOS became the software platform for the personal computer industry until Microsoft introduced Windows, which began to sell in volume in 1990.

Meanwhile, Microsoft built an industry-leading applications business, beginning with an early version of Excel in 1982, quickly followed by Word. In 1990, it launched the Office suite of applications. Together, sales of languages, operating systems, and applications pushed annual revenues over $100 million by 1985, helping Microsoft go public in 1986.[7] By 1987, Microsoft had passed rival Lotus (maker of the widely used spreadsheet, 1-2-3) to become the largest PC software products company in the world, with nearly $350 million in revenue.[8] Three years later, sales surpassed $1 billion.

The emergence of the Internet in the 1990s threatened to undermine the importance of the PC—the cornerstone of Microsoft's business. Gates responded by pouring resources into developing a Web browser and adding Internet functionality to nearly all of Microsoft's products. This strategy worked: Microsoft successfully beat back challenges from Netscape and other Internet firms to retain its position at the top of the software products industry.

In 2000, Gates stepped down as CEO, ceding the reins to his longtime friend and colleague Steve Ballmer. Gates remained Microsoft's chief software architect until 2006 and a full-time employee until 2008, when he began to devote most of his time to the Bill & Melinda Gates Foundation.[9]

Steve Jobs and Apple

Like Bill Gates, Steve Jobs was born in 1955 and grew up as the personal computer revolution was just beginning. The son of two students who met at the University of Wisconsin, he was adopted at birth by a working-class family who moved from San Francisco to Silicon Valley when the young Jobs was five years old. Jobs owed his early exposure to design and electronics to his father, a carpenter and mechanic, who liked to rebuild cars. A neighbor who worked for Hewlett-Packard fueled Jobs's growing fascination with circuitry by encouraging him to tinker with do-it-yourself electronics kits and introducing him to a company-sponsored program that brought HP engineers and local students together once a week.[10] A school like Stanford or Berkeley might have seemed the logical next stop for Jobs. Instead, he chose Reed College, a liberal arts school in Oregon famous for its counterculture atmosphere. Jobs enrolled at Reed in 1972 but dropped out after six months and spent the next few years auditing classes, hanging out with friends, and eventually traveling to India. Once back in Silicon Valley, he began to collaborate on projects with Steve Wozniak, an engineering wiz he had met while still in high school. In 1976, they started Apple Computer.

The company's first product, called the Apple I, consisted of a circuit board in a wooden case, which Jobs, Wozniak, and a friend put together in the Jobs family's garage. One year later came the Apple II, a fully assembled computer and keyboard housed in a sleek plastic casing. The Apple II became one of the earliest commercially successful personal computers and helped launch the new industry. Its success also led Apple Computer to go public at the end of 1980.

When IBM shipped its personal computer in 1981, Apple faced a giant new competitor. The IBM PC, running on an Intel microprocessor and using Microsoft DOS, soon became the dominant computing platform and surpassed the Apple II in market share. In an effort to change the game, Apple released the Macintosh in

1984. Although the "Mac" never seriously challenged the IBM PC and compatible computers (called "clones") in market share, it represented a decisive turning point for the industry. The Mac incorporated a graphical user interface (GUI) that made it much easier to use than the IBM PC. This innovation, later adopted by Microsoft with Windows, expanded the potential market for personal computers far beyond hobbyists and "geeks."

The Mac was a revolutionary product, but it got off to a slow start as an industry platform. Jobs had failed to cultivate a large ecosystem of application developers and kept the Mac priced too high for the mass market. Problems with Mac sales also led to a power struggle between Jobs and the CEO he had recruited from PepsiCo, John Sculley. After being fired as head of the Macintosh division in May 1985, Jobs stepped down as chairman a few months later, sold all of his Apple stock, and went on to found NeXT, a high-end computer workstation company. In 1986, he would also take over Pixar, the animation film studio.

Over the next decade, without Steve Jobs, Apple won a loyal following and dominated in niche markets such as desktop publishing and education. But the company lost significant share in the PC market and faced mounting losses by the mid-1990s. Efforts to launch a variety of consumer devices failed, and the core Macintosh software and hardware platforms were showing their age. As part of its turnaround strategy, Apple acquired NeXT and used its software technology as the basis for the next-generation Macintosh operating system. With NeXT, Jobs returned to Apple in 1997, first as an advisor and ultimately as CEO.

Jobs quickly refocused Apple on producing a small number of products, with the goal of making each one world-class. He started with a redesigned Macintosh called the iMac, which went on sale in 1998. Three years later, Apple released its breakthrough digital music player, the iPod, which became one of the defining products of the era. The iPod soon accounted for half the company's revenue.

With this new product, supported by the iTunes online music store, Apple moved beyond computers to consumer electronics. In recognition of this shift, Jobs dropped "Computer" from the company name and changed it to Apple, Inc. in 2007.

That same year, Apple released the iPhone, which became the top-selling smartphone in the world and a new platform for building "apps" sold through Apple's proprietary App Store.[11] Apple followed the iPhone with the iPad in 2010, a portable tablet computer that used the iPhone's operating system and applications, and enabled users to watch videos, play music, read and write email, and browse the Web. The iPad became an instant sensation, with sales reaching one million units in the first month and 15 million in its first nine months on the market.[12] On the strength of these new industry platforms, Jobs positioned Apple to attain the largest market capitalization of any company in history by the time he resigned due to illness in the fall of 2011.

Different People, Similar Approaches

As individual personalities, Gates, Grove, and Jobs could not have been more different. Grove was a disciplined engineer with a Ph.D. and the ultimate problem solver. At Intel, he initially took on the role of director of operations, despite the fact that he had no training in management. In the early years, his tasks included everything from reviewing engineering drawings and staffing levels to setting up Intel's post office box and ordering office furniture.[13] Those experiences turned Grove into an avid student of management and left a strong imprint on his style as CEO. For example, Grove insisted on formal systems for everything from employee reviews and exit interviews to long-range strategic planning.

A generation younger, Jobs was steeped in the counterculture of the late 1960s and driven to challenge the status quo. Sometimes described as "slightly loony," he frequently behaved as if the normal rules didn't apply to him. Jobs often showed up to meetings barefoot and unshaven (and sometimes unwashed, to the chagrin of colleagues and friends). He removed the license plates from his Mercedes and parked in handicapped spaces in Apple's parking lot. (Grove, by contrast, parked his car wherever he could find a space in the Intel lot, just like any other employee.) Yet despite the seeming casualness that marked his personal life, when it came to design, Jobs was a perfectionist, obsessed with elegance and simplicity. "If something isn't right, you can't just ignore it and say you'll fix it later," he maintained. "That's what other companies do."[14]

Jobs was probably thinking of Microsoft when he made this remark.[15] In comparison to Jobs, however, Bill Gates had impressive technical skills. While in college, Gates came up with an algorithm that not only solved a long-intractable combinatorial problem in applied math, but remained the most efficient solution to the problem for more than thirty years. He was known for dismissing others' struggles with technical hurdles by saying, "I could code that in a weekend."[16] But perfection was never Gates's goal. He was a pragmatist, focused on creating products and then industry platforms that were "good enough" to dominate the mass market.[17] If Jobs saw himself as an artist and a craftsman, Gates prided himself on being a software "hacker" and programmer, shipping products to market quickly and then improving them incrementally.

Despite their differences in background and personalities, Gates, Grove, and Jobs shared several key personal attributes. Most important, all three were enormously ambitious and dreamed big dreams—not so much for themselves as for their companies, their industries, and the world. They were determined to have an impact. For example, Gates recalled that when he and Paul Allen started Microsoft in 1975, "We talked about a computer on every desk and in every home."[18] And they were not thinking about just any computer, but machines running Microsoft software. For his part, Jobs genuinely believed that the products Apple was creating would, in his words, "make a dent in the universe."[19] His goal was not merely to build products that people would buy, but to change the way millions of people lived their daily lives. And none of these innovations would have been possible without the microprocessor, which Intel invented. Grove's stated ambition was to reshape the world's computer industry, putting Intel at its center.

In addition, Gates, Grove, and Jobs all had a ferocious personal work ethic, which they infused into the cultures of their companies. In 1981, in response to a downturn in the chip industry, Grove implemented what he called the "125% solution," asking Intel's salaried employees to work two extra hours a day for free.[20] Jobs pushed his product teams to work ninety-hour weeks and to strive for levels of achievement that most team members never thought possible. Gates was notorious for sending piercing emails at all hours of the day or night and for roaming Microsoft's hallways on weekends to see who was in the office. Even Gates noticed this resemblance with Jobs. Reflecting on their similarities, Gates commented that "[Jobs and I] were both hyperenergetic and worked superhard."[21]

All three leaders also promoted what Grove called "searing intellectual debates," which often escalated into shouting matches.[22] Supremely confident in their own abilities, none of the three spared much thought for the feelings of other executives or employees. Gates often shot down an idea he did not like by saying it was "the stupidest f***ing thing I've ever heard." One member of the original Macintosh team recalled that Jobs "had the uncanny capacity to know exactly what your weak point is, know what will make you feel small, to make you cringe."[23] Grove was more polite, but no less devastating. We do not recommend that other CEOs and leaders emulate their aggressive behavior, but they would do well to adopt the passion that drove the verbal attacks. Gates, Grove, and Jobs were all "truth-seekers," as an Intel colleague called Andy Grove.[24] And they respected colleagues with the intelligence, knowledge, and courage to prove them wrong. Jobs, for example, told an interviewer in 1995, "I don't care about being right, I care about success."[25] Recognizing both Jobs's capacity to intimidate and his willingness to back down, the members of Apple's Macintosh team even instituted an annual award for the person who did the best job of standing up to him.

Finally, all three CEOs harbored a healthy dose of paranoia, at least as far as their companies were concerned. Grove even titled his 1996 book on strategy *Only the Paranoid Survive.* Gates and Jobs could easily have written books with a similar title. They all understood that success in a rapidly evolving industry required constant vigilance. They were always looking over their shoulders for competitors gaining ground or new entrants appearing out of nowhere—just as they once did. In 1997, fresh from victory over Netscape in the browser wars, Gates wrote, "I see us as an underdog today, just as I've seen us as an underdog every day for the last twenty years. If we don't maintain that perspective, some competitor will eat our lunch. . . . One day somebody will catch us napping. One day an eager upstart will put Microsoft out of business. I just hope it's fifty years from now, not two or five."[26] Replace "Microsoft" with "Intel" or "Apple," and Grove or Jobs could have spoken the exact same words.

GUIDE TO THE BOOK

Based on our long study of Gates, Grove, and Jobs, we have deep respect and admiration for all three leaders, but we do not see them through rose-tinted glasses. None of the three was infallible. All three made mistakes when it came to both strategy and execution. All three championed products that flopped or came late to market and underperformed. All three were slow on occasion to seize strategic opportunities, although their companies' resources usually gave them the ability to catch up. And all three CEOs led their companies to run afoul of the law. Microsoft, Intel, and Apple each signed consent decrees with the U.S. Department of Justice or the Federal Trade Commission and faced antitrust scrutiny around the world.

Nonetheless, we believe Gates, Grove, and Jobs were three of the most successful CEOs and strategists in the high-tech world, and perhaps of all time. They were masters of strategy and surprisingly effective organization leaders. They set long- and short-term goals for their companies, positioned their organizations for success, led teams that executed with ruthless efficiency, and dominated the competition for an extended period of time. While their successes (and failures) are in the past, the lessons they offer are timeless. The five rules we use in this book to capture their approach to strategy and execution can help any organization leader navigate more confidently toward the future.

The first three chapters examine the basic strategy rules that helped drive Gates, Grove, and Jobs to their greatest successes. *Chapter 1 is about looking forward into the future and then reasoning back to actions that you must take today.* During their first five years as CEO, Gates and Grove both developed a distinctive view of the world; for Steve Jobs, that powerful vision did not emerge until his second go-round at Apple. Equally important, and seen much less frequently in practice, all three were able to figure out—in very detailed terms—what they needed to do immediately to turn their vision into reality. By anticipating customer needs, restricting competitor options, and altering industry dynamics in their favor, they turned ideas into strategies and actions.

Chapter 2 is about taking bold moves without being reckless and putting the company at unnecessary risk. High-technology markets driven by network effects can grow exponentially, producing big winners as well as big losers, often in the seeming blink of an eye. Gates, Grove, and Jobs each made huge strategic bets and had their fair share of mistakes. But they rarely took gambles that were excessively risky or irreversible. By timing, spreading, and diversifying their big bets, they successfully mitigated their risks.

Chapter 3 is about a relatively new approach to strategy that re-quires building platforms and ecosystems, rather than stand-alone products and companies. Technology-intensive industries often have special properties that require managers to think beyond best-of-breed products as well as outside the boundaries of their own firms. We learn from Gates, Grove, and Jobs how to balance the trade-offs between creating great products versus building industry platforms. While great products may stand on their own, industry platforms require complementary innovations by other firms to succeed in the marketplace.

The next two chapters analyze and illustrate the execution guidelines that Gates, Grove, and Jobs followed at the tactical and organizational levels. *Chapter 4 is about using both leverage and power to beat the competition, or what we call judo and sumo tactics.* Gates, Grove, and Jobs proved to be master tacticians, often turning op-ponents' strengths into weaknesses as well as, later in their careers, using the overwhelming resources of their companies to dominate competitors.

Chapter 5 is about building an organization around the leader's unique skills and business insights, or what we call a personal anchor. Gates shaped Microsoft around his deep understanding of software technology; Grove drove Intel to develop disciplined "engineering-like" processes to mass-produce complex semiconductor devices; and Jobs molded Apple around his obsession with elegance and sim-plicity in product design and the user experience. In addition, all three recognized and compensated for their weaknesses through the people they hired and the cultures, systems, and values they inspired and helped create.

Throughout these five chapters, we explore key episodes from the history of all three companies to show how Gates, Grove, and Jobs implemented the five strategy rules as well as where and why they sometimes went astray. Our goal is not to retell the full story of Microsoft, Intel, or Apple—a job that many others have accomplished well—but to focus on broader management lessons. As a result, our discussion sometimes moves around in time. In addition, we examine a few particularly important decisions in more than one chapter because they offer new insights when viewed from different perspectives.

The conclusion summarizes what it takes to master our five strategy rules. We recap the lessons learned from Gates, Grove, and Jobs and show how members of the successor generation—Mark Zuckerberg, Jeff Bezos, Larry Page, and Pony Ma—are already employing many of the same techniques. Finally, we identify some of the biggest mistakes Gates, Grove, and Jobs made during their tenures, including how they prepared their organizations for succession. We close with some suggestions for how senior managers and entrepreneurs can avoid or minimize similar errors while leading their own firms into the future.

CHAPTER 1

Look Forward, Reason Back

Nearly everyone is familiar with Edmund Burke's maxim, "Those who don't know history are destined to repeat it." And many of us have taken his admonition to heart. When facing big decisions, our first instinct is to look back at history and rely on its lessons as we think through the challenges that surround us today.

Strategy, however, is fundamentally forward-looking. It's about planning for the future. Understanding the lessons of the past is clearly important, but developing your playbook on the assumption that the future will be like the past is risky. As Andy Grove liked to say, quoting Einstein, "Visionary thought demands learning from the past while staying free of its limitations."[1]

Master strategists take a different approach. Rather than look backward and reason forward, they *look forward and reason back*. Part game theorist and part chess master, great strategists "look forward" to determine where they want their companies to be at a given point in the future and then "reason back" to identify moves that will take the business there. This focus on anticipating and shaping the future is particularly important in fast-moving industries, where the difference between being a half step ahead and keeping pace with the field can be the difference between greatness and failure. Bill Gates, Andy Grove, and Steve Jobs owed much of their success to this uncommon ability to stay ahead of their customers and competitors.

This ability should not be confused with clairvoyance. Master strategists do not have a crystal ball: Gates, Grove, and Jobs all made proclamations about the future that turned out to be wrong. But master strategists need to be relentlessly focused on the future, and they must constantly update their forecasts as new information becomes available, and competitors move or otherwise reveal their intentions.

Equally important, masters of strategy like Gates, Grove, and Jobs need to position themselves and their companies to take advantage of new opportunities as they emerge. We frequently give successful CEOs too much credit. With the benefit of hindsight, successful leaders tend to look like great visionaries who perfectly planned all their moves in advance. But in reality, most great strategists are opportunists as well as visionaries. They see early glimmers of an emerging market or identify gaps unfilled by the competition. Then they act, using educated guesses or intuitive leaps without becoming paralyzed by uncertainty or doubt.

For example, when IBM came looking for a new operating system, Gates's first response was that he wasn't in that business. However, he quickly realized that IBM was offering Microsoft an opportunity to control the platform for all PC software applications. Grove did not invent the microprocessor, but he was one of the first to understand its potential to reshape the computer industry. Apple did not come up with the idea of a graphical user interface, but Jobs was the first company leader to grasp its revolutionary potential.

In addition, all three CEOs developed and executed strategies for translating these visions into reality. The ability to see the future does not by itself make a great strategist. To be a great strategist, you have to figure out how to get from here to there. In this process, Gates, Grove, and Jobs all had the help of enormously talented executive partners and employees. Like most CEOs, they depended on their management teams and others in the company to propose a range of ideas and get the creative juices flowing. Once presented with a set of choices, they would assess their current positions, study the likely moves and countermoves of other players, and then propose a direction that tied the pieces together. They were "curators" and synthesizers as much as visionaries. If circumstances changed, they would adjust their visions and their plans. This is the hard work of strategy—not deciding where you want to be, but figuring out how to get there; not just looking forward, but also reasoning back and making adjustments as you go.

In this chapter, we make the hard work a bit easier. We break down the process of looking forward and reasoning back into four key components. By mastering these four principles, any manager can learn to plan more effectively for the future:

RULE 1: LOOK FORWARD, REASON BACK

1. Look forward to develop a vision of the future; reason back to set boundaries and priorities.
2. Look forward to anticipate customer needs; reason back to match with capabilities.
3. Look forward to anticipate competitors' moves; reason back to build barriers to entry and lock in customers.
4. Look forward to anticipate industry inflection points; reason back to commit to change—and stay the course.

ANALOGIES IN GAME THEORY AND CHESS

While few great strategists have been trained in game theory, and may or may not play chess, they practice the core tenet of these two disciplines: look forward, then reason back. Game theory, a branch of mathematics often used in economics, teaches that players must look to the end of the game, however that might be defined, find the best possible outcome, and then reason their way backward to discover the decisions required to produce that outcome. To solve a game, you must understand not only your interests but also those of your opponents, so that you can anticipate their moves. This is a relatively simple matter in stylized games, such as the famous Prisoner's Dilemma. However, in complex games or real-world situations, it can be impossible to calculate all the possibilities or outcomes. Therefore, great game theorists, just like master strategists, must rely to some extent on experience and intuition to win.

Chess masters also look forward to identify the positions they hope to create on the board and then reason back by calculating "lines" of play—if I make this move, then my opponent will probably do this, and then I will do that. Chess masters start with a vision of where the game is heading. The challenge is that, at the outset, the number of possible permutations in each line of play is far beyond human ability to calculate. So world-class chess players learn to "prune," quickly eliminating inferior moves to reduce the number of lines they need to consider. Even Deep Blue, the IBM supercomputer that defeated world champion Garry Kasparov in 1997, did not have enough computing capacity to calculate every possible position in a game. Although Deep Blue could analyze 200 million moves per second, its algorithm incorporated the ability to recognize and discard obvious bad moves.

Now when we see new things or opportunities, we can seize them. . . . A creative period like this lasts only maybe a decade, but it can be a golden decade if we manage it properly.[2]
—STEVE JOBS [2000]

LOOK FORWARD: START WITH A VISION OF THE FUTURE

In business, as in game theory and chess, all great strategies start with a vision of the future. In one sense, the recipe is simple: it should include a sense of where the organization should go, what customers are likely to pay for, and how the organization can offer a unique product or service that customers will buy. The devil, of course, lies in the details.

In order to get those details right, successful CEOs rely on both extrapolation and interpretation. Extrapolation is the relatively easy part: analysts, research firms, and academic research can help company leaders identify industry patterns and trends based on current data. However, someone then has to interpret that information—that is, identify the key opportunities and threats created by these trends. Extrapolation alone can be generic and easily imitated. Interpretation is where visionary CEOs make their mark.

Andy Grove based his vision for Intel on an extrapolation known as "Moore's Law." In 1964, Gordon Moore, later one of Intel's co-founders, predicted that the number of transistors on an integrated circuit would double every 18 to 24 months. The industry had delivered on this prediction for more than two decades when Grove began to articulate his vision of the future in the late 1980s. While some saw Moore's Law as just another example of progress in engineering, he interpreted it as a strategy that would transform the structure of the computer industry. Grove argued that if Intel could continue to drive Moore's Law, competitors would need massive scale economies to produce integrated circuits, or chips. Inevitably, this would topple the vertically integrated giants that had dominated the sector for decades. At the time, the leading computer companies, led by IBM and Digital Equipment Corporation (DEC), produced everything, from soup to nuts. They manufactured their own semiconductors, built their own hardware, wrote their own operating systems, and distributed their products through in-house sales forces. Several years before it became obvious to the world, Grove foresaw the overthrow of this system and the rise of an industry organized in horizontal layers—chips, hardware, operating systems, applications, distribution—each of which would be dominated by a small number of powerful companies. Based on this vision, he focused Intel's strategy and organization entirely on achieving leadership in the microprocessor segment.

Bill Gates also built his vision of the future on the trend described by Moore's Law, but he interpreted the repeated doubling of computing power as a force that would turn hardware into a commodity, leaving software as the true source of value in the industry. In a 1994 interview, he recalled his thinking:

> When you have the microprocessor doubling in power every two years, in a sense you can think of computer power as almost free. So you ask, why be in the business of making something that's almost free? What is the scarce resource? What is it that limits being able to get value out of that infinite computing power? Software.[3]

This insight was revolutionary and prophetic, as was Gates's conviction as early as 1975 that there would one day be a personal computer on every desk and in every home. Steve Jobs had a similar vision just a year or so later, when he and Steve Wozniak founded Apple Computer in 1976. Both Microsoft and Apple emerged from

The Transformation of the Computer Industry

(not to scale)

The Old Vertical Computer Industry—Circa 1980

	IBM	DEC	Sperry Univac	Wang
sales and distribution				
application software				
operating system				
computer				
chips				

The New Horizontal Computer Industry—Circa 1995

sales and distribution	Retail Stores	Superstores	Dealers	Mail Order
application software	Word	Word Perfect	Etc.	
operating system	DOS and Windows	OS/2	Mac	UNIX
computer	Compaq	Dell	Packard Bell	Hewlett-Packard	IBM	Etc.
chips	Intel Architecture	Motorola	RISCs	

SOURCE: Re-created with permission from Andy Grove's Intel presentation.

this vision at a time when industry luminaries believed the home computer was a silly idea. Gordon Moore once told us that, in the 1970s, he could not see any use for a computer in the home other than for storing recipes in the kitchen. And in 1977, Ken Olsen, the CEO of the world's second-largest computer company, Digital Equipment Corporation, publicly said, "There is no reason for any individual to have a computer in his home."[4] Obviously, Bill Gates disagreed, and, in 1975, he dropped out of Harvard to start Microsoft with Paul Allen and make this vision of the future happen. Paul Maritz, who ran Microsoft's operating system business from the late 1980s through much of the 1990s, later told us how strongly Gates's original vision influenced the entire company:

> The notion that we were part of creating this new platform that was going to deliver extraordinary functionality and benefits, both in personal lives and in enterprise work environments, was very much on everybody's mind. And we viewed it as a great mission to be on. We were going to take down the bad guys. We were going to take down the old, proprietary, expensive mainframes, minicomputers, and deliver [new] things.[5]

Later in his career, Gates delegated some of the work of extrapolating from the present. According to Russ Siegelman, who worked directly for Gates in the early 1990s, "[He] wouldn't say, 'Here's where the future is. Gates hired people like Nathan [Myhrvold] to do that.'"[6] And indeed, Myhrvold, Microsoft's chief technology officer and the founder of Microsoft Research, was a prolific writer of memos about future trends. But Gates remained firmly in control of Microsoft's vision and led the way when it came to interpreting the impact these trends would have on the company's products and competitive position.

While Gates's vision included a PC in every home, his natural inclination was to build products for other programmers and enterprise customers, not the average consumer. By contrast, Steve Jobs was inspired by the same heady advances in computing power to change the life of the average person. Jobs's vision was to use technology to fulfill unmet and even unidentified consumer needs. From the very beginning of his career, Jobs was dedicated to transforming mundane computers into "insanely great" products. Eventually, his vision for Apple expanded beyond creating individual products to designing the entire digital experience. Like many others in the industry, Jobs realized that the explosion of digital devices in the 1990s was creating a digital Babel, made worse by poor usability and connectivity. But, unlike others, he had a solution. In 2001, Jobs told Macworld attendees that the Mac "can become the 'digital hub' of our new emerging digital lifestyle, with the ability to add tremendous value to these other digital devices."[7] With its focus on the user experience, Apple was uniquely suited to deliver on this vision.

Jobs's vision of a digital hub set Apple on a new path. As former Apple head of hardware Jon Rubinstein recalled, after Jobs articulated the digital hub strategy internally in 2000 and externally in 2001, he and his team "spen[t] a lot of time brainstorming about what other devices we should go do" and considered personal digital assistants, cameras, and phones, before deciding that the iPod presented the best short-term opportunity.[8] More broadly, Ron Johnson, then head of retail, explained:

> [The digital hub vision] created a mental roadmap for products, software products, how Apple would win in the marketplace. Apple had been locked into a PC model for most of its history, and this [vision] liberated the company to be relevant in all emerging categories from music players, to cameras and beyond. It really became how we allocated resources.[9]

We find each of these visions noteworthy not only for the audacious ambition they represented, but for the clarity and simplicity with which Gates, Grove, and Jobs communicated their goals. They used only a few words and occasionally pictures to present their ideas to employees, customers, and partners. Perhaps as a result, audiences, both inside and outside each company, hung on every word when these CEOs explained their views of the future.

However, clarity is not the same as immutability. These visions did not spring fully grown from the minds of their creators like Athena emerging from the head of Zeus. They were continuously revisited, revised, and redefined as new events and information emerged on the horizon. Grove, for example, refined his vision over five years as he transformed Intel from a classic semiconductor company making commodity products into a central player in the new computer industry. When he first became CEO, he envisioned Intel as the world's leading broad-line semiconductor manufacturer.[10] He only "gradually concluded we needed to reposition the company from broad semiconductors to desktop focus," as he admitted to his management team in 1990.[11]

Under Bill Gates, Microsoft moved in the opposite direction, broadening its scope over time while maintaining a tight focus on software. Microsoft's original products were programming languages, followed by operating systems and then applications. Later Gates expanded his vision to include a wider range of products, such as software for communications networks, data servers, multimedia applications, and Internet servers and applications. Similarly, Jobs's vision for Apple evolved continuously, focusing first on computers, then on the Mac as a digital hub, and, by the end of the 2000s, on the "cloud." This ability to update in response to changes in the environment, while preserving clarity at the core of their strategy, was an important strength all three CEOs shared.

REASON BACK:
SET BOUNDARIES AND PRIORITIES

Former IBM CEO Lou Gerstner once said, "Vision is easy. It's so easy to just point to the bleachers and say I'm going to hit one over there. What's hard is saying . . . how do I do that."[12] In other words, vision is never an end in itself. Leaders must translate vision into a strategy that defines the scope of a company's activities—what it will and, perhaps even more important, what it will *not* do. This pruning process, which provides the foundation for wise resource allocation, is an essential element of reasoning back.

Let's return to Grove. In a nutshell, his vision for Intel was to become one of the most powerful companies in computing by harnessing the potential of Moore's Law. As a result, Intel's top priority was to drive the engineering and manufacturing innovations needed to double the transistors on an integrated circuit every 18 to 24 months. Moore's Law, and its implications for investment in process technology and capital expenditure, were discussed more often by the Intel board during Grove's tenure than probably any other subject. Year in and year out, nothing was more important for strategy, planning, and resource allocation than making sure Intel stayed on the trajectory predicted by Moore's Law.

But validating Moore's Law was not the ultimate goal. The goal was to position Intel to thrive in an industry formed of horizontal layers. Grove believed that firms able to achieve massive scale economies would dominate each layer; those that didn't would flounder or fail. This vision had no place for companies that tried to do it all. Intel had to get out or stay out of businesses in which it could not succeed and commit to being first and foremost a microprocessor company. This evolution in Grove's thinking and the transformation of Intel did not happen all at once. In 1987, Grove's first year as CEO, he proclaimed that 50 percent of Intel's business should be "systems," or fully assembled computers. Two years later, he set the

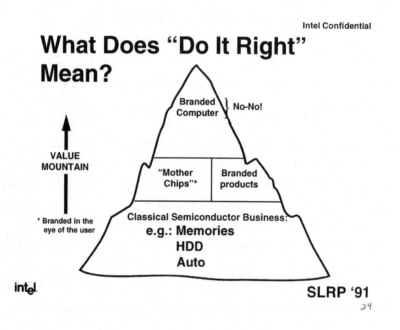

SOURCE: Andy Grove's SLRP presentation to Intel, 1991, re-created with permission.

goal of making Intel the "TOP 5 IN SYSTEMS."[13] But by 1990, he realized that the company needed to exit the systems business to focus on its core strength. In the future, it would make products, such as motherboards—printed circuit boards containing the CPU, memory, and other components—that would help sell microprocessors. It might enter markets for related products (modems, for example) where fixed costs were relatively low. But it would steer far away from layers of the computer industry dominated by other large players with scale economies on their side. In particular, as Grove told his team in 1991, getting into the branded PC hardware business—which would mean competing directly with Intel's customers—was now a definite "No-No!"[14]

Bill Gates took the same disciplined approach when mapping out Microsoft's strategy. Cofounder Paul Allen originally wanted to produce hardware and software, and Microsoft did design some mice and keyboards, but the company's energy and resources were focused overwhelmingly on software. Gates was adamant about the importance of focus, later explaining, "[Y]ou have to have as much of a single strategy as possible. There are separate businesses and there are separate competitive battles, but it's got to be within one jihad."[15] The central goal of Microsoft's jihad was to dominate the operating system market, first through DOS and then with multiple versions of Windows. Secondary fronts focused on desktop productivity applications (Word, Excel, and PowerPoint), a Web browser (Internet Explorer), an operating system for servers (Windows Server), and other complementary software products. Microsoft largely ignored hardware until the launch of Xbox in 2001, more than a quarter century after the company's founding.

Similarly, Steve Jobs saw pruning as a central element of his job as Apple's chief strategist. Toward the end of his tenure, he explained, "[T]he way we've succeeded is by choosing which horses to ride very carefully."[16] Unfortunately, Apple did not always follow this rule. When Jobs returned in 1997 after a twelve-year exile, he found the company's product portfolio in disarray. Never one to mince words, he complained, "[T]he products SUCK! There's no sex in them anymore!"[17] Why? Mostly because there were too many of them. Apple's leadership had already started a major restructuring and downsizing of the company before Jobs was reappointed CEO.[18] The printer division, the low-end Macs, and Apple's advanced technology group were all shut down. But Jobs still felt lost in the thicket of Apple's products.

Fed up, Jobs drew a simple grid of two rows and two columns. He labeled the columns "Consumer" and "Professional" and the rows "Desktop" and "Portable." He insisted that the company focus on just four products, one computer for each quadrant in the grid. And even within the professional segment, according to former Apple CFO Fred Anderson, Jobs told company executives to abandon the enterprise market and instead emphasize the markets for education as well as design and publishing professionals.[19]

Jobs was known to say, "I'm as proud of what we don't do as I am of what we do."[20] One of the things Apple never did on his watch was enter the low end of the computer market by making inexpensive machines to compete with Dell, Compaq, and the like.[21] Jobs brought the same focus on a few great products to Pixar, the animation studio he acquired in 1986. Pixar maintained a relatively slow release schedule for its films, rather than putting out multiple movies per year. This pace meant that there would be no "B teams." Every film would get the best of Pixar's animators, storytellers, and engineers. Said Jobs, "Quality is more important than quantity . . . one home run is much better than two doubles."[22] Although the metaphor was imperfect (one home run produces the same result as two consecutive doubles), Jobs clearly believed in swinging for the fences.

You can't just ask customers what they want and then try to give that to them. By the time you get it built, they'll want something new.[23]
—STEVE JOBS [1989]

LOOK FORWARD:
ANTICIPATE CUSTOMER NEEDS

In order to start and then run a business successfully, you need to understand customer needs and try to improve the value you give customers every day. So you get feedback on your existing products and services. You listen (we hope) to what your customers are saying. You look for their pain points and try to make them go away.

In order to develop a strategy for the future, you have to do all that and more. You have to look beyond what customers want today and figure out what they will want tomorrow. This is challenging because customers often don't know what they want before they see it. And the difficulty is even greater in the high-tech world because few laypeople understand the potential of emerging technologies. In this environment, surveys and focus groups are of little help. Instead, great strategists use their superior knowledge of technology trends to create products and services that satisfy needs and desires customers never knew they had. In the process, they both anticipate and shape customer preferences.

Bill Gates and Paul Allen looked forward in 1975 when they saw a new PC hobbyist kit for sale and anticipated the need this would create for programming language products and other software development tools. In subsequent years, however, Gates was generally a fast (and sometimes not so fast) follower: with operating systems, applications, servers, and Internet browsers, as well as other products and services, Microsoft's strategy was largely to wait until a mass market was about to emerge, copy the basic features of industry leaders, and then enter with "good enough" products that the company then improved incrementally.[24]

In contrast, Steve Jobs mastered the art of anticipating and shaping customer needs. As he told his biographer, "Some people say, 'Give the customers what they want.' But that's not my approach. Our job is to figure out what they're going to want before they do. I think Henry Ford once said, 'If I'd asked customers what they wanted, they would have told me, "A faster horse!" ' "[25] Jobs didn't waste time asking customers what they wanted. He saw himself as the prototypical customer and assumed that products that met his exacting standards would be embraced by the marketplace at large. As Fred Anderson recalled, Jobs "didn't believe in market research.

He believed that the consumer really didn't know what the next great thing was. . . . Steve took pride in his ability and vision to see the next great thing and pursue that with a passion."[26]

The development of the original Macintosh computer illustrates Jobs's approach. Before Apple created the Mac, most computers had a command-line interface: that is, they were controlled by typing in textual commands. In the early 1970s, Xerox's Palo Alto Research Center (PARC) created the first graphical user interface (GUI), which replaced arcane text commands with more intuitive icons, menus, and windows, but Xerox failed to commercialize its innovation. That role fell to Apple. After visiting Xerox PARC in late 1979, Jobs did not need to do any market research to conclude that he had seen the future of computing.

Jobs immediately focused Apple on the task of designing a mass-market computer with a graphical user interface. Throughout this often frenzied process, he personally determined the smallest details of the Macintosh, from the design of the mouse to the way text scrolled on the screen.[27] He based these design decisions not on customer feedback but on his own strongly held beliefs about the nature of good design. As Jobs later told Apple CEO John Sculley, he saw no alternative to this method: "How can I possibly ask somebody what a graphics-based computer ought to be when they have no idea what a graphics-based computer is? No one has ever seen one before."[28]

Jobs's decisions fundamentally shaped the way in which people think about how a personal computer should look and work. Similarly, while Apple did not invent the MP3 player, the smartphone, or the tablet, Jobs played a crucial role in defining—or, more often, redefining—how customers use these products. In the process, he served essentially as a "one-man focus group."[29] As Apple's many triumphs show, Jobs had a rare talent for anticipating customer wants and needs. But there was a downside to relying almost exclusively on one person's taste. As Anderson commented, "more times than not

[Jobs] was right, but there were some failures."[30] These ranged from the expensive Lisa, Apple's first GUI-based computer, to the weirdly shaped Macintosh Cube and Apple's first, disastrous cloud service, MobileMe. Steve Jobs was not infallible, and other CEOs should not necessarily try to replicate Jobs's approach. The best product ideas at Apple, as well as Microsoft and Intel, often emerged from internal debates and competitions, not marketing studies or one person's insights. Intense debates, used to explore and then refine a wide range of product ideas, followed by a clear decision, make it more likely the company will identify future customer needs—long before customers do so themselves.

Andy Grove was less idiosyncratic than Jobs in his approach to anticipating and shaping customer preferences, but he was equally committed to this task. The challenge he faced was similar to Apple's: technology was advancing faster than customers' perceived needs. Moore's Law meant that Intel could double the amount of processing capacity it delivered to customers every other year. This created an obvious problem: what do you do with that additional processing power? Personal computer users had no idea. In the 1980s, for example, many people were skeptical that anyone would ever need a chip more powerful than the Intel 80386, introduced in 1985. Even worse for Intel, many of its direct customers—the companies that made personal computers—actively resisted the company's efforts to add new capabilities to each generation of chips. Given limits on how much consumers would pay for a PC, as the value of the CPU increased, the value captured by the PC maker, such as Dell or Compaq, fell.

In order to get personal computer makers to buy its new, more expensive chips every 18 to 24 months, Intel had to convince consumers to buy the new, more expensive PCs built around those chips. And to persuade consumers to upgrade their PCs, Intel had to convince them that the new, more expensive machines offered them capabilities and functions that would improve their lives at work and at home. To solve this problem, Grove developed a catchy mantra: he demanded that Intel drive the "power spiral" and find "MIPS-sucking applications" that would take advantage of the increased power offered by each new chip. (MIPS are millions of instructions per second.)

Since Intel did not develop consumer software, this led to a *platform* and not just a *product* strategy, as we discuss in Chapter 3. Intel had to engage actively with many other firms to build those MIPS-sucking applications. In addition, company engineers started designing new functions into its chips, such as instructions that accelerated multimedia. These functions would support novel and exciting PC applications that customers didn't know they wanted—playing music, watching and editing videos, playing games, making telephone and video calls—but would soon find they couldn't live without. Intel played an active role in promoting these applications, although other companies sold them. In 1994, for example, Intel funded a large-scale advertising campaign that featured eight cutting-edge consumer and business software programs. This campaign was an important driver of demand for the Pentium, Intel's newest and most powerful chip.[31]

REASON BACK:
MATCH NEEDS WITH CAPABILITIES

The danger of looking forward is that the future is an alluring place, and it is easy to get lost in dreams of what could be. That may be fine for a futurist, but it can spell disaster for a strategist. In order to steer your company safely from the present to the future, and build a viable business, you must determine the steps that will transform today's vision into tomorrow's reality.

First, this means ensuring that your company has or can build the capabilities it requires to meet future customer needs. These capabilities can include talent, technology, facilities, partnerships—anything you need to bring planned products and services to market ahead of the competition. A company must sometimes make these investments many years in advance.

In the late 1980s, for example, Bill Gates began to invest in an operating system to replace Windows, which was then only a few years old. The original Windows was basically a graphical user interface built on top of DOS. Gates wanted the new version—eventually named Windows NT—to be robust enough to serve the more demanding needs of corporate users, as well as future consumers. To build a new OS from the ground up, he hired engineers with extensive experience at companies like DEC and AT&T. Microsoft shipped the first version of Windows NT, which targeted businesses, in 1993, but it took the company another eight years to replace the old code base and ship an operating system for the home market—Windows XP—based on the Windows NT code base.[32]

Matching capabilities to needs can also mean revamping the company's structure to bring it into alignment with the new strategy. As Ron Johnson recalled, around the same time that Apple started to work on tablets, senior executives were thinking how to reorganize the company to support the "digital hub" vision that Jobs began to articulate in 2000. "We need a software division. We need an apps division. We need device divisions," Johnson said, summing up the main threads of that discussion.[33] These conversations ultimately led to a new device group, which focused on the iPod, and a new software application division.[34]

But the process of reasoning back shouldn't stop at a company's borders. In order to succeed, strategists often must ensure that other firms' capabilities and objectives support their plans for meeting customer needs. This is especially true in platform industries or businesses with complex supply chains. Even the most visionary CEOs will stumble if they fail to recognize not just their companies' limitations, but those of their suppliers and ecosystem partners.

Andy Grove, for example, was absolutely convinced in the early 1990s, long before the days of Skype, that PC videoconferencing would be the next big thing. Hundreds of millions of dollars later, Intel's videoconferencing system, called ProShare, failed. Why? Because in the 1990s, videoconferencing required expensive hardware and a complicated, slow, and often unreliable ISDN (Integrated Services Digital Network) telephone line.[35] Pat Gelsinger, ProShare's project manager, explained, "Betting on ISDN was a fundamentally bad decision." And to make matters worse, even as it became clear that ProShare was not going to succeed, Grove's "passion to create a new application category" made it almost impossible for Gelsinger to say, "Andy, this isn't going to work."[36]

Apple faced a similar challenge early in the 2000s. According to Avie Tevanian, company engineers built iPad-like tablets as early as 2002 and 2003.[37] The tablets, he said, were fine: the processor, user interface, touch capabilities—everything worked. But company executives realized that, even so, they wouldn't satisfy customer needs. The problem, Tevanian noted, was the network: "WiFi was just starting, so I couldn't connect to anything. What good is it to have this device if I can't connect?"[38] Apple held off on releasing the iPad until the infrastructure capabilities were in place to deliver fully on its vision.

These examples suggest that CEOs and entrepreneurs must avoid becoming overly enamored with "rocket science"; otherwise, they risk getting too far out in front of customers and the industry at large. In order to avoid this scenario, master strategists must constantly link a tight focus on the near future with their longer-term vision. As Jon Rubinstein said of Jobs, he had a clear vision for Apple, but much of the time, "Steve was just focused on the next thing—which gave him some real advantages in that the world's a lot clearer when it's a year away than when it's three years away."[39] Similarly, Les Vadasz, a senior Intel executive and one of Andy Grove's closest friends, emphasized Grove's ability to tie the future back to the present (ProShare notwithstanding). Vadasz told us, "There are many managers who make that five-year plan and then around year three they start to think about the next five-year plan. Not Andy." Grove, he noted, understood a basic truth:

> You can only look so far, and so you better just keep looking frequently. That's the most important element of strategy: You understand the direction you're going, but you also know what you're going to do in the next six months. Most companies will do a pretty good job many times about the direction, but then they never break it down to shorter metrics. Intel did a super job on that. When you ask why [we] succeeded, this is one of the reasons.[40]

Grove, like Jobs, understood the importance of keeping two key ideas in mind at the same time—the future and the present. In order to succeed, company leaders must be able to track both simultaneously. It is not a question of either/or—either you look to the far horizon or you focus on the day-to-day. You must do both. If you focus exclusively on challenges over the next six months, you won't know where you are going; if you focus exclusively on the long term, you may never get there. If you tie the two tightly together with a series of frequently updated plans or ideas, you'll increase your odds of navigating successfully through the present and into the future.

> Microsoft has had clear competitors in the past. It's a good thing we have museums to document that.[41]
> —BILL GATES [2004]

LOOK FORWARD:
ANTICIPATE COMPETITORS' MOVES

When you look forward, anticipating customer needs is the fun part of the job, especially in industries where emerging technologies seem poised to change the world. It is easy to dream up a future where products are flying off the shelves, customers are lining up around the block, reviewers are raving, and your rivals are quietly sobbing into their drinks. But those dreams will quickly turn into nightmares if you fail to anticipate your competitors' moves. This was a lesson that Gates, Grove, and Jobs learned early and never forgot.

Perhaps Andy Grove's most famous phrase was "only the paranoid survive," the title of his bestselling 1996 management book. Grove begins the book with the following commentary:

> I'm often credited with the motto "Only the paranoid survive." I have no idea when I first said this, but the fact remains that, when it comes to business, I believe in the value of paranoia. Business success contains the seeds of its own destruction. The more successful you are, the more people want a chunk of your business and then another chunk and then another until there is nothing left. . . . I worry about competitors. I worry about other people figuring out how to do what we do better or cheaper, and displacing us with our customers.[42]

Every year as CEO, Grove held a two-to-three-day management meeting, called SLRP (Strategic Long-Range Planning, pronounced "slurp"), where he gave his paranoia free rein. In his words, Grove designed these meetings to answer a fundamental question: "What do I have to do *today* to solve—or better, avoid—*tomorrow's* problem?"[43] At each SLRP, Grove spoke for two hours or more on Intel's position vis-à-vis the competition. In 1991, for example, he characterized Intel as a castle besieged by competitors on all sides.[44] He went on

Competitors Attack the Intel "Castle"

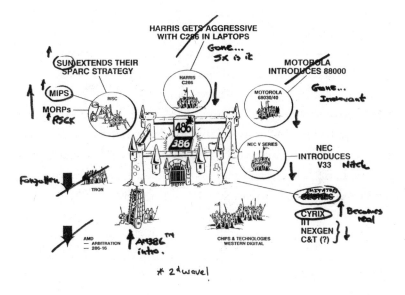

SOURCE: Andy Grove's SLRP presentation to Intel, 1991, reproduced with permission.

to describe where potential competitors were making inroads, where new entrants were offering new approaches, and what it meant for Intel at the time. Intel developed road maps for future products in parallel with this type of competitor analysis. When management saw potential holes in product lines, which a competitor like AMD or others might exploit, Grove would demand an acceleration of the road map or new products to fill those holes before the competition.

If there was any other CEO as paranoid as Grove, it was Steve Jobs. When it came to product plans, Jobs may have been the most secretive man on the planet. His reasoning was simple: competitors are imitators. Give them a glimpse of your product vision, and they won't simply copy it; they'll steal it. (As proof, this was exactly what Jobs did after first seeing the graphical user interface developed at

Xerox PARC in 1979.) Apple products were designed in "intense secrecy," as one of Jobs's biographers wrote about Apple's operating system OS X, in order to prevent competitors—notably Microsoft—from ripping them off.[45]

Bill Gates worried less about imitation than Jobs, but he was equally concerned about competition and what the future might hold. In the mid-1990s, he shared some of his fears with us: "We don't know what the business model looks like in the future—can content providers hold us up? With the information highway, maybe no one will make money because everything will become a commodity. I also worry that, as we branch out, we may be getting outside our circle of competence."[46] Out of the public eye, he regularly sent alarmist emails to his direct reports, warning that new competitors were challenging Microsoft's hegemony. For example, in 1996, Gates told his team that they needed to be more systematic in their analysis of Netscape. His email noted:

> One exercise that would be helpful to me is to take our plans and lay them out next to Netscape's current products and whatever we know about their future plans. We have most of this information but it isn't brought together into one place at a high level on paper. . . . I think we need to look hard at whether we are being creative.[47]

One year later, Gates turned his attention to a new prospective enemy: "The biggest threat is absolutely the JAVA phenomenon and the ISV [Independent Software Vendors] excitement that has grown up around that. We have to come in every day knowing that we have NOT solved this problem and in many ways we get weaker every day."[48]

At the time, Microsoft was one of world's most successful companies and Gates one of the world's richest men. Yet like Grove and Jobs, he never felt secure or became complacent. Even when at the top of their game, all three CEOs feared that competitors could destroy them practically overnight, if they were not sufficiently diligent. As a result, they cultivated the mind-set of an underdog even when the rest of the world saw them as industry giants. They forced their executive teams and, to a large extent, even the lowest-level employees, to constantly anticipate competitors' future moves.

REASON BACK:
BUILD BARRIERS TO ENTRY, LOCK IN CUSTOMERS

The purpose of thinking systematically about future competitor moves is to reason back to what your company should do today. Good strategists calculate their competitors' most likely actions and figure out how to counter those moves. A master strategist goes one step further and figures out how to change the nature of the game, typically by altering the other players' options and payoffs. Often these game-changing moves involve building barriers to entry or locking in customers before competitors have a chance to act. As explained by Bruce Henderson, the founder of the Boston Consulting Group and one of the earliest gurus of modern strategy, the goal is to "induce your competitors not to invest in those products, markets and services where you expect to invest the most. That is the fundamental rule of strategy."[49]

Intel took a classic, deep pockets approach to building barriers to entry. Under Andy Grove, the company developed a strong lead in silicon technology, advances in design, and a growing patent portfolio. By the early 1990s, Intel had also begun to build brand preference, but the competition kept on coming, in the form of both imitators, such as AMD, and alternative architectures, such as IBM's PowerPC chip. In 1993, Grove decided to get a jump on the competition by investing heavily in manufacturing capacity in advance of proven demand. He told his senior management team that it had cost $1 billion in capital to make the 486, but that he was prepared to invest $5

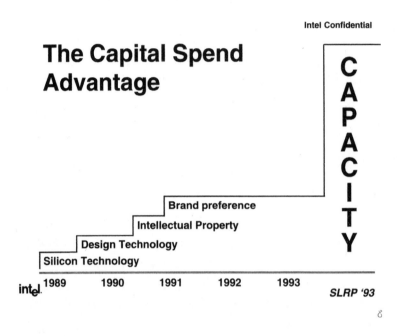

The Capital Spend Advantage

Intel Confidential

CAPACITY

Brand preference
Intellectual Property
Design Technology
Silicon Technology

intel. 1989   1990   1991   1992   1993

SLRP '93

SOURCE: Andy Grove's SLRP presentation to Intel, 1993, re-created with permission.

billion in plants to manufacture its successor, the Pentium. The impact of this decision on the competitive landscape was profound. In the early 1990s, the "entry fee to be a major player in the global semiconductor market" was already "$1B—payable in advance," in Gordon Moore's words.[50] Intel's commitment to massive capacity investments caused this entry fee to grow dramatically over time, and, as it did, the number of potential competitors shrank. Grove's decision to bet on capital expansion—two or more years ahead of demand—raised a hurdle that other firms found increasingly difficult to clear.

Bill Gates similarly focused on building barriers to entry from day one. In negotiating Microsoft's original contract to provide DOS to IBM, he fought hard to keep control of the right to license the OS to other companies. In return for this right, he was willing to give IBM a sweetheart deal—a low fixed fee, with no ongoing royalty charges. His goal, Gates later explained in 1994, was to control access to DOS, build volume, and keep prices low, thereby making life very difficult for potential competitors:

> Our restricting IBM's ability to compete with us in licensing MS-DOS to other computer makers was the key point of our negotiations. We wanted to make sure only we could license it. . . . We knew that good IBM products were usually cloned, so it didn't take a rocket scientist to figure out that eventually we could license DOS to others. . . . Subsequently . . . there were people coming out with completely new operating systems, but we [had] already captured the volume, so we could price it low and keep selling.[51]

Using pricing to lock in customers was a tactic to which Gates returned time and time again. When licensing DOS and Windows to computer makers, he gave customers a choice: pay a high price per operating system installed or pay a much lower royalty to Microsoft based on the number of computers shipped—ostensibly because tracking software installations was too hard. Virtually everyone opted for pricing based on hardware shipped, which forced computer makers to pay twice if they wanted to ship a competitor's operating system—once for DOS/Windows and once for the OS that was actually installed, such as IBM's OS/2, Novell's DR DOS, or some flavor of UNIX. The U.S. Department of Justice banned this practice in 1994, precisely because it locked in Microsoft's dominant position.[52]

Strategic pricing also helped Microsoft win and keep customers in the desktop productivity market, where it was a late entrant. Throughout the 1980s, Microsoft Word and Excel lagged far behind market leaders like Lotus 1-2-3 and WordPerfect. To catch up, in 1990, Microsoft bundled Word, Excel, and PowerPoint as the Office suite and offered it at a large discount. (Other products such as Outlook and Access were later added to the suite.) Sales of applications exploded, from $567 million in 1990 to almost $4 billion in 1995.

A simple example demonstrates the power of bundling. Imagine a world with two users: a reporter and a financial analyst. The reporter is willing to pay top dollar—let's say $100—for a great word processing program but will pay only $20 for a spreadsheet, which he uses far less often. The financial analyst, on the other hand, wants a great spreadsheet, for which she will pay $100, but will pay only $30 for a word processor. If you are Lotus, and you dominate the spreadsheet business, your best pricing strategy is to charge $100 and get the financial analyst; and if you are WordPerfect, and you dominate the word processing sector, your optimal price is also $100. This strategy works beautifully until Microsoft combines a comparable word processor and spreadsheet into a single product for $120. This is a much better deal for both potential customers than buying two separate products from the competition.[53] Since the marginal cost of software is close to zero, it is also a profit-maximizing strategy. Microsoft employed this approach repeatedly over the years, often going so far as to bundle key applications—such as Internet Explorer with Windows—at no additional cost.

Unlike Microsoft, Apple did not rely heavily on pricing as a game-changing tool. Apple products typically commanded a premium, and discounts were few. However, Jobs was no less focused than Gates on building barriers to entry and imitation. Throughout Apple's history, he was known for filing broad patents, frequently including his own name, and suing anyone he suspected of copying the company's product designs, including partners (such as Microsoft), suppliers (such as Samsung), and even customers.

More important, Jobs's focus on providing consumers with a tightly integrated, user-friendly experience tended to lock them in for years. His strategy for music was a case in point. By Jobs's own admission, he was slow to wake up to the significance of digital music, but he more than made up for his tardiness once he decided to enter the game. In January 2001, Apple launched iTunes, which gave Mac users the ability to copy music from their CDs, arrange it into playlists, and burn CDs. Nine months later, Apple released the iPod, which dominated the portable music player market for a decade.[54] Part of Apple's success was due to superior product design. By most accounts, iTunes was a superior music-management software platform and the iPod a better digital music player than alternatives on the market. But it was the tight integration of Apple's products that largely accounted for the persistence of the iPod's market share.

With the launch of the iTunes Music Store in 2003, Apple adopted a proprietary technology for music downloads. Since Jobs refused to license Apple's encoding and copy-protection technology to other music vendors or device makers, music downloaded via iTunes would only play on an iPod, and an iPod could only play generic MP3 recordings or iTunes tracks. Apple users who switched from the iPod to another device would lose access to their music libraries. So, the more music they downloaded through iTunes, the less likely they were to leave the Apple universe for another platform—a clear example of a simple "network effect," as we discuss in Chapter 3. Until Apple abandoned this system in 2009, customers were locked in, thereby creating a huge barrier to entry for potential rivals.

When a change in how some element of one's business is conducted becomes an order of magnitude larger than what that business is accustomed to, then all bets are off. There's wind, then there's a typhoon, there are waves and then a tsunami. A 10X change.[55]

—Andy Grove [1996]

LOOK FORWARD:
ANTICIPATE STRATEGIC INFLECTION POINTS

One of the toughest problems facing any strategist is identifying and preparing for shifts that could fundamentally alter your industry's structure—what Grove called a "10X" change. These 10X changes are both the biggest opportunities and the biggest threats any business can face. In some industries, they come every 20, 30, or even 100 years; in others, they can happen every five or ten years. Since 2007, for example, the smartphone and the tablet have launched typhoon-force winds through the communications and computer industries. Going back further, the Apple II and then the Macintosh had a similar impact on the personal computer industry, which then underwent another fundamental transformation as horizontally focused competitors like Microsoft and Intel replaced vertically integrated monoliths. The failure to anticipate or adapt quickly to this 10X change meant death for Digital Equipment Corporation and all of the minicomputer companies and a greatly diminished presence in the PC industry for both IBM and Apple, the latter of which languished with a tiny share of the PC market before remaking itself as a blockbuster consumer electronics company. In contrast, Microsoft and Intel turned this seismic shift into an opportunity to build two of the greatest franchises in business history.

Whether we call these 10X changes "disruptive innovations," to use the terminology of Clay Christensen, or "strategic inflection points," in Andy Grove's words, the master strategist's role is to identify and then devise strategies to handle these transformative periods. Recognizing a 10X change after the fact can be the kiss of death; recognizing it in time is a matter of awareness, timing, and preparation. As Grove notes in *Only the Paranoid Survive*, you have to act "when not everything is known, when the data aren't yet in. Even those who believe in a scientific approach to management will have to rely on instinct and personal judgment."[56] Making such judgments is extremely difficult. At these moments, the noise-to-signal ratio is very high. In the end, the master strategist must rely on judgment and intuition, fed by experience.

Jobs, as we discussed earlier in this chapter, drove four 10X changes in his tenure: the graphical user interface in PCs; the iPod and iTunes revolution in digital music; the iPhone and App Store revolution in smartphones; and the iPad revolution in tablet computing. Grove and Gates shared at least two 10X changes during their CEO tenures. The first was the emergence of the horizontal PC industry. The second was the rise of the Internet as a consumer phenomenon. In 1994, Grove's technical assistant, Sean Maloney, sat him down at a computer terminal and introduced him to the Internet. Grove later told his board of directors that he didn't really understand it, but somehow he knew it was important. As he prepared to move Intel into an Internet-centric rather than a PC-centric world, he organized a two-hour tutorial for the Intel board, where all the directors sat at computers with tech-savvy Intel managers at their sides. He wanted his board to understand that this was an inflection point, which demanded a shift in strategy.

As Grove thought more about the Internet, he came to realize that the merging of communications and computing created both opportunities and threats for Intel. In the mid-1990s, he began to give speeches proclaiming Intel was providing "free" MIPS—by which he meant extremely low-cost computing—and in the very near future, the communications industry would provide "free" bauds—by which he meant extremely low-cost data transmission. In combination, these two developments could drive an explosion in demand for computing power as exciting new applications emerged.

Yet the Internet also threatened to commoditize the PC and, by association, Intel's bread and butter—the x86 line of microprocessors. In the mid-1990s, there was much talk of PCs being replaced by "thin clients" or "Internet appliances"—stripped-down computers—connected to the Web. When industry leaders, such as Oracle's CEO

Larry Ellison, began to preach the gospel of the "network computer" and Intel competitor AMD started aggressively cutting prices, senior executives at Intel feared that prices for PCs and CPUs would collapse. In the spring of 1997, Grove told his team that this phenomenon, which he termed "gravity," was the biggest threat Intel faced. Management, he chided, is "not taking this seriously."[57] Fortunately, however, Grove had a plan for countering gravity, as we discuss in Chapter 4.

Like Grove, Gates saw the Internet as a source of tremendous opportunity as well as potent threats. In early 1995, he made the Internet the focus of his annual "Think Week"—a hiatus of several days when he took time off from Microsoft to read books and research coming out of universities and bring himself up to date on trends in technology. The output from that week was a May 1995 memo titled "The Internet Tidal Wave," which he sent to his executive staff and direct reports. In this document, Gates made it clear that the growth of the Internet was leading to a strategic inflection point and that Microsoft desperately needed to get out in front of this new parade.

> Developments on the Internet over the next several years will set the course of our industry for a long time to come. . . . I want to make clear that our focus on the Internet is critical to every part of our business. The Internet is the most important single development to come along since the IBM PC was introduced in 1981. It is even more important than the arrival of the graphical user interface (GUI). . . . Our products will not be the only things changing. The way we distribute information and software as well as the way we communicate with and support our customers will be changing.[58]

Gates realized that consumers might no longer need an expensive, complex program like Microsoft Windows to run their computers if they could access applications through a Web browser instead of storing and running them on their PCs. But if Microsoft could control the browser and integrate the Internet into Windows and

Office, he could neutralize this threat and Microsoft could extend its dominance from the desktop to the Internet.

Gates and Grove were particularly adept at recognizing strategic inflection points, in part because of their deep paranoia that their businesses were always at risk. They coupled their relentless focus on the future with a mastery of history. They were keenly aware that the vast majority of technology firms over the prior thirty years had died unceremonious deaths. Firms ranging from DEC to Wang had disappeared because of their inability to adapt to 10X changes, such as the emergence of the personal computer. As a result, Gates and Grove rarely discounted industry challenges, and they always created time in their hectic schedules to study, probe, and explore how they might respond to each new threat.

> You can't judge the significance of strategic inflection points by the quality of the first version. You need to draw on your experience . . . you must discipline yourself to think things through and separate the quality of the early versions from the longer-term potential and significance of a new product or technology.[59]
> —ANDY GROVE [1996]

REASON BACK:
COMMIT TO CHANGE—AND STAY THE COURSE

Recognizing strategic inflection points is essential for long-term success, but it's just the first step. You then have to develop a response—

and do so quickly. When you believe an inflection point is on the horizon, you have to commit to change *today*. The "same old" strategy will no longer work. This task can be particularly challenging because inflection points, by their nature, involve great uncertainty. You essentially have to act now to head off future threats or seize future opportunities that others may not see.

Given the magnitude of the change involved, your company's first steps down a new path may be wobbly and uncertain. Early versions of new products and services may not be up to snuff. Critics will pounce, and even supporters may wonder if you know what you're doing. But if you have faith in your vision, you need to hang tough and avoid getting knocked off course by bumps along the way.

Bill Gates's leadership of Microsoft exemplified this approach. The first versions of Microsoft products tended to have few fans but, once Gates decided something was a strategic priority, he didn't let poor reviews or low sales change his mind. For example, there were few takers for Windows 1.0 when it launched in 1985, and Windows 2.0 in 1987 fared only marginally better. But Gates understood that Microsoft would soon be history if it failed to produce an operating system with a good graphical user interface. He continued to invest heavily in improving Windows, and in 1990, with version 3.0, Microsoft finally got it right.

Gates showed the same persistence when he decided to push Microsoft into the market for server software in the late 1980s. He realized that, as people increasingly used their computers to access data and applications stored on remote servers, those machines were going to become an ever-larger part of the computing landscape. If servers ultimately became more important than PCs, other firms could eclipse Microsoft's preeminence as the software platform leader. The server edition of Windows NT was his answer to this threat.

Russ Siegelman, who worked directly for Gates, recalled, "When I first got there, we weren't in the server business . . . [but Bill] had this notion, 'Look, we're gonna have to win in the networking business by being an application server company.' "[60] And he was willing to invest heavily to bring this strategy to fruition: "Bill was definitely willing to make big financial commitments, like building Windows NT. . . . [No matter] how long it took, how much money it took, how many people, his best people, we were going to make NT successful." And ultimately it was. In 2014, Windows NT ran around 65 percent of corporate servers.

Similarly, when Gates saw the Internet Tidal Wave heading toward his company—and with it, the threat that the ability to build applications accessible through Web browsers could make Windows almost irrelevant—he committed massive resources to building a Web browser. Internet Explorer 1.0 and 2.0, both launched in 1995, were widely reviewed as inferior to Netscape's Navigator. When IE 3.0 shipped in 1996, however, Microsoft finally had a superior browser, and the improved IE 4.0, introduced in 1997, sealed Netscape's fate.[61] Looking back, Jon Shirley, Microsoft's first president and chief operating officer, argued that Gates's long-term vision was Microsoft's real advantage: "It is not cash, because others have it." Instead, it was "Bill's willingness to stick with technologies for a long time, no matter what the short-run return," that separated Microsoft from the crowd.[62]

Steve Jobs was just as committed to getting it right. In 2008, for example, Apple launched MobileMe, the company's first attempt to deliver cloud computing. By then, Jobs's original vision of the PC as a digital hub had evolved, with the "cloud" becoming the hub and the PC just another device. MobileMe was supposed to bring this vision to life by allowing users to store their content—pictures, videos, an address book, or calendar—on a company's servers and access it from any device. However, MobileMe was expensive and did not work well. Walter Mossberg, the veteran technology columnist, concluded, "If Apple does get MobileMe working smoothly, it could be a terrific service. But it's way too ragged now."[63] Jobs was furious about MobileMe's failure and replaced much of the team that worked on the service, including the project leader. But he remained committed to his vision of the cloud as a digital hub and worked for three more years to get it right with iCloud in 2011.

It can be difficult to stay the course when a strategic inflection point is in the offing and you've chosen a new path. The stakes are unusually large at such moments in a company's history, and risk is everywhere. But precisely because the stakes are so high, you can't wait for the uncertainty to resolve or for the engineering team to design the "perfect" product. Once the fog lifts and the future is clear enough for all to see, it will be too late to act. If you want to lead change and are convinced that your direction is right, you have to act now by committing to a vision and staying committed to improving new products or services incrementally in order to make that vision work.

LESSONS FROM THE MASTERS

Every day, there is a new fire to put out. The demands of current customers and employees can consume all of your time. To be a great strategist, however, you need to step back from the burdens of today and the constraints of yesterday, and set aside time to *look forward* to the future of your company, your customers, your competition, and your industry. Then you need to *reason back* to the actions you need to take today. CEOs and other senior executives should repeat this exercise periodically—at least every six months in the fast-changing tech world. This process requires you to walk a fine line—making sure not to look too far ahead or to fall too far behind. It is a difficult balance, but one that Gates, Grove, and Jobs achieved most, although not all, of the time.

Our three CEOs developed distinctive visions that set boundaries and priorities for their firms. They all had the imagination to anticipate customer needs, as well as the discipline and flexibility to revise their ideas as new and better information emerged. They also sought to match customer needs with the capabilities required to satisfy them, although this proved at times to be a particularly difficult task.

Gates, Grove, and Jobs were especially astute at anticipating competitors' moves and then heading them off. Their collective track record makes it clear that paranoia pays off. If you are not careful, competitors will copy or steal your ideas. If you don't build barriers to entry and lock in relationships with customers and partners, competitors can take away those early advantages in the blink of an eye. Therefore, master strategists practice constant vigilance to avoid following in the footsteps of onetime greats such as IBM, DEC, or Netscape.

Finally, Gates, Grove, and Jobs excelled at identifying major inflection points in their industries and then formulating responses that turned potential threats into opportunities. They were not always the first to see every shift, but they were usually early enough to respond effectively. Equally important, they had the fortitude to stay the course, despite initially weak products and other disappointments along the way. A 10X change in the environment may require an equally large change in your strategy and capabilities. With change of this magnitude, you won't necessarily get the strategy and the products exactly right the first time. When an ordinary product fails, it may make sense to scrap it. If the first shot in your campaign to reshape the future falls short, you may have to double down. The challenge is to know the difference between doubling down on a sound strategy or direction and recklessly betting your company's future—the strategy rule we tackle in the next chapter.

CHAPTER 2

Make Big Bets,
Without Betting the Company

Strategy is not for the faint of heart. Great strategists do the non-obvious, the difficult, and the counterintuitive in order to alter the competitive landscape in their favor. Often this means making big bets, whether in the form of huge financial commitments or competitive gambits, such as an all-out attack on the leaders in the field. The scale of these gambles may intimidate colleagues and partners as well as the competition. When executed skillfully, however, they deliver suitably outsized rewards.

In the early 1980s, when Bill Gates decided to develop Windows and compete head-to-head with IBM, he put his young company up against the powerhouse that had virtually invented the world's computer industry. Gates won his bet, and Microsoft went on to become the most powerful software company in the world. When Andy Grove decided in 1985 that Intel would change its licensing policies and become the "sole source" for its next-generation micro-processor, he rewrote the industry's rules and, not incidentally, committed to billions of dollars in capital spending. The gamble paid off, transforming Intel from a small, entrepreneurial firm into the giant of its field. In 2005, Steve Jobs risked the future of the Macintosh franchise when he decided to replace the Mac's PowerPC chip with Intel technology, but the success of this gambit gave the Mac and ultimately Apple a new lease on life.

These examples demonstrate that great strategists need to be willing to make courageous bets, but without putting their companies at risk of collapse. Gates postponed the break with IBM until Microsoft's other lines of business were strong enough to keep the company afloat. Grove reduced the riskiness of his biggest bet by phasing in capital investment over time. And Jobs astutely timed his bet to lessen the company's exposure to risk.

The common theme is to be bold, but not reckless. Merriam-Webster defines *bold* as "fearless before danger: intrepid; showing or requiring a fearless daring spirit."[1] Too many firms get derailed by meek strategists who are unable or unwilling to make hard choices. Great leaders, in contrast, are prepared to make bold decisions in order to launch, reinvigorate, or reinvent their businesses. In the case of Gates, Grove, and Jobs, these decisions reflected four principles, which helped drive their success:

RULE 2: MAKE BIG BETS, WITHOUT BETTING THE COMPANY

1. Bet big to change the game.
2. Don't bet the company.
3. Cannibalize your own business.
4. Cut your losses.

We learned that high market share was critical for success, and that to get market share we had to be willing to invest in manufacturing capacity. Such investments involve big bets because they have to be made in advance of actual demand.[2]

—ANDY GROVE [EARLY 1990S]

BET BIG TO CHANGE THE GAME

Making big bets is one of the toughest jobs in strategy. The natural instinct of many managers and entrepreneurs is to plan, analyze, plan some more, and then move incrementally down the chosen path. Lesser strategists often hedge, delay, defer, and refuse to commit. Others take reckless positions that promise great rewards if successful, but risk bankrupting the organization over time. Great strategists must avoid both traps. They must be willing to "go for the big win" and have the courage and conviction to follow through on their plans.

Bet Big on New Technologies

Of the three CEOs, Steve Jobs was temperamentally most open to big bets. Some of his moves seemed almost quixotic at the outset. Typically, though, Jobs prevailed in the end through a combination of "pure staying power, persistence, continually believing in something, dogged stubbornness to get things done, and continual optimism," as one former staffer said.[3] An early example was Jobs's decision to abandon his most successful product, the Apple II, once he discovered the graphical user interface (GUI) in December 1979. As soon as he saw it, Jobs said, he knew immediately that the GUI was the key to making computers easy to use and truly accessible to the mass market. As Xerox PARC engineers demonstrated their technology, Jobs exclaimed, "Why aren't you doing anything with this? This is the greatest thing! This is revolutionary!"[4] He later said, "It was like a veil being lifted from my eyes. I could see what the future of computing was destined to be."[5]

Jobs went back to Apple and pushed the company to bet on the GUI as the future of personal computing. He initially seized on the Lisa, then in the early stages of development, as the computer that would bring the GUI revolution to the world. Apple had originally designed the Lisa with a traditional text-based, command-line interface, but Jobs quickly decided it should have a graphical user interface and a mouse. He reportedly said, "We'll make [the Lisa] so important that it will make a dent in the universe."[6] If anything, the Lisa, which cost an estimated $50 million to develop, put a dent in Apple's finances. Launched in 1983 at a price of $9,995, it failed to find a market and was discontinued two years later. But by then, Jobs was no longer associated with the Lisa. After getting kicked off the project, he had joined the team building the Macintosh, which debuted in 1984. Despite a rocky start, the Macintosh ultimately turned Jobs's dream of revolutionizing computing into reality. For neither the first nor the last time, Jobs had bet big and won.

When Jobs left Apple in 1985, he spent the next decade wagering his personal fortune on NeXT, a computer workstation company that never developed significant sales, and Pixar, which ultimately became wildly successful. These experiences did little to diminish Jobs's appetite for risk. After returning to Apple in 1997, he made another big bet on the Macintosh when he agreed to switch to Intel chips.

By the late 1990s, Apple had been struggling for several years. Failed product launches, inconsistent pricing strategies, and internal turmoil had all taken a toll. In the early to mid-1990s, Apple had three CEOs in four years and shed 9 percent of its workforce over the same period. From 1992 to 1996, the company's market value plunged by nearly 50 percent, and 1996 operating losses totaled nearly $1.4 billion. Most disturbing, Apple's share of the U.S. personal computer market fell from nearly 14 percent in 1993 to just over 6 percent in 1996.[7] Apple's premium pricing and struggles to maintain inventory helped account for the decline. But more important, the Macintosh was running out of steam. Apple computers were becoming less and less competitive with "Wintel" machines— PCs running Microsoft Windows and using Intel microprocessors.[8] The Mac's operating system was aging, and its microprocessor— IBM's PowerPC—could not match Intel's chips when it came to raw performance or, in the case of laptops, battery life.

Jobs's strategy to reboot the Mac by building the next-generation Macintosh around an Intel microprocessor was a huge bet. The PowerPC's weaknesses had been apparent for some time. Intel chips would improve the Macintosh's performance and, maybe equally important to some users, allow them to run both Windows and Mac software on their Apple machines. But adopting a new microprocessor was not a simple matter of swapping out one chip for another. Not only did Apple have to rewrite its operating system to run on Intel chips—a process that Jobs secretly began soon after returning to Apple, with the first version of OS X— but Macintosh developers, including those working at Apple, also had to rewrite their applications software to take advantage of the performance offered by the new processor. Together, the cost of redesigning both hardware and software could cost Apple close to $1 billion at a time when the company's total spending on research and development was under $500 million and profits were only $276 million.[9]

Apple had already negotiated one such transition successfully, switching from the Motorola 68000 series microprocessors to the

PowerPC chip in 1994–95. But switching architectures was a risky business. Even if the technological transition went smoothly, Apple could suffer a short-term hit to sales as potential buyers, not wanting to buy an obsolete Mac, delayed purchases until the new Intel-powered computers became available. (After Jobs announced the switch in June 2005, a *Macworld* survey found that the announcement made one-third of potential purchasers less likely to buy a Mac in the next twelve months.)[10] And in the longer run, Apple faced the danger that customers would jump ship to a new platform altogether, once they realized that their old software would need to be replaced.[11] As one analyst warned, "I don't know that Apple's market share can survive another architecture shift. Every time they do this, they lose more customers [and developers]."[12]

Jobs fully appreciated these risks, but he also understood that Apple had fallen woefully behind its Wintel competitors in technology and market share. To have any chance of success, Apple had to break with its existing platform and try to leap ahead. The situation justified what CFO Fred Anderson called a "burn the boats" strategy. Once Apple had decided to switch to Intel, "there was no turning back," he recalled.[13] Jobs's approach probably cost Apple executives more than a little heartburn, but, once again, his willingness to bet big paid off. Introduced in 2006, the Intel-based MacBook laptop turned out to be the best-selling Macintosh in the company's history.[14] Overall, the Macintosh doubled its market share over the next five years.[15]

Sometimes Jobs was almost cavalier in his approach to risk. His decision to enter retail distribution was a case in point. Retail was "beyond his skill base," noted Ron Johnson, who was in charge of launching Apple Stores. Yet Jobs's lack of retail expertise had no impact on his determination to bet on stand-alone Apple stores. According to Johnson, Jobs maintained, "If you believe in something as the right thing to do, you've got to go make it work. You don't test. Testing is for people that don't have conviction."[16] And conviction was one thing Jobs never lacked. According to Jon Rubinstein, head of hardware engineering at NeXT and then Apple, "Steve would take risks that I wouldn't take . . . the guy had balls—he didn't always decide the right thing, but he made decisions."[17]

If Apple's first stores had failed, the financial impact would have been small, but the public relations fallout would have been substantial. And the precedents were not encouraging. At the time, Gateway Computer's Country Stores were failing miserably. Yet Jobs forged ahead with his retail plans. The first Apple retail store opened in Tysons Corner, Virginia, in 2001. At the time, many analysts predicted the stores would fail, but, ten years later, they had higher sales per square foot than any other retail business in the United States. Once again, Jobs's bet had paid off.

Bet Big on Market Leadership

Like Jobs, Bill Gates made a series of big bets throughout his tenure as CEO of Microsoft. These included early decisions to provide an operating system for the IBM PC, even though the company had previously focused on programming languages; produce applications for the Macintosh, when most of the industry thought it was a toy; maintain a decade-long commitment to build Windows, despite opposition from IBM; force his applications group, "against their will," to write for Windows before anyone knew if Windows would succeed; and then drive the Internet into every corner of Microsoft's business after 1995.[18]

However, Gates's biggest bet may have been his 1990 decision to end the partnership with IBM that had given Microsoft its big break. Since the 1981 launch of IBM's PC, Microsoft and IBM had worked closely together to expand the personal computer market and move PC technology forward. In 1985, they signed a joint development agreement to create a next-generation operating system, released two years later as OS/2. Gates felt so wedded to IBM that he proposed that the giant computer company buy 30 percent of Microsoft in 1986.[19] "It was a real turning point when IBM said no," Gates later commented. "We thought, "Hmmm, I wonder why they're saying no?'"[20] Nonetheless, the two companies remained partners, releasing a graphical user interface for OS/2 in 1988 and touting it as the PC software "platform of the future."

Throughout this period, Gates's biggest fear remained a breakdown in Microsoft's relationship with IBM. According to Paul Maritz, the head of the operating system group at the time, "we used to go to executive retreats and list what were the nightmare scenarios, and always the number one was divorce from IBM."[21] As Russ Siegelman, later head of Microsoft Network (MSN), explained, "Microsoft's early success was so predicated on IBM and the relationships and dependence were so deep, there was a fear that a break would make IBM want to kill Microsoft."[22] He added, "IBM had its hooks into every large company, and they could have gone all out to wage war if they had wanted to."[23] For Microsoft, this was a frightening prospect. IBM had been the eight-hundred-pound gorilla of the computer industry for more than three decades. It had set the standards for every generation of computing, from mainframes to minicomputers to personal computers. In 1990, IBM had $69 billion in revenue and $6 billion in profits. Microsoft was a minnow by contrast, with $1 billion in revenue and less than $300 million in profits.

However, Microsoft was slowly developing the assets that would allow it to survive a split. Working independently of IBM, Microsoft released its first version of Windows, which layered a graphical user interface onto DOS, in 1985. Microsoft also became a leading developer of application software for the Macintosh. Initially, Gates proceeded cautiously with these ventures, fearing a backlash from IBM. But the situation changed in the spring of 1990, when Microsoft released Windows 3.0, the first version of Windows to win widespread praise. By the end of the year, Microsoft had sold

2 million copies of Windows 3.0, and third-party developers had written hundreds of applications for the new OS. Based on this success, Gates and his team decided to quit hedging, focus on Windows, and abandon OS/2. Gates and Steve Ballmer still publicly supported OS/2 as late as January 1991.[24] And behind the scenes, Gates tried to negotiate a deal with IBM that would extend their partnership. But IBM demanded the same terms for Windows that it had received for DOS—a perpetual low-cost, royalty-free license. Faced with this demand, "Gates said 'no,'" Maritz recalled. "Gates was willing to risk the number one nightmare scenario of the company and put his full force behind Windows."[25]

The collaboration between the two companies, never smooth, came apart over the next two years and ended formally in June 1992, with IBM taking over all responsibility for OS/2. The divorce Microsoft had long feared had finally happened but without the dreaded results. Windows 3.0 established Microsoft's dominance on the desktop, a position cemented with the release of Windows 3.1 in 1992 and then Windows 95 in 1995. For almost two decades, Windows retained more than 90 percent of the PC operating systems market and generated roughly half of Microsoft's profits. While IBM aggressively pushed OS/2 in the early 1990s, the company's new CEO, Lou Gerstner, eventually decided to steer the company away from PCs. OS/2 gained only a niche audience, and IBM stopped selling it in 2005.

Bet Big on Changing Industry Structure

Taking on the industry leader was no small matter, but Andy Grove's biggest bet may have been even more audacious than Bill Gates's challenge to IBM. In the mid-1980s, he bet that Intel could force a change in the structure of the semiconductor industry and drive change in the PC sector as well. Until then, every computer and electronics company had insisted on having multiple suppliers for key components in order to ensure both price competition and reliable supply. This meant that semiconductor companies had to license their designs to competing firms. As former Intel CEO Gordon Moore explained, "we had to have multiple sources in CPUs to get wins, so we [worked with] Advanced Micro Devices, Fujitsu, Siemens, and others."[26] Intel licensed a dozen companies to produce the 8088 microprocessor, which powered the original IBM PC; as a result, it collected only 30 percent of the revenue generated by microprocessors based on its own design. For the next generation, the 80286, introduced in 1982, Intel cut the number of licensees to four. Even though AMD was the only licensee to produce in volume, Intel still had to share a significant portion of the revenues and profits with its competitors. "We were losing lots of profits while getting nothing in return," Moore complained.[27]

Intel's licensees, in contrast, were getting a good deal. According to then–general counsel Tom Dunlap, in exchange for a license, Intel required a company to provide a combination of "some tangible value (e.g., money and/or products) and the intangible value of becoming a second source."[28] Management believed that the intangible value of being a second source was a significant part of the compensation for the first generation of microprocessors for the IBM PC because every customer wanted a second source, which meant that the second sources greatly expanded the total market. Therefore, licensees were required to provide Intel with relatively little in the way of tangible value. Once the platform architecture was established, however, the value of a second source for the 80186 and 80286 dramatically declined.

When it came time to launch production of the 80386, which Intel spent four years and $200 million to develop, the executive staff hotly debated whether a second source was required. Ultimately, Grove decided, according to Dunlap, that a second source was "of minimal intangible value and that Intel would require full tangible value before it would license the 386."[29] In other words, licensees would have to pay much higher royalties than in the past. Not surprisingly, possible licensees rejected the new terms. As Grove later wrote, "Our competitors were reluctant to pay for technology that we used to give away practically for free."[30]

So Grove and his management team decided that it was time to go it alone. Rather than go back to AMD, "we told IBM that we won't second-source with AMD," Moore explained. "Instead, we'll build another plant in New Mexico. We thought we'd just do it ourselves, even if we don't meet market demand. This was the first time that we were the sole producers of CPUs."[31] But IBM wasn't interested in the 386, raising serious concerns about overall demand. According to Grove, in 1985 "the 386 was a year away from volume production and IBM had already positioned it as a niche product and were committed to buy only 7,000 the next year."[32] Moreover, IBM had internal plans to develop its own microprocessor. In an interview a few years later, a senior IBM executive confided that his firm was hoping to use its own CPU (later called the PowerPC) to eliminate Intel from the equation.[33]

Nonetheless, Intel pushed ahead. Since IBM wasn't buying, it turned to Compaq Computer, a leading maker of IBM PC clones, to showcase the 80386 in a new line of personal computers. At the time, moving forward without IBM was a bold—some might say foolhardy—decision. Without the support of market leader IBM, demand for the new chip was difficult to predict, and Intel had to invest in production ahead of proven demand. Reflecting back, Grove commented that if the 386 had failed, "Intel would have been less capable of shaping the industry."[34] Grove's dream of a horizontal industry structure might never have materialized, at least not with Intel playing a leading role. In addition, unutilized capacity would have triggered a huge hit to profits. Many executives would have found it tempting to stick to the safe strategies of the past but, as Frank Gill, who ran Intel sales at that time, commented, "Andy [Grove] had the courage of a lion."[35]

That courage paid off. Compaq's DeskPro 386, which debuted in 1986 and showcased the new 386 chip, was the first PC designed by a company other than IBM that moved the platform forward technologically. IBM gave in and brought out its own 386-based PC seven months later, but, by then, Compaq had already seized market leadership. After an extended legal battle, AMD ultimately released a clone of the 386 chip in 1991. In the meantime, Intel reaped the financial benefits of more than five years as the sole supplier of the market-leading microprocessor.

Despite an initially slow ramp for Intel's 80386, the bet on a sole-source strategy was a defining decision for Grove and Intel. When Grove reflected on this move many years later, he identified it as a key inflection point in Intel's history. Grove had struggled for years to figure out how to escape a miserable industry structure: "We decided a dozen [second sources for the 8086] was too many, and four [with the 286] didn't work. We tried high royalties and the other companies laughed us out of the business, thinking that we were going to collapse." In the end, Intel settled on a sole-source strategy largely in response to a series of opportunities and tactical interactions, rather than as the result of a high-level plan. Nonetheless, on reflection, Grove called the decision "monumental."[36]

Grove later mused, "There is at least one point in the history of any company when you have to change dramatically to rise to the next level of performance. Miss that moment and you start to decline."[37] The bet to sole-source the 386 was the moment for Grove and Intel. For Gates and Microsoft, it was the decision to push forward with Windows and break with IBM over OS/2. For Jobs and Apple, it was a series of moves to create the Macintosh and keep it alive through successive architectural evolutions (the Motorola 68000 to the PowerPC and then to an Intel microprocessor) until the company could break out of the personal computer industry and refocus on consumer electronics.

■

> Dylan and Picasso were always risking failure. This Apple
> thing is that way for me. I don't want to fail, of course. . . .
> If I try my best and fail, well, I've tried my best.[38]
> —STEVE JOBS [1998]

DON'T BET THE COMPANY

Big bets are probably the most important strategic moves any CEO
or entrepreneur can make. But not every big bet is a winner. Even
the best strategists make mistakes. The future almost never turns
out exactly as you expect. So when making a big bet, you need to
keep the potential downside within an acceptable range. Gates,
Grove, and Jobs (during his second stint at Apple) all accepted risk
on a scale that many CEOs would have been unable to stomach, but
without betting the company on a single move. Instead, they timed
and segmented their biggest bets to mitigate the risk they faced at
any one time.

Even Steve Jobs, who sometimes seemed to turn recklessness into
an art, eventually learned that betting the company is a bad idea.
As a general rule, Jobs did not believe in hedging his bets. As Jon
Rubinstein told us, "There was never Plan B. Steve only had one
plan, and we were going to go execute that plan, which would cause
you to always deliver on Plan A."[39] Until Jobs was fired in 1985 for
his big bet on the Macintosh, he seemed to ignore risk completely.
For example, Jobs completely disregarded the rest of Apple's business
when he was building the Mac, ruthlessly raiding the Apple II and
Lisa teams for resources and personnel. Andy Hertzfeld, an early
Apple engineer, recalled a conversation with Jobs in 1981 about his

interest in working on the Mac. When Hertzfeld asked for a couple of days to hand off his current project—a new version of the operating system for the Apple II—Jobs replied, "You're just wasting your time with that! Who cares about the Apple II? The Apple II will be dead in a few years. Your OS will be obsolete before it's finished. The Macintosh is the future of Apple, and you're going to start on it now!" Jobs reached over and pulled the plug on Hertzfeld's Apple II, causing him to lose the code he was writing. Telling Hertzfeld to follow, he picked up his computer, loaded it into the trunk of his car, and drove Hertzfeld to his new office with the Mac team.[40]

Yet ironically, it was the Apple II's success that made it possible for Jobs to bet on the Macintosh without betting the company. By the end of 1982, Apple had sold 600,000 Apple II computers, giving it the largest installed base in the PC industry.[41] And although engineering resources were increasingly being diverted to the Mac (much to the chagrin of Apple cofounder Steve Wozniak), Apple continued to bring out new versions of the Apple II, including the IIe in January 1983. Just prior to the Mac's launch in 1984, the Apple IIe was selling nearly 75,000 units per month, giving Apple an installed base of 2 million PCs.[42]

The relationship between the Apple II and the Mac did not pass unnoticed within the company. One night a shouting match broke out at a pub near the Apple campus. According to an observer, "The Mac guys were screaming, 'We're the future!' The Apple II guys were screaming, 'We're the money!' "[43] Both were right: Apple II's steady revenue stream made it possible for Apple to continue investing heavily in the Macintosh despite disappointing initial sales. Although the Mac had the splashiest launch in the history of the industry, it found few early buyers because of its sluggish performance and the scarcity of Mac-compatible software. Without the continuing success of the Apple II, Apple would probably not have survived. Mac's cumulative sales only reached the 500,000 mark in September 1985 and did not pass the one million mark until March

1987.[44] As late as 1985, the Apple II line continued to account for 70 percent of company revenues, and it outsold the Mac through most of 1987—giving Apple the money and time it needed to fix the Macintosh and entice developers to write applications. [45]

Time Your Bets

With the Macintosh, Jobs inadvertently avoided betting the company. But he seemed to have learned a crucial lesson from that episode more than fifteen years later when he had to choose between switching to Intel chips or sticking with the PowerPC. Intel had been trying to persuade Apple to adopt its technology since Jobs reemerged on the scene, but Jobs initially balked. In the late 1990s, Apple remained so dependent on Macintosh revenue that any serious disruption to Mac sales could have doomed the company. Sales of Macintosh computers and software represented more than 80 percent of the company's revenue. Moreover, as much as Intel wanted to win Apple over, it was not offering particularly appealing terms. Rubinstein described the economics of doing a deal with Intel as "horrible" at that time.[46]

By June 2005, when Jobs announced at a developer conference that Apple would be switching to Intel processors, the situation had changed dramatically. Sales of the iPod, which launched in 2001, started to take off in 2004, greatly reducing the extent to which Apple's future depended on Macintosh sales. In the two quarters before Apple finalized the decision to migrate to Intel, it sold nearly 10 million iPods.[47] Not only did this provide Apple with a financial cushion, but it also helped Jobs negotiate with Intel from a position of strength.

As one industry analyst commented that summer, "with iPod sales exploding and Mac sales riding an apparent halo effect, it's hard to imagine a better time for Apple to make this risky move."[48] In the last three months of 2005, Apple sold 14 million iPods, three times the volume of the previous holiday quarter, and the company's revenue grew 63 percent year over year.[49] The success of the iPod protected the company against a possible downturn in Mac sales. As Apple completed the transition to Intel technology in 2006, the iPod continued to buoy its growth. By then, less than 40 percent of the company's revenue came from the Macintosh business, with Apple's music business accounting for most of the rest.[50]

Diversify Risk

While Apple's financial vulnerability forced Steve Jobs to postpone his bet on Intel technology until the timing was right, Microsoft enjoyed the luxury of strong cash flow from the mid-1980s onward. As a result, Bill Gates could make big bets without facing the threat of bankruptcy. Nonetheless, he mitigated the risks the company faced—and increased his ability to take big gambles—by broadening and diversifying Microsoft's business model.

Early in Microsoft's history, Gates reduced the company's dependence on the operating system business by developing application software, such as Word and Excel, which provided Microsoft with a second revenue stream. In addition, he made Microsoft applications available not just on Windows and OS/2, but also on some of his competitors' platforms, including Apple's Macintosh. As Jon Shirley admitted, Gates did not immediately grasp the advantages of this strategy but, once he did, he acted decisively to implement it: "Bill missed the application business for the original IBM PC, but the discontinuity created by the Macintosh gave Microsoft the opportunity to win the space."[51]

By writing applications—particularly for other platforms—Gates ensured that, even if Windows failed and OS/2 or Apple prevailed, Microsoft would still have a healthy business. This strategy also kept the company's options open while Windows slowly built market share. Although Gates believed Windows would eventually defeat OS/2, he was never sure how long this would take. In a talk at the Boston Computer Society in 1993, reflecting on the decision to build Windows, Gates admitted, "Microsoft bet the company on graphical interfaces. . . . [But] it took much longer than I expected for the graphics interface to move into the mainstream."[52] So while waiting, he tried to avoid a total break with IBM. As Shirley later revealed, Gates even left the door open to a "common migration strategy": he was prepared to make all of Microsoft's applications run on OS/2, if IBM made OS/2 into a great success.[53]

Spread Bets Out Over Time

Gates had little control over how long it would take his bet on Windows to play out. In contrast, Andy Grove deliberately controlled the timing of his bet on a sole-source strategy as a means of mitigating risk. Over the long term, Intel's commitment to supply the entire world with microprocessors would require tens of billions of dollars in capital spending. However, the company invested only a fraction of this sum at the outset. As Intel prepared to manufacture the 386 microprocessor, Grove committed the company to building a single new factory. During the two years it took to complete the new plant, Intel's capital expenditures never rose above historical averages. Intel regularly spent 15 percent to 20 percent of revenue on capital expenditures in the decade prior to the 386. In the four years after the introduction of the new chip, capital spending was 13 percent to 16 percent of revenue. The same restraint governed Intel's approach to production and sales of the 386. By 1988, 386 chips generated less than half of Intel's revenue. In 1989, four years after 386 manufacturing began, 286 chips were outselling the 386 more than two to one.[54] By 1992, when Grove decided to scale up manufacturing and dramatically increase capital spending, the risks of the sole-source decision were long behind the company.

Of course, not all of Grove's bets paid off. One notable example was the early 1990s Itanium project—a joint venture with Hewlett-Packard to create a new "64-bit" microprocessor. As we discuss in Chapter 3, the project was several years late, and sales never lived up to expectations. However, Itanium did not consume enough resources to ever put Intel or its main product lines at risk.

A Cautionary Tale: Nokia's Bet on Windows

Nokia's ill-fated bet on Windows powerfully illustrates the danger of betting the company. In 1999, Nokia was the most valuable company in Europe, with a market capitalization of €200 billion (around $250 billion). Over the next decade, Nokia dominated the global cell phone industry. In 2010, three years after the introduction of the iPhone, Nokia still held 37 percent of the smartphone market. But a decade of bad decisions was catching up to the company. Nokia had failed to turn its operating system, Symbian, into a viable competitor to Apple's iOS or Google's Android. The company had also abandoned the United States before it emerged as the leading smartphone market in the world. With Nokia's sales and stock price falling, CEO Stephen Elop openly admitted in February 2011, "We fell behind, we missed big trends, and we lost time."[55] Three days later, he announced that Nokia was betting its future on his previous employer, Microsoft. Rather than jump on the Android bandwagon, or hedge by developing phones for multiple software platforms, Elop bet that he could differentiate Nokia by committing his company to Windows. Within ten months, it became apparent that Elop had made a disastrous decision: Sales of Nokia's Symbian phones collapsed, and the company's Windows phones failed to take off, winning less than 4 percent of the market by 2013. Sales declined, losses grew, and Nokia's market value dropped almost 90 percent from the time of Elop's announcement to around €4 billion ($5.2 billion). Desperate, Elop sold Nokia's core handset business to Microsoft for €5.4 billion ($7 billion) in September 2013.

One of Jobs' business rules was to never be afraid of cannibalizing yourself. "If you don't cannibalize yourself, someone else will," he said.[56]
—WALTER ISAACSON [2011]

CANNIBALIZE YOUR OWN BUSINESS

Making big bets often requires the willingness to cannibalize your
own business. This principle may seem obvious, but it is agonizingly
hard to carry out. The obstacles are both external and internal. Cannibalization can mean trading known success for an unknown future; trading highly profitable sales for unknown margins; and even
trading dollars for dimes, especially in the world of high technology,
where commoditization sets in quickly. Making the problem worse,
cannibalization creates winners and losers within an organization.
If a new product group takes sales away from an old product group,
then its star will rise as the other's falls.

Faced with these challenges, many managers find excuses for
avoiding cannibalization. In contrast, great strategists embrace and
sometimes even seek to accelerate the process. At Intel, for example,
making your own products obsolete has been an underlying principle of company strategy. Andy Grove told his board of directors
numerous times throughout the 1990s that, when given a choice between giving incremental revenues to your competitor or capturing
them yourself, the answer is obvious. Chris Peters, a former senior
developer at Microsoft, similarly recounted, "Bill always understood
and internalized, that you [must] . . . radically change things and
really have big plans. . . . A classic example is, DOS was doing great.

[We could have said,] 'Let's just come out with new versions of DOS. Why make Windows?'"[57] But that would have left the door open for IBM or Apple to supplant DOS. Rather than take that risk, Microsoft decided to a build a DOS killer itself.

Be Your Own Substitute

Steve Jobs sometimes took this approach to extremes. Donna Dubinsky, an early Apple employee and later CEO of Palm, recalled Jobs's all-or-nothing approach to the launch of a new dot-matrix printer in the 1980s. In a planning meeting, Dubinsky recommended reducing the price of the older daisy-wheel printer and selling the two simultaneously so that customers could choose between the older, cheaper product and the newer, more expensive one. This would allow Apple to clear out its obsolete inventory at a modest cost. But Jobs didn't even wait to hear her out. Apple should scrap its old inventory, he declared, interrupting her presentation, and sell only its latest product.[58]

Similarly, in 2005, Jobs insisted on killing the iPod Mini before launching its successor, the Nano. Although demand for the Mini remained huge, Jobs wanted to move to the next device before it had been market-tested. Rather than continue selling the Mini, and allow the next generation product to win the market gradually, Jobs demanded killing the Mini immediately. Jon Rubinstein recounted, "We had to deliver the Nano for Christmas, a very high-risk program. And Steve instructed me to shut down the Mini, six months in advance. If I hadn't made the schedule, we would have been out of the iPod business, because we would have missed Christmas."[59] Fortunately, Rubinstein did make the schedule, in what he described as "a miracle," and sales of the Nano exploded, proving Jobs's hunch had been right. "That happened all the time," Rubinstein recalled. "Steve would bet all the chips—he would just push all the chips in the middle of the table and go 'let it ride.'"[60]

Bet followed bet. Soon the iPod itself was a candidate for canni-balization. Even as iPod sales were going through the roof in 2005, Jobs warned Apple's board, "the device that can eat our lunch is the cell phone. . . . Everyone carries a cell phone, so [building music players into cell phones] could render the iPod unnecessary."[61] Con-vinced that a killer smartphone would render the iPod obsolete, Jobs was determined that Apple be the company to build that phone.

Jobs turned Apple upside down to launch the iPhone. The iPhone became, like the Mac in the 1980s and the iPod in 2001, the com-pany's top-priority product and the home of Apple's elite. Racing to meet an ambitious schedule, the iPhone group raided other groups within Apple for talent, especially the Mac software development team—and delayed the latest version of the Mac OS as a result.[62]

When Jobs unveiled the iPhone in January 2007, he pitched it as a combination iPod, cell phone, and Internet communication de-vice. In fact, he called it "a wide-screen iPod with touch controls" and "the best iPod we've ever made."[63] Given this pitch, few people seemed likely to buy both an iPhone and a full-sized iPod (unless they owned more music than the iPhone could hold). Instead, they might buy the smaller, cheaper iPod Shuffle or Nano along with the iPhone. To cushion the financial blow of lost iPod sales, Apple built the price of an iPod into the iPhone. When Jobs announced pricing for the iPhone, he explained that it combined the price of the most popular iPod ($199) with the price of a typical smartphone ($299 in his estimation). That came to $499 for the basic iPhone and more for higher-end models with more memory. (Analysts and consumers immediately complained that this price was too high and compared it unfavorably to the price of other smartphones. And Apple found that it had to bend to the criticism, cutting the price of the 8GB model from $599 to $399 just a few months after launch, while eliminating the cheaper 4GB model.)

The iPhone became a runaway success within eighteen months, and, in the process, it ate into iPod sales. Shipments of iPods began to plateau after Apple released the iPhone in June 2007. Between the last quarter of 2007 and the last quarter of 2008, iPod sales grew only 3 percent. By late 2012, quarterly iPod sales, at $820 million for the third quarter, had fallen below $1 billion for the first time since 2005, while sales of the iPhone during the same quarter surpassed $17 billion.[64]

Three years after the iPhone's launch, it was the iPad's turn to raise concerns about cannibalization. Despite tepid early reviews, the iPad was an enormous success, even by Apple standards. Sales reached one million units in the first month and 15 million by March 2011, nine months after the iPad's release.[65] By then, it was clear that iPads were cutting into Mac sales. In July 2011, Apple COO Tim Cook told analysts, "Some customers chose to purchase an iPad instead of a Mac." On the bright side, he added, "even more decided to buy an iPad over a Windows PC. There are a lot more Windows PCs to cannibalize than Macs."[66] From April through June 2011, sales of Mac laptops were basically flat at 2.8 million units, while Apple sold more than 9 million iPads. In dollar terms, iPad sales surpassed sales of Mac desktops and laptops combined.[67] Once again, Jobs's big bet on cannibalization had paid off.

Control the Pace of Cannibalization

For Apple, cannibalization concerns typically arose when the company introduced new products but, for Intel, cannibalization was a way of life. The company was founded on the idea that cannibalization was not only inevitable but should proceed at high speed. Moore's Law predicted that semiconductor performance would double roughly every two years. This meant that each new generation of products had a built-in obsolescence date. And even before that date came, cutthroat competition would bring about sharp declines in price.

The key to surviving and thriving in this environment lay in

Cannibalize Your Own Business

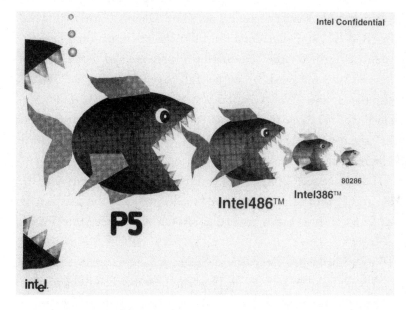

SOURCE: Andy Grove's SLRP presentation to Intel, 1993, reproduced with permission. (P5 was the soon-to-be named Pentium.)

learning to drive and manage cannibalization, rather than leaving its pace up to chance. As Paul Otellini, Grove's technical assistant in the early 1990s and later Intel CEO, commented in a 2000 interview, "We believe very strongly that the best business model for us is a large market segment share because then you can manage transitions. And the key to Intel's business model is cannibalizing your own product line."[68] In his 1993 SLRP presentation, Grove illustrated this philosophy with an image that showed each new microprocessor gobbling up its predecessor.

Yet, even in a company built on the principle of cannibalization, the strategies used to manage this process could generate controversy. This was the case with one of Grove's most innovative moves—the decision to brand the microprocessor. Before the mid-

1980s, microprocessors had never been a branded product. But in an effort to push aside the 286 chip and promote its successor, the 386, Grove and his former technical assistant, Dennis Carter, launched the "Red X" campaign. Intel ran full-page ads in national newspapers that featured "286" covered by a spray-painted red X; each of these ads was followed by another full-page ad touting the 386SX, with the tagline: "Now Get 386 System Performance At A 286 System Price." Their goal was to get consumers to demand computers with the new 386 chip, which most PC companies were only slowly bringing out.

The success of "Red X" led to expanded efforts to promote the 486 and Pentium chips and, more broadly, to brand the company itself with the "Intel Inside" campaign. As Grove described Intel Inside:

> It was the biggest campaign the industry had ever seen—in fact, it ranks up there with the big time consumer merchandising campaigns. Its aim was to suggest to the computer user that the microprocessor . . . *is* the computer. . . . By 1994, our research showed that our logo had become one of the most recognized logos in consumer merchandising, up there with names like Coca-Cola and Nike.[69]

Intel Inside was far from popular within the company. While cannibalization itself raised few concerns, branding was viewed with deep skepticism by many managers and members of the board of directors. The "chip heads" at Intel were mostly engineers and scientists who believed that superior engineering and great products would win the day. Grove recalled that the very first time he put money for brand advertising—$50 million—in Carter's budget, Intel chairman Gordon Moore and Craig Barrett, later Intel CEO, took it out while Grove was on vacation.[70] (Livid, Grove restored the funds.) Even as the brand campaign built momentum in the early 1990s, Intel's chief financial officer continued to argue that advertising would never see a return and was an incredible waste of money: a semiconductor was a semiconductor and ultimately winning would come down to the best product at the lowest price.[71]

Equally important, many of Intel's customers—computer companies such as IBM and Compaq—opposed the campaign. Why, they asked, should a supplier tell their customers which PC to buy? IBM, for example, wanted to continue selling its 286 machines. The last thing it wanted was Intel telling PC buyers to upgrade to a 386-based computer. And even Compaq, which benefited from the 386 campaign, turned against Intel Inside. At an industry conference in 1994, CEO Eckhard Pfeiffer angrily proclaimed, "I'd like to make three points to Intel: don't impose products and prices on us, don't be our competitor, and don't use Intel Inside."[72] Nonetheless, Grove believed strongly that the branding campaign—even though it focused on a component few consumers would ever see—would lead customers to demand a PC with Intel inside. And he was right.

When the basics of the business are undergoing profound change, [existing management] must adopt an outsider's intellectual objectivity . . . unfettered by an emotional attachment to the past.[73]
　　—ANDY GROVE [1996]

CUT YOUR LOSSES

So far we have focused on the importance of the fortitude to make big bets and the savvy to calibrate them to your company's ability to bear risk. But what if something goes wrong? What if new information or developments emerge that upset your plans? Even great strategists cannot foretell the future. Everyone makes mistakes, and Gates, Grove, and Jobs were not exceptions to this rule. Each of them made bad bets on occasion or stumbled in ways that could have significantly weakened their companies. However, when facing a dead end, all three had the discipline and flexibility to admit their mistakes and cut their losses. As their colleagues commented, Gates, Grove, and Jobs were "intellectually honest."[74] Admitting errors wasn't easy for any of them, but the ability to do so and change course was one of the critical characteristics that distinguished them from run-of-the mill CEOs.

Admit Mistakes

Andy Grove faced one major disaster during his tenure as CEO. Shortly before Thanksgiving 1994, a math professor discovered an error in Intel's new Pentium processor: a small design flaw produced a rounding error when one very large number was divided by another. Engineers concluded that the rounding error would occur roughly once every nine billion calculations. The average spreadsheet user would suffer this mistake once every 27,000 years. Intel executives believed that the error was so minor, so unlikely, and so obscure that it was not an urgent problem. Intel might replace the motherboard for computer users working on mission-critical tasks, like programming the launch of the space shuttle, but otherwise the company would fix the problem with the next version of the Pentium.

But discussion boards on the Internet saw the issue differently. An error was an error, and Intel should fix it for everyone who had bought a computer with a Pentium processor. When the debate moved first to CNN and then to every major U.S. newspaper and eventually every media outlet in the world, this obscure error became a cause célèbre and a growing public relations disaster. In a phone meeting with Intel's board, Grove reiterated his public position: no electronic calculation device was perfect, so Intel should hold its ground. But then IBM escalated the attack on Intel by announcing that it would stop shipping Pentiums and "all hell broke loose," according to Grove.[75] One of Intel's largest customers would not sell its newest product. If other customers jumped on the bandwagon, the company could be irreparably damaged.

As a board member, David Yoffie tried to call Grove shortly after the IBM announcement. Grove's assistant told him that the CEO was unavailable, not taking any calls or returning calls. David was stunned. In the midst of a crisis, the CEO was not willing to talk with his board? As the crisis deepened, Grove retreated into a virtual bunker, speaking to nearly no one. However, five days after the IBM announcement, Dennis Carter, now the company's chief marketing officer, called Grove for a one-on-one talk. Carter told Grove that he was destroying the brand and all the consumer goodwill Intel had built over the prior five years. It no longer mattered who was right and who was wrong. Consumers would vote with their feet. Exhausted, Grove relented. Three days later and six weeks after the start of the crisis, Intel published full-page ads in major U.S. newspapers, apologizing for its initial handling of the Pentium processor flaw and offering every Pentium owner a new motherboard.[76]

The $475 million write-off was one of Grove's better investments. His public mea culpa renewed consumer confidence in Intel products. Almost immediately, demand for the Pentium exploded. In an ironic twist, the crisis had turned "Pentium" into a household name, much like the firestorm of protest that greeted the launch of "New Coke." Helped further by the introduction of Windows 95 eight months later, Intel had one of its best years ever. Revenue grew 40 percent in the twelve months following the resolution of the crisis, and profits jumped 56 percent.

Write Off Sunk Costs

At Microsoft, perhaps Bill Gates's biggest mistake was his failure to appreciate the significance of the Internet in 1993 or 1994. By 1995, when Gates recognized that the Internet was an unstoppable force, companies such as Netscape had already captured the imagination of the world and a big head start in the market for Internet software. In the meantime, Microsoft had invested huge sums in its online business, Microsoft Network (MSN), and in other content services, such as MSNBC, Microsoft's joint venture with NBC. Before MSN launched in August 1995, Gates told MSN head Russ Siegelman, "My number one concern is not short-term financial returns, but that Microsoft not get a black eye."[77] Then–executive vice president Steve Ballmer expected the company to incur $1 billion in losses on MSN and related ventures over the next three years.[78]

MSN offered subscribers dial-up access to a private network offering MSN-only information, entertainment, and shopping services, as well as email, newsgroups, chat forums, and the like. MSN provided access to the Internet, but the service was not built on Internet protocols. The infrastructure that underpinned the network was based on an older communications standard known as x.25. Microsoft had spent lavishly on deals with telecom companies around the world to offer MSN on their dial-up, x.25 networks. But the true key to its strategy lay in marketing. By bundling MSN with Windows 95, Microsoft could reach millions of potential customers for free.

Unfortunately, by the time MSN debuted, it was already out of date. The writing was on the wall for proprietary online services. CompuServe and other networks had flourished in the late 1980s and early 1990s when the Internet was a bare-bones, text-dominated service that was not particularly attractive or easy to use. They offered easy access to curated content and communication services at a time when few customers wanted to explore the Internet on their own. But with the invention of the graphical Web browser in 1993 and the proliferation of free online content, Internet use took off. Some 15 million people had Internet access by 1995, and their numbers were expected to double every year.[79] Rather than pay a premium for proprietary online content, many of these users preferred to buy cheaper Internet access and find their own way on the Web.

Microsoft had bet big and bet wrong. Admitting a mistake of this magnitude is no easy matter. But to his credit, Gates recognized in the fall of 1995 that defending MSN was the wrong strategy. The right way forward was to walk away from the sunk costs embodied in MSN and embrace the Internet, where the competition now focused on the race to dominate the Web browser market. So, after spending $25 million to build a proprietary, dial-up infrastructure, Siegelman recounted, "We killed it. Bill never said, 'Oh yeah, we should keep it around. We made a big investment.' It was like, 'Tell BT [British Telecom] we're not going to use their network.' End of story."[80] Microsoft also gave away all the proprietary technology it had designed to make MSN special, such as tools for creating advanced multimedia content. Gates even sacrificed MSN's last potential competitive advantage—exclusive distribution with Windows—in order to hasten victory in the browser wars. In 1996, in return for AOL's agreement to promote Internet Explorer almost exclusively, Microsoft granted AOL a coveted place on the Windows desktop. In combination, these moves quickly paid off. Internet Explorer, which had only 3 percent of the browser market in 1995 compared to Netscape Navigator's 80 percent, was the market leader by the end of 1998.[81]

Bill Gates did not let Microsoft be swamped by the disruptive forces of the Internet barreling down upon it. Instead, he changed direction and rode its momentum to even greater success. Similarly, Steve Jobs, although known for his stubbornness, knew it was time to give way to a superior force once developers started to "jailbreak" the iPhone so that it could run software Apple had not approved.

Jobs's initial vision for the iPhone called for Apple to write all the apps. Conventional wisdom at the time held that third-party applications could introduce viruses into the network or instability into the device and user experience, which most consumers would find unacceptable. Although Apple board member Art Levinson and senior vice president Phil Schiller pushed Jobs to open up the platform, he held firm. At the iPhone's January 2007 launch, Jobs argued, "You don't want your phone to be an open platform. You need it to work when you need it to work. Cingular [AT&T] doesn't want to see their West Coast network go down because some application messed up."[82] Consistent with Jobs's philosophy of emphasizing products over platforms, which we discuss in Chapter 3, the iPhone initially came with only a handful of apps, including text messaging, Web browsing, a clock, email, and Google Maps. However, developers soon began to modify the iPhone's software in order to allow it to run unauthorized applications. Bowing to the inevitable, Jobs announced in June 2007 that third-party developers would be allowed to create iPhone apps. Apple's App Store opened one year later with about 550 company-approved offerings; three years later, 200 million users had downloaded more than 15 billion copies of the available apps.[83]

If Jobs had insisted on sticking to his decision not to allow third-party applications, the iPhone might have been doomed to a small niche. If Android and other mobile operating systems, such as Windows or BlackBerry, had taken the lead in applications, Jobs would have missed his opportunity to redefine the smartphone industry. Instead, as smartphones increasingly looked like commodity devices, a million iPhone-specific applications continued to separate Apple from the competition. By pivoting to accept the open-platform model, Jobs had turned what he once saw as a source of weakness into one of the iPhone's greatest sources of strength.

LESSONS FROM THE MASTERS

Big, bold bets are easy to discuss in theory and even easier to justify in retrospect, but extremely hard to execute in real time. Making game-changing decisions requires a high tolerance for both risk and uncertainty along with the ability to act even when you know you may be wrong. Gates, Grove, and Jobs all possessed these attributes in spades, as those who worked closely with them can attest. Renée James, who rose from the position of Grove's technical assistant to Intel president, said of Grove: "What he used to say was, 'I might be wrong but I'm never confused.' He would just [take a position] that a lot of people didn't have the guts to do."[84] Avie Tevanian spoke in similar terms of Jobs: "Most people would say, 'Oh, gee, I don't know. This is kind of risky.' Whereas Steve was, 'We're going to just go for it, and this is going to be huge.'"[85]

This decisiveness was a key factor in all three CEOs' ability to cannibalize their own businesses, as many big bets require. Deciding to overthrow your own business can be a gut-wrenching choice, but, when executed deftly, it's a strategy—or even a philosophy—that can deliver rich rewards. A big part of what kept Microsoft, Intel, and Apple on top was Gates's commitment to winning in new arenas, even if it meant undercutting existing revenue streams; Grove's drive to kill the prior generation of his company's processors; and Jobs's focus on the next product, no matter what the consequences.

Equally important, while taking some of the biggest bets their industry had ever seen, Gates, Grove, and Jobs all found ways to avoid the threat of bankruptcy if they failed by carefully timing their bets, diversifying their risks, or spreading their bets out over time. Making big bets shouldn't mean betting the company because, for even the best strategist, there is always a chance that something—sometimes everything—will go wrong. If and when that happens, it can be difficult to recover. All too often failure leads to paralysis or a stubborn refusal to admit past mistakes. But Gates, Grove, and Jobs all understood the importance of cutting their losses and moving forward. Unsparing critics of those around them, they were no less rigorous when it came to their own performance. This intellectual honesty was an essential ingredient of their success.

CHAPTER 3

Build Platforms *and* Ecosystems— Not Just Products

Strategy operates at many levels. It starts with defining your firm's unique value proposition, market position, and competitive advantage. This is basic strategic thinking, lesson number one. But, in order to become a true master of strategy, managers need to think much more expansively. Building a competitive advantage that can last for years often requires influencing the world beyond the boundaries of a single firm. Great strategists, especially in technology markets, don't just try to build great products or even great companies. Their goal is usually to build industry-wide *platforms* that bring together a broad *ecosystem* of partners engaged in complementary product and service innovation, as well as in related marketing, sales, service, and distribution.

We hear the word "platform" nearly every day, in many contexts. We catch a train at a platform. A politician recruits supporters based on a platform formed of campaign commitments or ideals. Companies build families of related products around platforms—common components that different teams of engineers can use without having to reinvent the basic infrastructure. In more recent years, we have heard about programmers writing applications or "apps" for software platforms like Microsoft Windows, Google Android, and Apple iOS.

Platforms bring individuals or groups together for a common purpose, usually with access to some shared resource. This definition also applies to the platforms that Bill Gates, Andy Grove, and Steve Jobs championed. Microsoft, Intel, and Apple established *industry platforms* that bring together users and companies creating complementary products and services. Such complements can make a platform more useful and valuable—sometimes exponentially so. However, Gates, Grove, and Jobs arrived at their understanding of industry platforms at different times and with different emphases. Their varied approaches reflect the spectrum of priorities, nuances, and trade-offs that spans the distance between "platform" and "product" thinking.

For example, in 1980, when IBM executives came to Microsoft looking for an operating system for their new personal computer, Bill Gates immediately thought "platform first, product second." He retained the right to sell DOS and then Windows to other companies and thereby use the operating system as a foundation for various hardware companies to build personal computers as well as for both Microsoft and other software firms to build complementary applications. By contrast, it was another ten years before Andy Grove fully understood the importance of an industry platform and the role of Intel's main product—the microprocessor. As for Steve Jobs, his thinking always seemed to be "product first, platform second," starting with the Apple II in 1978 and the Mac in 1984 through the iPhone in 2007. We know that Jobs understood the power of industry platforms: he did cultivate outside software companies and other firms to help him. He also spent many years battling Microsoft's dominant position in computing, even though Apple had what most observers agree was a far superior product in the Macintosh. But Jobs believed that cultivating ecosystem partners was less important than maintaining tight control over product design and the user experience. Even though Apple's products increasingly depended on software or services provided by other companies, including Microsoft, Jobs's embrace of platform thinking remained halfhearted at best. As a result, Microsoft with the DOS-Windows ecosystem, and later Google with the Android ecosystem, were able to overtake Apple in personal computers and then smartphones, as well as erode Apple's leading market share in tablets.

In this chapter, we examine how Gates, Grove, and Jobs grappled with the tensions inherent in creating industry platforms rather than stand-alone products. We focus on how they negotiated these trade-offs and what they did to promote their platforms and build industry partnerships. While each CEO had a distinctive approach to platform strategy, the following four principles capture the challenges they all had to resolve:

RULE 3: BUILD PLATFORMS *AND* ECOSYSTEMS—NOT JUST PRODUCTS

---

1. Think platforms, not just products.
2. Think ecosystems, not just platforms.
3. Create some of your own complements.
4. Evolve and invent new platforms to avoid obsolescence.

INDUSTRY PLATFORM DYNAMICS

In their 2002 book, *Platform Leadership*, as well as in a number of articles, Michael Cusumano and Annabelle Gawer have argued that industry platforms can become much more valuable and lasting than stand-alone products or company platforms due to the power of complementary innovations and network effects (also referred to as network externalities).[1] In platform markets, these concepts go together. For example, a simple network effect exists when the value of a product grows with the number of people who use it—think of the telephone as a communications mechanism or Facebook as a social media sharing site. One user is not very useful; two are more useful, and so on. Now think about how much more attractive and valuable these platforms can become if other companies create hundreds, thousands, or even millions of complementary products and services. Depending on the type of platform, these outside innovations can range from devices like fax machines that make the telephone system more useful, to software applications that help Facebook users share photos and music or play games with their friends. As the number of complements grows, the platform becomes increasingly useful, which attracts more users. More users, in turn, attract more producers of complementary innovations or other market actors, such as advertisers and different service providers. In extreme cases, industries with powerful network effects have been known to "tip," delivering the bulk of the market to a single firm in what is often called the "winner take all" phenomenon.[2]

Although we talk about it as something very new, managing industry platforms, complementary innovations, and network effects is actually an old phenomenon. The great railroad companies in nineteenth-century America and Europe had to deal with network effects, literally and figuratively, when they built railway track systems and tried to convince other companies to adopt a common gauge standard. A railroad network that went only from, say, New York to Philadelphia became much more valuable when it could link to other railroad networks. It was the same with the telephone companies. Local systems had limited value; nationally and then globally linked networks became far more valuable and useful, not to mention more profitable. The power grid also involved platform concepts and network effects. In the late 1800s and early 1900s, General Electric had to establish a set of standards and get agreement from many different companies and municipalities in order to establish its alternating current (AC) technology as a national platform for bringing energy into homes and businesses. Similarly, the Yellow Pages, shopping malls, and credit cards brought together buyers and sellers long before we had Internet search engines and e-commerce sites to help us with shopping.

John Donne famously wrote, "No man is an island, entire of itself, every man is a piece of the continent, a part of the main."[3] The same can be said of companies and, as these examples demonstrate, this has long been the case. However, as products and services have become increasingly complex and interconnected, the importance of managing the world outside a firm's boundaries has grown. To their credit, Gates, Grove, and Jobs all realized, at different times and to different degrees, that cultivating outside partners was better than trying to do all the potential innovation themselves—surely an impossible task. The industry platforms and ecosystems that emerged from this strategy set in motion extraordinarily powerful network effects and global communities of innovators. Platform and ecosystem thinking not only helped Microsoft, Intel, and Apple dominate their competition and generate spectacular financial returns; the innovations they fostered forever changed the way we all live, work, and communicate.

■

We look for opportunities with network externalities— where there are advantages to the vast majority of consumers to share a common standard. . . . The key to our business is building annuities, by tapping into the broad revenue streams that will rely on our software expertise.[4]

—BILL GATES [1994]

THINK PLATFORMS, NOT JUST PRODUCTS

Bill Gates has often been criticized for not being a true visionary. Indeed, Microsoft has usually been a fast follower rather than an inventor of breakthrough products. Yet when it came to understanding the importance of the personal computer and software products as well as the role of industry platforms, complementary innovations, and network effects, Gates was clearly ahead of the crowd. The concept of an industry platform did not become commonplace, even in the high-tech world, until the Internet boom of the late 1990s. However, Gates revealed his understanding of platforms and network effects not only in the 1994 interview cited above, but also through the strategy he pursued more than a decade earlier with DOS.

Put Platform before Product

The story of how Microsoft came to provide DOS to IBM is well known: IBM executives visited Gates in July 1980 looking for an operating system for their new PC. Not having an operating system in the works, Gates demurred and suggested they talk to Gary Kildall, CEO of Digital Research. When Kildall decided he didn't want the business, IBM returned to Gates. After some internal debate, Gates decided to do the deal with IBM. He paid a small Seattle company $75,000 for a rudimentary operating system; he and his engineers fixed it up for IBM; and Microsoft went on to dominate the PC software platform business for the next three-plus decades.[5]

Many observers have argued that Microsoft was lucky. IBM's decision to approach and then come back to Gates was, indeed, a stroke of luck. But Gates also had the clarity of vision to seize the opportunity when IBM came to him a second time. Moreover, he had the foresight to treat the IBM deal not simply as a "product design win," but as a chance to build an industry platform. In the short term, Gates could have maximized Microsoft's revenues and profits by selling DOS for a large lump sum or asking IBM to pay a royalty on every copy of DOS it shipped with a PC. But he was thinking much more broadly. Gates knew that a "clone" industry of compatible machines had emerged around the IBM mainframe, and he believed this could also happen with the IBM personal computer. If he preserved the ability to sell DOS to makers of PC clones, Microsoft would own not just a component of an IBM product, but an essential element of the foundation for an entire new industry. With this goal in mind, Gates—pretty much on his own—got IBM to agree to the following contractual terms:[6]

1. Microsoft would receive a small payment from IBM (around $50,000) to get DOS ready for the mass market and to provide some programming languages and small applications that IBM would bundle with its new PC.
2. Microsoft retained the right to license DOS to other companies—which would become the PC clone makers. This right was crucial to Microsoft's ability to expand the business beyond IBM.
3. IBM would not pay any royalty fees for using DOS, which it rebranded as PC-DOS when bundled with IBM PCs.

IBM executives probably thought this was a pretty good deal. IBM had always made most of its money from selling hardware, and it would make even more if its PC operating system were royalty-free. Moreover, IBM executives expected few other companies to be in the market for DOS. IBM had built a special chip that enabled the operating system to communicate with the hardware components; without this IBM chip, a PC wouldn't work. However, in 1982, Microsoft helped Compaq and then other companies reverse-engineer the chip, build PCs, and load the machines with DOS.[7] These "IBM compatibles," running a generic version of the operating system, would soon turn DOS and later Windows into *the* industry software platform for personal computing.

Compatibility Trumps Performance

Like Microsoft, Intel played a central role in the story of the first IBM PC, which was built around Intel's 8088 microprocessor. At the time, though, Intel executives did not recognize that they could use the IBM deal to build an industry platform of their own. Very different from Bill Gates, Intel CEO Gordon Moore and then-president Andy Grove saw the IBM contract as an important, but not extraordinary, product sale. Moore commented in 1999: "Any design win at IBM was a big deal, but I certainly didn't recognize that this was more important than the others. And I don't think anyone else did either."[8]

At the time, Moore and Grove were focused on developing path-breaking *products*. Since Intel's founding in 1968, its innovations had ranged from the world's first memory chips (DRAMs, SRAMs, and EPROMs) to the first microprocessors and microcontrollers. In order to help customers figure out how to use Intel chips in their products, the company also developed complementary software and hardware. But Intel's goal remained selling products to keep its factories operating at full capacity. Moore and Grove were not thinking—yet—of enabling a third-party ecosystem around their microprocessors that would lead to much more explosive growth in demand for the personal computer than Intel or its direct customers could have generated on their own.

It took Grove another ten years after the IBM deal to realize that Intel could become a global powerhouse by making sure its products remained an essential part of the PC platform. The turning point came around 1990, when Grove faced a fundamental decision about the future of Intel's core business, the x86 microprocessor family. Since 1980, Intel had followed the 8088 with the 286, 386, and 486 chips. Each was more powerful than its predecessor. Since they shared the same architecture, they were also "backward-compatible": that is, each new chip could still run the software supported by the previous generation, including DOS, Windows, and all the applications written for the two operating systems. Nonetheless, by the late 1980s, the x86 architecture was under attack. Its design depended on an approach known as "complex instruction-set computing," or CISC. A decade earlier, IBM had developed a competing approach called "reduced instruction-set computing," or RISC. RISC chips were reputedly faster and cheaper to design and manufacture.

Within Intel, a renegade team had designed a RISC processor, called the i860, that expert reviewers considered one of the best in its class. Intel announced the availability of the i860 chip in 1989, and new customers started knocking on its door. But Andy Grove was genuinely torn over what to do, as he revealed in a long conversation with David Yoffie outside the boardroom in 1990. Most of Grove's own technical people, his best customers, and many of his partners, wanted Intel to embrace RISC. But Intel's current road map around the x86 was just picking up momentum, and adopting RISC would require splitting resources behind "two competing horses." Grove explained his dilemma to a class at Stanford Business School at the time: "I have three options. I can tell [software developers] that we lean heavily on x86, that the x86 is forever. Or I can tell them that RISC is important and that Intel wants to be the premier company in RISC. Or I can tell them we will support both CISC and RISC and let the market sort it out."[9]

Many CEOs would have gone for option 3—let the market decide. Others might have chased option 2—the "best" technology. But after more than a year of internal debate, Grove decided to stick with the x86 and essentially abandon RISC. Some insiders argued that Intel could close the technical gap with RISC over time by incorporating some RISC features into the x86 designs (and indeed, it did, as we discuss in Chapter 4). Equally important, though, Grove had to weigh the value of maintaining compatibility with previous generations of Intel chips. If Intel put its full resources behind RISC, the market would either tip in that direction or split between RISC and CISC. Many software developers would be stranded because their programs would not run on new RISC-based PCs, and millions of PC users would find themselves in the same fix. Dennis Carter, then head of marketing, became nearly "hysterical" at the prospect of Intel abandoning consumers in this way, especially since Intel had begun to invest heavily in its brand, starting with the "Red X" campaign that promoted the 386 chip.[10] Craig Kinnie, who headed Intel's architectural research lab, and Pat Gelsinger, the young manager of the 80486 project, also rejected the RISC strategy, arguing that RISC's technical benefits were grossly overstated. As Gelsinger later recalled, he and Kinnie "were absolutely adamant that compatibility carries the day."[11]

When Frank Gill, head of Intel's system business in the 1990s, reflected on this debate, he concluded that rejecting RISC was possibly the most courageous decision Grove had ever made. Despite a chorus of experts saying that RISC was the future, Gill recalled, "Andy, by himself, said no, we're not going to do that. He's not a computer architect. He's not a software engineer. But he just intuitively knew the best path for us. He had the courage to go against everybody."[12] When Grove looked back, he highlighted not the courage it took to make that decision but how obvious it seemed in retrospect: "How [could I] even have considered walking away from our traditional technology that then had . . . phenomenal headroom and momentum?" he wondered.[13] With hindsight, Grove believed that, if he had adopted RISC, he would have cost Intel the spectacular run it enjoyed in the 1990s.

By avoiding the trap of chasing the next great technology, Grove cast a decisive vote in favor of a platform rather than a product strategy. This move showed that he finally understood that long-term backward and forward compatibility was a key part of what defined a platform and made it so valuable for an entire industry. In the future, preserving that compatibility and trying to "grow the pie" for the broader PC ecosystem would be the cornerstones of Intel's strategy and business model.

Go for the Mass Market

Andy Grove took a decade longer than Bill Gates to conclude that his company should focus on building industry platforms, not just stand-alone products; Steve Jobs took more than twenty years to come to a similar realization. This should not be surprising. Jobs was a classic "product guy." The best way to win customers, he believed, was to build great products, and the best way to build great products was to maintain complete control over their design and performance. Jobs prided himself on Apple's self-sufficiency: "We're the only company that owns the whole widget—the hardware, the software, and the operating system," he explained. "We can take full responsibility for the user experience. We can do things the other guy can't do."[14] Giving up any of this control, he argued, would result in inferior products:

> If you have an extreme passion for producing great products, it pushes you to be integrated, to connect your hardware and your software and content management. You want to break new ground, so you have to do it yourself. If you want to allow your products to be open to other hardware or software, you have to give up some of your vision.[15]

Ironically, the success of Apple's products always depended on the availability of software developed by third parties. Apple II sales took off only with the emergence of a "killer app"—VisiCalc, the first electronic spreadsheet made by Software Arts. And the Macintosh might have disappeared from the market (like Sony's

Betamax VCR) if Microsoft, Adobe, and a few other companies had not provided key applications for word processing, spreadsheets, and desktop publishing.[16] Nonetheless, Apple did little to promote the Macintosh as a broad industry platform. Apple under Jobs refused to license the operating system to other hardware makers and kept its prices high, about twice that of a PC. High prices translated into fewer Mac purchases, which meant in turn that fewer developers invested in building Macintosh applications. This process drove Apple's share of the personal computer market down to the low single digits in the 1990s, while sales of PCs based on Windows software and Intel hardware soared. The Macintosh managed to live on only because it retained a small cadre of loyal users, largely in schools and desktop publishing.

Jobs applied the same "product over platform" mentality to his second act, NeXT Computers. David Yoffie discovered this at a dinner with Jobs and Andy Grove in the early 1990s. Partway through the meal, Jobs posed a question: "I'm going to start selling my operating system separately. What do you think is the right price?" David thought for a minute and said DOS was selling to computer companies for about $15 and Windows was roughly a $15 add-on—so NeXT should sell for $25 to $35 if it wanted to get broad adoption and become an important platform. Jobs felt that was insane: He believed that NeXT's OS was so much better than Windows that NeXT should charge $500 or even $700 per license. David, of course, lost the argument, but a few years later—when Jobs sold the company to Apple—NeXT was virtually dead.

By then, Jobs had matured as a strategic thinker. Nothing illustrated this transformation more dramatically than his eventual acquiescence—even if it was "kicking and screaming"—in the decision to pursue a platform strategy for Apple's hot new product, the iPod. Introduced in 2001, the early iPod won praise for its slick design, large memory, and ease of use. Yet sales remained small because iTunes, the software used to download, convert, organize, and transfer files to an iPod, worked only on Macintosh computers. The decision to ignore the true mass market—the 95 percent of personal computer users who owned Windows machines—was pure Jobs. He believed that the iPod was such a great product that it would force Windows users to become Macintosh users. He also wanted the iPod to be part of an Apple "digital hub" tied to the Macintosh platform and ecosystem, so that Apple could continue to control all aspects of the user experience. Initially, he argued, the strategy was working. In the early months after the iPod's release, Jobs claimed, "keeping the iPod for Mac only . . . was driving the sales of Macs even more than we expected."[17] But other company executives were less sanguine. Although Apple sold 125,000 iPods during the 2001 holiday season, sales fell below 60,000 units in each of the next two quarters.[18]

Jobs's continued refusal to make the iPod compatible with Windows PCs pitted him against all his senior executives. Fred Anderson, former Apple CFO, recalled that the senior leadership wanted to "open up the iPod to the broader world," but Jobs said, "No, I don't want to do that."[19] Jobs reportedly declared at one point that Windows users would get iPods "over my dead body."[20] As senior Apple engineering executive Jon Rubinstein explained to us, "Steve didn't do things for the PC—the PC was the enemy. . . . Steve said, 'No, no, we're not doing it; this is the digital hub strategy.'" Eventually, however, Jobs's executive team wore him down. After yet another heated argument, he hurled an expletive at the assembled managers, yelled, "Do whatever you want, you're responsible," and stormed out of the room.[21]

Taking Jobs at his word, Apple engineers shipped a Windows-compatible iPod in September 2002, almost a year after the release of the original device. Initial sales were weak, primarily because it used a third-party program, called MusicMatch, that was noticeably inferior to iTunes. Jobs had hoped to keep iTunes, if not the iPod, solely for Macintosh users, but the failure of the Windows iPod finally made him a convert to the platform strategy. He recognized that, if Apple insisted on providing only a second-rate version of the iPod to the Windows world, the iPod would never really take off. And even the best iPod was not compelling enough to drive the Macintosh market share beyond 5 percent, where it had languished for years. Consumers were not going to give up their Windows PCs and purchase Macs in order to take full advantage of the iPod. But if they purchased iPods to go along with their Windows PCs, then Apple would own a new global platform for music and other digital media.

Bowing to reality, Jobs approved a project to build iTunes for Windows, which he described, with typical modesty, as the "best Windows app ever written."[22] With the October 2003 release of iTunes for Windows, Apple's fortunes changed forever. As a huge market became accessible, iPod sales exploded. By June 2003, Apple had sold one million iPods in the eighteen months since its release, a respectable number, but still a niche business. Between June 2003 and the end of 2005, it sold 12 million.[23] By late 2007, Apple had sold some 100 million iPods at a time when the Macintosh installed base remained about a quarter of that number.[24]

Jobs (and Apple?) Never Fully Committed to Platform Thinking

The decision to go after Windows users largely drove Apple's explosive growth from 2004 to 2011. Yet Steve Jobs never fully committed to an industry platform strategy. His instincts continued to put products before platforms. Of course, this approach had its own logic. Jobs pushed his team to design devices that were optimized for new markets. If sacrificing compatibility with Apple's existing platforms produced better products, that was an acceptable trade-off to Jobs. Superior design and performance remained the hallmarks of Apple's product line.

While Jobs's strategy made the iPhone and the iPad into spectacular revenue- and profit-generating products, they have been less successful as broad industry platforms. A mass-market platform needs to be relatively cheap and easily accessible in order to attract increasing numbers of users and complementors, both of which generate those all-important network effects. In addition, most successful industry platforms are relatively "open" and "modular," which make it easier for producers of complementary products and services to add their own innovations.[25] In terms of price, openness, and modularity, the iPhone and iPad ranked low compared to phones and tablets based on Google's Android operating system, which debuted in 2007. Perhaps most important, Android software was open source and free to license; Apple would not license iOS for *any* price.

The success of Apple's App Store, built on what we might call a "closed, but not closed" platform strategy (as opposed to Microsoft's "open, but not open" strategy, which we discuss below), helped turn the iPhone and iPad into platforms far beyond what the Macintosh ever achieved. However, Jobs maintained tight control over Apple's ecosystem. Apps for the iPhone and iPad could only be purchased through Apple's App Store, and developers had to follow strict guidelines and pay Apple a 30 percent commission. Art Levinson, an Apple board member, described the App Store as "an absolutely magical solution that hit the sweet spot. It gave us the benefits of openness while retaining end-to-end control."[26] The early explosive growth was indeed magical, but those tight controls made it a mixed blessing for developers—and eventually for Apple as well.

Jobs's reluctance to embrace a broader platform and ecosystem strategy limited Apple's long-run market share in these new markets. As Google's Android operating system improved in functionality, manufacturers around the world imitated and enhanced Apple's revolutionary product designs. Developers followed in their wake and began to write increasingly popular Android apps, free of the restrictions Apple imposed. Predictably, the smartphone and tablet platform battles came to resemble the Macintosh-PC wars (or the Betamax-VHS battles) of years past. After initially achieving a dominant position in both markets, Apple struggled to maintain market share in the low teens in smartphones. In tablets, the iPad lost roughly 65 points of market share in the two years after Jobs's death in 2011. By 2014, Android had captured roughly 80 percent of the worldwide smartphone market and more than 60 percent of the tablet market. Samsung replaced Apple as the world leader in smartphone shipments.

We are seeing the same type of "product over platform" strategy with Apple's highly anticipated new product, the iWatch. This "wearable" is a potentially new computing and communications platform. Software companies could write applications that enable the iWatch to check the wearer's health and activity levels, and perform other functions now available on smartphones and tablets with the ease of simply looking at your wrist. However, just like the original iTunes and iPod, which worked only with a Macintosh computer, Apple designed the iWatch only for an iPhone. Unless management changes course in the future, the user base will always be limited by the market share of the iPhone. A true industry platform strategy, by contrast, would make the iWatch compatible with the industry leading platform, Google Android, and go for the majority of smartphone users.

Microsoft is the company that has worked with independent software developers more than any other company. . . . Why did we beat other operating systems? Because we worked with independent software companies to get them to write applications.[27]

—BILL GATES [1991]

THINK ECOSYSTEMS, NOT JUST PLATFORMS

David Johnson, who headed the Intel Architecture Lab in the late 1990s, described the fragile position of a platform company: "[At Intel,] we are tied to innovations by others to make our innovation valuable. If we do innovation in the processor, and Microsoft or independent software parties don't do a corresponding innovation, our innovation will be worthless."[28] In other words, prosperity in a platform business depends not simply on the strength of one's own products but on the innovations of other firms, sometimes including bitter rivals. Even Steve Jobs, who hated depending on others, reluctantly came to accept this truth. At Macworld in August 1997, he explained: "Apple lives in an ecosystem. It needs help from other partners; it needs to help other partners. And relationships that are destructive don't help anybody in this industry."[29] At the time, Jobs was justifying his decision to drop Apple's lawsuits against Microsoft for copying the Macintosh interface and to accept a major investment from his archrival Bill Gates.

For Intel and Microsoft, the strategic problem was simple: If Intel sold a great microprocessor and Microsoft sold a great operating system that went into an inferior computer, few people would buy it. Without the right memory configuration, bandwidth, and critical software drivers and applications, the user experience would be terrible. Apple sold complete systems but faced a similar conundrum: Even if company engineers designed great computers, without great peripherals (for example, printers and software drivers), great third-party software applications, and a well-oiled supply chain for components and assembly, Apple could not offer the consumer a complete solution and great user experience.

The response to this strategic problem was equally straightforward, at least in principle: Gates, Grove, and Jobs all made it part of their mission to facilitate innovation and cooperation throughout their ecosystems. However, each leader took a distinctive approach to this task, reflecting the differences in their priorities and the range of options available to those who follow a platform strategy. Platform versus product is not simply black versus white; there are many shades of gray.

Grow the Whole Pie

Intel, for example, had a long history of educating industry participants about its leading-edge products. As early as the late 1970s, we noted that Intel created software and hardware tools to make it easier for companies such as Microsoft and IBM to adopt its microprocessors. But the company's efforts basically stopped there. As Grove acknowledged in a 2003 interview, Intel executives in the 1970s and early 1980s were "chip heads" who did not truly understand the importance of industry platforms and ecosystem software partners like Microsoft.[30] Grove himself was largely stuck in the "product model" of strategy, rather than the "platform model."

By the late 1980s, however, after Intel introduced the 386 microprocessor, Grove was beginning to understand that his company needed to engage at a higher level with other firms that were crucial to Intel's long-term success. The impetus behind this shift was Grove's realization that the PC was a flawed technology. On the hardware side, conflicting standards, limited functionality, and technical "system bottlenecks," in Grove's words, made it hard for programmers to write compelling applications. The relative scarcity of compelling software, in turn, limited demand for new PCs, which limited Intel's ability to sell its microprocessors.

Grove's new strategy was to upgrade the PC as a system. Rather than just supply PC makers with chips, Intel would take direct responsibility for solving many of the PC's hardware problems and work more closely with ecosystem partners, especially in software. As a first step, Grove appointed Craig Kinnie in 1991 to head the new Intel Architecture Lab and make Intel "the architect for the open computer industry."[31] He charged Kinnie and his team with finding ways to overcome the technical deficiencies in the PC that made it difficult to deploy new applications. As a sign of his commitment to this effort, Grove empowered Kinnie to expand the lab, which grew to five hundred engineers (mostly software programmers) under his successor, David Johnson, by 2001.[32]

The lab's first big effort was the Peripheral Component Interconnect (PCI) initiative. In order to improve the PC's ability to handle graphics, help it connect easily with printers and other peripherals, and resolve related performance issues, Kinnie's engineers designed a new bus architecture and chipset to work alongside Intel's microprocessor. A "bus" is a hardware and software system that transfers information between components within a computer. A special chipset then manages communication between the microprocessor and the rest of the computer. Intel had traditionally not been involved in either area. As Grove recalled in a 1998 interview, "The notion that a silicon producer could define a computer bus architecture was a very strange thing. But nobody was doing it. . . . So around 1990, we started a pretty major effort to develop our own chipsets as well as the bus architecture. . . . It was a pretty controversial move."[33] Large computer companies like Compaq were particularly unhappy with Intel's PCI initiative, which they saw as a move onto their turf. Yet according to Grove, smaller PC makers, which did not have the engineering resources to design their own chipsets, welcomed the move: "For the smaller OEMs, this was wonderful because it gave them an opportunity to compete for a larger audience on the same footing [as the bigger PC makers]."[34]

The PCI initiative was only the beginning. Following the release of the first PCI bus in 1992, Intel engineers set out to identify other technical bottlenecks in the PC system. Over the next several years, these efforts led to the universal serial bus (USB), the accelerated graphics port, and new technologies such as Internet telephony. Modern consumers take these capabilities for granted, but they might not exist in personal computers running Windows without Intel's efforts. Intel's USB technology was an especially important breakthrough.[35] Before USB, connecting any peripheral to a PC had been a nightmare because each manufacturer had different standards and plugs. (Apple, in contrast, had one proprietary standard.)

Grove's philosophy, as described to us by his former technical assistant Renée James, was simple: "If you grow the whole thing and we take our fair share, then the whole industry grows."[36] This led to Grove's decision to make most of these innovations relatively "open" and often free. Intel patented but did not charge royalties for most of the essential platform-related technologies it developed. Intel also arranged cross-licensing agreements to seed its innovations throughout the industry. Grove's goal was to get as many companies as possible working together to improve the functionality of the PC, and thereby attract more complementary innovations and, ultimately, more users. With 80 percent or so of the PC microprocessor market, Intel would benefit disproportionately if these efforts to "grow the whole pie" succeeded. And the Wintel ecosystem did grow significantly, at least until smartphones and tablets started to eat away at PC sales. As PC shipments slowed through the mid-2000s, Intel eventually reorganized the lab and tied R&D more closely to its own products and non-PC platform initiatives.

Steve Jobs also understood the importance of growing the pie, but he took a different tack toward his ecosystem partners: he wanted to solve their problems and then charge for the privilege of using Apple's tightly controlled platforms and elegant technical solutions. Jobs's ecosystem partners ranged from music labels and video content producers to accessory manufacturers and book publishers. In each case, Jobs dictated pricing (always high for Apple, but low for complementors), commissions (usually 30 percent for Apple), branding, and promotion, and then told his "partners" to take it or leave it.

Of course, Jobs had a rare advantage: In the 2000s, Apple came up with three revolutionary products, the iPod, iPhone, and iPad, that evolved quickly into fast-growing industry platforms. This meant that almost everyone in the ecosystem wanted to work with Apple. Equally important, Jobs was solving difficult problems. For example, Apple's digital rights management system offered the first viable solution to music piracy, which was destroying the music industry before the introduction of iTunes. In addition, while Jobs demanded very low, unbundled pricing from his partners, he was one of the few players in the music ecosystem who could deliver meaningful revenues. Similarly, book publishers found that Apple offered them one of the only viable alternatives to Amazon. With the introduction of the iPad, Jobs gave them an opportunity to break Amazon's hold on the industry (albeit at a steep price), as we discuss in Chapter 4.

Apple's App Store was an equally important solution for software distribution. Every other major platform company would go on to copy this idea. Rather than go to hundreds or thousands of company websites to find a software application—which might or might not work with a specific device—consumers could simply visit the App Store, which centralized and simplified the entire process. Apple took 30 percent of the revenues, but, in return, it helped grow the pie for everyone by showcasing applications, enabling a simple payment and pricing system, and providing a trusted distribution channel for consumers.

Open, but Not Open

Microsoft, like Intel and Apple, depended heavily on complementors. If ecosystem partners did not design new hardware around DOS and Windows, or develop new software applications that ran on Microsoft's operating system, customers would have little reason to buy new computers or upgrade their operating systems, and demand for Windows would stagnate. Recognizing this relationship, Gates adopted a strategy that, on the surface, resembled Grove's:

both invested in new technologies and promoted standards in order to move the PC forward and expand the market. But Gates's approach really fell somewhere in between the strategies that Grove and Jobs pursued. Intel mostly gave away its technology while Apple kept its technology expensive and exclusive. Gates, by contrast, offered just enough "openness" to provide incentives for other companies to work with Microsoft, while keeping many aspects of Microsoft's technology "not open" and proprietary.

Gates clearly understood what he was doing, even in the very early years. On the one hand, it was crucial for Microsoft to convince other hardware and software companies to invest in new versions of DOS and then Windows. Starting with the first version of DOS in 1981, Microsoft encouraged such investment by essentially giving away its software developer kits, which provided enough information and sample code for manufacturers to build PCs and for software developers to write applications. Like Intel, Microsoft also introduced innovations that benefited the entire industry, such as technologies that facilitated networking or sped up the software-writing process by making it easier to reuse large pieces of code.[37] These efforts helped drive the proliferation of millions of Windows applications by the end of the 1990s.

On the other hand, Gates never wanted Microsoft to be completely open, which could make it easier for customers to switch to non-Microsoft technology. After all, in the applications market, Microsoft competed directly with many of the software companies it was trying to help. Gates and his team had a natural advantage in this competition because they knew where Microsoft's operating system road map was headed. In the mid-1980s, for example, Microsoft had a big head start when it came to rewriting the Excel and Word applications for Windows—an advantage amplified when some competitors refused to have anything to do with the new platform. Notably, Jim Manzi, the CEO of Lotus, proclaimed that he would not rush out Lotus 1-2-3 for Windows because Microsoft was the enemy.[38] This proved to be a disastrous mistake, and Lotus ended up being acquired by IBM in 1995.

At times, the "not open" side of Microsoft's strategy caused the company to cross over into illegal behavior. In the late 1990s, the U.S. Department of Justice accused Microsoft of giving special advantages to Microsoft's own applications developers—a charge that gained plausibility from Gates's admission, in a 1995 media interview, that there was "no Chinese wall" between Microsoft's operating systems and applications groups.[39] Competitors, including IBM, Lotus, WordPerfect, and Netscape, all claimed that they received information on new versions of Windows later than Microsoft's application groups. When Microsoft agreed to settle the government's antitrust case in 2001, the court appointed technical experts to limit illegal monopolistic behavior in the future. Nonetheless, similar charges have continued to emerge, leading to lawsuits and penalties, especially in Europe.[40]

Despite these legal setbacks, Microsoft benefited enormously from Gates's "open, but not open" platform strategy. In contrast to Andy Grove, who invested heavily to grow the overall pie for everyone, and to Steve Jobs, who fought to preserve Apple's exclusivity and control, Gates managed to have the best of both worlds for a very long time. He kept Microsoft "open" enough to attract thousands of complementors and cement its position as an industry platform, but simultaneously "not open" enough to maintain an edge over rival application developers.

Tensions exist. . . . Somebody who is doing videoconferencing wants to keep a [coder/decoder] proprietary to the videoconferencing product. The people who are responsible

for microprocessors want to give those videoconferencing products away for free. [We give it away and] the world trusts us. . . . But they trust us because we have not created an additional business that was successful.[41]
—ANDY GROVE [1998]

CREATE SOME OF YOUR OWN COMPLEMENTS

Few successful platform companies rely completely on their ecosystem partners for complementary innovations. Third parties are not always capable of delivering new products or services in a timely fashion. This dynamic creates a classic "chicken-and-egg" problem: without critical complements, customers will not buy a new platform, and without the promise of high sales volume, third parties might not invest in complements. Strategy in a platform business, therefore, may sometimes require you to create some of your own complements to get the market going. However, when platform leaders decide to play on both sides of the market—platform *and* complements—they run the risk of creating major conflicts with their partners, violating their trust, and making them less likely to invest in a business over which they have little control. If complementors feel that the owner of their target platform is becoming their primary competitor, they may switch to another ecosystem or even attempt to create a new platform of their own.

Gates, Grove, and Jobs all came to understand that creating an industry platform and a vibrant ecosystem was not always enough to stay ahead of the competition and keep growing. Sometimes they had to produce their own complements to stimulate demand for new versions of their platforms. This decision not only addressed the chicken-and-egg problem, but also encouraged ecosystem partners to move faster with their own product development. As a result, all three CEOs chose to play on both sides of the market, although to different degrees. In distinctive ways, Gates, Grove, and Jobs each discovered how to maintain ecosystem partnerships while sometimes competing with these same firms.

Attack the Chicken-and-Egg Problem

Of the three companies, Intel probably faced the biggest platform-related dilemma in the mid-1990s. The company was making massive capital investments to build new microprocessors. Those new, more powerful microprocessors could not simply be slipped into existing PCs and shipped. Computer companies needed to design and build new motherboards that would be ready to go when Intel's chips were ready to ship. All the pieces had to come together at the right time. If the timing was off, even by a few months, Intel would have expensive factory capacity left idle and its financial performance would suffer dramatically. This problem became especially acute when the Pentium came to market in 1994, precipitating the biggest production expansion in Intel's history until that time.

Grove's answer was for Intel to cut the time-to-market for new PCs by manufacturing some motherboards itself. Getting into the motherboard business, which had razor-thin margins, was not the end goal. Instead, Grove wanted to attack Intel's chicken-and-egg problem. Grove told us in 2013 that his initial instinct was to go for 80 percent of the motherboard market, which would have meant going full-scale into a new business. However, he was "talked down" to a lower number by his finance people. By the time the Pentium shipped, Intel offered a "Burger King strategy," noted Frank Gill, Grove's lieutenant in charge of the business. "We told the customers, 'Have it your way.' Have a chip. Have a chip plus chipsets [motherboard components]. Have a board or have a low-volume system [an unbranded PC]."[42]

This approach solved an especially vexing problem for smaller companies, such as Dell, Packard Bell, and Gateway. They did not have the expertise to design the motherboard for the new, higher-performance Pentium. A few years earlier, computer makers had balked at Intel's efforts to move beyond designing and building microprocessors. But by 1993, as Grove told his senior leadership team, the attitude of all but the largest companies had changed to "if not Intel, who else will do it?" As a result, Intel shipped almost 50 percent of its Pentium chips with Intel-made motherboards, accelerating the time-to-market for this new product and generating dramatic profits for both Intel and its leading PC customers.[43]

Bring the Big Profit Centers In-House

While Grove moved Intel into producing complements primarily to solve its chicken-and-egg problem, Gates saw the market for complements to Microsoft's operating system—notably applications software—as a huge profit center in its own right. Mike Maples, then a Microsoft executive vice president, made the company's position clear at a 1991 gathering for reporters: "If someone thinks we're not after Lotus and after WordPerfect and after Borland, they're confused. My job is to get a fair share of the software applications market, and to me that's 100 percent."[44]

Gates believed that Microsoft should dominate the biggest segments of the applications market; other developers could have the rest. And he succeeded in achieving this goal. Although Excel initially lagged behind Lotus 1-2-3 and early versions of Word were much less popular than WordPerfect, Microsoft captured as much as 95 percent of the desktop productivity applications market after bundling Word, Excel, and PowerPoint to create Office in 1990.[45] Eventually, applications became Microsoft's largest and most profitable business. In the 2013 fiscal year, when Microsoft still broke out its results by products, the Office group accounted for 30 percent of company sales and 45 percent of operating profits. This compared to 23 percent of sales and 33 percent of operating profits for desktop Windows.[46] But not all of Microsoft's application ventures succeeded. The personal finance product Microsoft Money, for example, failed to make much of a dent in the market share of Intuit's accounting software, Quicken. Intuit had built a loyal installed base and managed to stay one step ahead of Microsoft on features and functions. Similarly, in business applications, multimedia, and Internet content, Microsoft often fell behind more focused competitors.

Unlike Grove, Gates did not hesitate to build his own complementary products, even though he fully understood the importance of cultivating ecosystem partners. When he saw significant sales and profit potential or strategic value, he invested aggressively. Microsoft was able to take this approach because Windows became so dominant as a software platform that other developers had to support it, even when Microsoft launched application products that directly targeted theirs.

Build Complements Critical to the Customer Experience

Like Microsoft, Apple was heavily involved in creating complementary applications. Unlike Gates, however, Jobs was motivated primarily by his desire to control the customer experience and only indirectly by incremental sales and profits. Over time, Jobs learned to rely more heavily on third parties in such areas as manufacturing as well as applications and content development. Yet when he believed a complement was essential to the customer experience, he insisted on bringing it in-house.

iTunes was perhaps the leading example of Jobs's approach. Other companies that built digital music players, such as SanDisk, never developed their own music management software. Instead, they relied on applications from third parties, including RealNetworks,

MusicMatch, and Microsoft. But Jobs believed that iTunes was an essential complement to the iPod, as well as a new platform for content distribution. If it didn't work well, the iPod would fail. So this was something Apple had to do itself and do right.

In addition, Jobs believed strongly that Apple should create critical applications that showed off the distinctive features of his designs. With the Macintosh, for example, Jobs insisted that Apple bundle unique programs, such as MacWrite and MacPaint, that made the computer immediately useful and obviously different from the IBM PC. In his second stint at Apple, he returned to this theme, directing Apple engineers to develop iLife—a suite of applications that worked only on the Macintosh. These programs showed off Apple's ease of use and multimedia capabilities.

Similarly, when Apple shipped the iPhone, Jobs included a few critical complements, such as a weather app, to highlight the user experience. And when the iPad shipped in 2010, Jobs did not wait for third parties to deliver basic productivity software. The App Store sold Apple's internally developed Pages, Numbers, and Keynote programs—for only $10 each, a fraction of the $100 or more Microsoft demanded for Word or Excel on PCs.

This insistence on low pricing for complements—or even giving them away for free—was an essential part of Jobs's version of platform strategy. He understood that platform markets had different "sides" and he could choose which to monetize. Jobs chose to make money on the hardware and use cheap, ubiquitous complements to help drive demand for Apple computers and devices. This strategy worked very well for several years, though maintaining high prices for its products limited Apple's market share and became increasingly difficult as competitors copied Apple's hardware (and software) designs.

Our vision for the last 20 years can be summarized in a succinct way. We saw that exponential improvements in computer capabilities would make great software quite valuable. Our response was to build an organization to deliver the best software products. In the next 20 years the improvement in computer power will be outpaced by the exponential improvements in communications networks. . . . The Internet is a tidal wave. It changes the rules. It is an incredible opportunity as well as an incredible challenge.[47]

—Bill Gates [1995]

EVOLVE AND INVENT NEW PLATFORMS TO AVOID OBSOLESCENCE

Although "hit" products come and go, industry platforms, once they gain a significant market share, are difficult to dislodge. They owe much of this persistence to investments by customers that "lock them in." For example, a large organization that has invested millions of dollars in Microsoft software licenses and training is unlikely to decide overnight—or ever—to swap out its Windows PCs for Macs. In order to maintain this lock-in effect as a platform evolves, companies typically build in backward compatibility—ensuring, say, that older versions of Word and Excel or database products will still run on newer versions of Windows. But this close connection to the past creates an "innovator's dilemma" for platform strategists: how to preserve what is important to existing customers and complementors without becoming obsolete.[48]

Gates, Grove, and Jobs all worried about how much and how quickly to evolve their platforms. If they moved too quickly, they could disrupt relationships with existing customers and complementors. If they moved too slowly, they might find themselves outstripped by the competition. While maintaining a tie to the past, they also had to focus on the future. As Jobs said, quoting hockey great Wayne Gretzky, their job was to "skate where the puck's going, not where it's been."[49]

Extend Platform Capabilities and Features

At Intel, the challenge of evolving the platform meant not just making faster chips or adding more memory. It had to overcome system bottlenecks and build new features into the microprocessor that helped software programmers write more and better applications. The ultimate goal was to enable consumers to get more value out of their PCs—and not buy Macs, RISC workstations, or cheap Internet appliances. Under Grove, one of the most successful of these initiatives was development of the MMX instruction set, introduced in 1997 with the Pentium chip. Intel designed MMX to improve the microprocessor's ability to handle multimedia content, including audio and video. IBM had not designed the original PC to run graphics-intensive games or play music and video clips. By adding fifty-seven new instructions to the microprocessor, Intel enabled developers to write much faster and higher-quality multimedia applications.[50]

Intel spent tens of millions of dollars to develop and test MMX. In addition, Grove allocated roughly $100 million to underwrite new software that took advantage of the instruction set and another $150 million to market the Pentium with MMX as a brand-new microprocessor that would drive consumers and businesses to buy new PCs. These investments soon paid off: Sales of Pentium processors with MMX exploded, making it the most successful extension of

Intel's platform in the 1990s. It took Intel nearly a decade to find an equally successful platform extension—the Centrino, introduced in 2003, which enabled PCs to take advantage of Wi-Fi.

Of course, not all of Intel's efforts to evolve the platform were successful. A notable failure was Grove's initiative to change the basic architecture of Intel microprocessors. Starting with the 80386, Intel's CPUs were "32-bit," whereas the highest performance processors at the time had become "64-bit." A 32-bit system could handle less data and less memory and was generally slower than a 64-bit system. Recognizing this weakness in the product line, Grove became convinced in the early 1990s that Intel needed a 64-bit solution. Hewlett-Packard promised to deliver some of the critical ingredients, so the two companies joined forces to create a new microprocessor, the Itanium. Intel and HP expected the new chip to leapfrog the competition in the market for servers, which primarily used RISC microprocessors.

The future did not unfold as planned. The Itanium came to market three years late in 2001 and was plagued by high costs, low production volumes, and poor performance. Pat Gelsinger, who at one point managed the project, confided that the real problem was "a bad strategy." He explained, "The technical benefits of the Itanium were overstated, [and] the strength of an HP partnership was radically overestimated. We underestimated the strength of an architectural ecosystem and the costs of an architectural conversion."[51] Grove knew that the project was going badly, but, as he later acknowledged, he did not understand all the technical details, and his managers were unwilling to pull the plug on their own. Ultimately, Intel did establish a dominant position in servers and data centers with its x86 Xeon line of microprocessors, which won some 90 percent of the market worldwide. The Itanium, however, as columnist John Dvorak wrote in 2009, went down in computer industry history as "one of the great fiascos of the last 50 years."[52]

Intel and Grove bore primary responsibility for Itanium's failure. But in another well-known case, the fault lay at a partner's door. Intel introduced NSP (Native Signal Processing) in the mid-1990s as part of its efforts to improve multimedia and graphics processing on the PC. The main innovation of NSP was that it allowed application developers to bypass the Windows layer and give instructions directly to the microprocessor. As a programming technique, NSP sped up the performance of graphical applications. Microsoft, however, interpreted the technology as an invasion of its territory and refused to support it in Windows 95. Bill Gates made his position in "the Wintel partnership" clear, stating "we are the software company here, and we will not have any kind of equal relationship with Intel on software."[53] Ultimately, Intel caved. "We did not adequately appreciate Microsoft's business model at the time," Grove admitted. "Introducing a Windows-based software initiative that Microsoft doesn't support . . . well, life is too short for that."[54]

Gates was not opposed to change, but he wanted it to take place on his terms. Throughout his tenure, Microsoft invested heavily in improving the performance and functionality of its operating systems. In the 1980s, in response to competition from the Macintosh, Microsoft engineers successfully leveraged their knowledge of the Mac GUI to create the Windows layer on top of DOS. This evolution in scope and capabilities was an unqualified success. The move to Windows maintained backward compatibility but extended the platform in new directions that reduced any major threat from the Macintosh. Windows dramatically grew the market for both Microsoft and Intel because less sophisticated customers found the graphical user interface much easier to use than DOS, even if Windows was still less intuitive to use than the Macintosh.

Gates also made sure that Microsoft successfully adapted Windows to incorporate Internet functionality. To be sure, he trailed visionaries such as Marc Andreessen of Netscape and Jeff Bezos of Amazon in recognizing the importance of the Internet. He was even a year or more behind some of his own engineers. But when Gates wrote his Internet memo in May 1995, relying heavily on analyses by younger Microsoft engineers, he was still early enough to respond effectively. Microsoft went on to dominate the Web browser market by bundling Internet Explorer with Windows and cutting distribution deals with competitors like AOL. In short, while Gates may have been late, he was not too late and he acted without hesitation—sometimes even breaching antitrust regulations in his haste. Looking back in 1999, Gates recalled: "By the time we went public with our Internet strategy in December 1995, it was damn the torpedoes, full speed ahead. As I've said several times since, if we go out of business, it won't be because we're not focused on the Internet. It'll be because we're *too* focused on the Internet."[55]

Recognize the Need for New Platforms

Both Gates and Grove fell short, particularly in comparison to Jobs, when it came to seizing the opportunity offered by the rapid growth of new non-PC platforms. Both men recognized the potential explosion in Internet appliances and handheld consumer devices. Grove, for example, bought an ARM microprocessor license from DEC in 1998, and started Intel down the path of low-powered CPUs for smart devices. Gates, in late 1997, sent this memo to his executive staff:

> After my latest trip to Japan I came away with a huge concern about non-PC devices. With great progress in screens, digital audio, digital video, speech, handwriting and the Internet, there is HUGE risk that we will not be called to provide the OS for these devices. . . . The high price of Windows for $500 machines does make these non-PC devices more attractive. I need some piece of Windows CE that is super cheap. . . . We need a clever solution.[56]

Awareness, however, is not the same as commitment. Intel was never fully devoted to ARM and sold off its ARM business after Grove retired as chairman in 2006. At Microsoft, engineers tried to force-fit a version of Windows ("Windows CE") onto smaller devices rather than build a new operating system from scratch. At the time, Gates may have been distracted by Microsoft's legal battles; in any case, he failed to marshal the resources to act effectively on his realization that new platforms were on the horizon. According to Paul Maritz, who headed Microsoft's Windows division in the 1990s, it was not that he, Gates, and others didn't see new platforms emerging; they did. But it was hard to give up on the PC and enterprise sales of Windows and Office while they were generating so much money. Microsoft executives saw the transitions coming "through a PC lens" and thought the new devices were less urgent than the current business. In only one case did Microsoft find "the courage to do something that wasn't PC-centric"—the Xbox gaming platform, developed beginning in the late 1990s and first released in 2001.[57] Like Intel, Microsoft ended up missing or coming late to many of the most important new platform introductions of the next decade, notably in digital-media players, smartphones, and tablets, as well as software as a service and cloud computing.

During this same period, it was Apple that moved most nimbly to introduce new platforms. This may seem ironic, given Jobs's "product first" orientation. But in fact, the success of Apple's new platforms was directly related to the weakness of its old ones. Jobs and other company executives found it easier to innovate radically because they had much less to lose by breaking with the past. The Macintosh during the 1990s and early 2000s was a far distant second in computing, with only 3 percent to 5 percent of the global market. As a result, Apple could aggressively move into new product categories with much less concern for platform compatibility, cannibalization, or the impact on its relatively small number of ecosystem partners and customers.

It was also easier for Jobs to champion new platforms because he had never displayed much interest in maintaining compatibility with the past. His former software chief, Avie Tevanian, even described Jobs as having a "no lifeboats" philosophy. Tevanian explained: "Lifeboats cause people to get lazy and depend on them. If you want developers to use something new, don't let them use something old."[58] This philosophy became evident with Jobs's first break with the past—the introduction of the Macintosh in January 1984. The Mac did not run any existing Apple II applications when it debuted. Not until November 1985 did Apple release an emulation program that allowed Macs to run a few noncopyrighted Apple II applications.[59]

With subsequent platform changes, Apple made slightly greater efforts to ease the transition for customers, but they paled in comparison to the full-scale commitment to backward and forward compatibility demonstrated by Microsoft and Intel. In March 2001, when Apple released OS X to replace the aging Macintosh operating system, it made available an emulation program that sat on top of OS X and imitated the classic Mac OS. This made it possible for consumers to continue using their old Mac software, but at much slower speed due to the extra programming layer that was involved.[60] Similarly, in 2006, when Jobs ended Apple's twenty-year partnership with IBM and Motorola in order to switch to an Intel chip, Apple bundled emulation software with its new Macs so that users could run their old software. However, users who upgraded to the new machines still had to learn a new interface, and developers once again had to learn a new programming environment, as they had just five years earlier with the release of OS X.

When the iPod and iPhone were in development, Apple engineers wanted to base iOS on a mobile version of Linux, which would have tapped into the existing ecosystem of open-source programmers. But Jobs rejected this approach because his dream was to have "one OS across everything," according to Jon Rubinstein.[61] What's more, he "hated open-source." As Rubinstein explained, "He was very worried about IP, that someone would come after us later on and we'd have to give away our technology." Consequently, Apple engineers created iOS by removing multitasking and other features from the Mac OS X. These decisions initially limited iOS functionality and made the new operating system incompatible with Macintosh applications. Over time, Apple has slowly and cautiously expanded the functionality in iOS and moved to unify some aspects of the iOS core software and user interface with the Mac OS.

Today, Apple and Microsoft continue to play by the rules Jobs and Gates set down. Apple remains committed to designing great products and consumer experiences, and will break with the past when necessary. Microsoft remains committed to the Windows platform and continues to rely on Windows desktop and servers as well as Windows applications (mainly Office) for most of its revenues and profits. Operating under these constraints, both companies are playing catch-up in the mobile platform world now dominated by Google's Android. Unconstrained by legacy, Google and its Android partners have successfully played the platform game that Gates and Grove pioneered in the 1980s and 1990s.

LESSONS FROM THE MASTERS

Platform markets are industries characterized by a foundation technology and network effects driven by increasing numbers of users and complementary products and services. In such markets, whether we are talking about video recorders, personal computers, or smartphones, history suggests that the best platform, and not the best or the first product, generally wins in the long run. Over their careers, Bill Gates and Andy Grove devised what is now the classic playbook for such markets: First, think platforms before products when making key decisions on design, performance, and price. Second, encourage the growth of a strong ecosystem of complementors by promoting their success and facilitating access to your platform. Third, attack the chicken-and-egg problem and drive demand for new platform versions by creating some complements yourself. Finally, don't stand still for too long and simply be content with selling the old technology, even if customers continue to buy it. Evolve the platform at least incrementally by incorporating new ideas and features, especially from competitors who threaten your position.

This last point touches on the innovator's dilemma for platform leaders. Successful industry platforms like DOS/Windows or the Intel x86 microprocessor line create huge recurring revenue streams—what Bill Gates in 1994 referred to as "annuities" resulting from "network externalities." The more successful the platform, the more difficult it becomes to risk the revenues and profits it generates by making major changes or moving on to something entirely new. Meanwhile, customers as well as third-party complementor firms become invested in the existing platform, together generating those powerful network effects that bring exponentially increasing utility, value, and customer lock-in. Yet everyone knows that, eventually, there will always be a better mousetrap. With the right strategy, new platform leaders can emerge that either fragment the existing market or displace the old guard, sometimes in the seeming blink of an eye. This is what Nokia and BlackBerry experienced when the iPhone trounced their once-dominant cell phone platforms. It is also what Apple began to experience when Google gave away the Android software and built up its partner ecosystem.

Although leading companies are likely to hold on to their old platforms for too long, there is also a paradox here: The less successful a platform is in terms of broad industry adoption, the greater the incentives for the platform company to innovate and try something new. As we saw with the iPod, iPhone, and iPad, it is sometimes far more rewarding financially for a company to break with the past and create new platforms for new markets where they have another shot at winning.

Overall, we learn from Gates, Grove, and Jobs that platform strategy is really about understanding choices and trade-offs—whether to put more emphasis on stand-alone products or on partnerships that could grow the pie for everyone and potentially lead to a more dominant and enduring market position for the platform leader and its partners. In sorting through the options, the key question is *when to do what*. In the long run, for markets defined by complements and network effects, establishing the best platform—the one that is most open and accessible to the largest numbers of users and complementors—should be the best way to compete. On other occasions, such as when technological disruptions are on the horizon, or if a firm truly has a breakthrough category-defining design, it may be better to put "product over platform," at least in the short term. In such cases, companies need to get the new product right. It is also useful, however, to make the product design and business model flexible enough to support an industry platform strategy should the opportunity appear to open up and move in this direction.

CHAPTER 4

Exploit Leverage *and* Power—
Play Judo *and* Sumo

Thinking strategically is the fun part of business. Great strategists think big thoughts about the purpose of their enterprises, the long-run visions for their firms, the big bets they plan to make, and the products, platforms, and ecosystems they hope to build. But it is not enough to think big thoughts. To become a great strategist, you must turn your vision and high-level ideas into tactics, actions, and organizations that reach the customer and fend off the competition. In this chapter, we explore the tactical link between thinking strategically and delivering real outcomes; in the next, we talk about building organizations that embody the distinctive competitive edge of the leader.

Arthur Rock, one of Silicon Valley's most famous venture capitalists and an early investor in both Intel and Apple, once wrote, "[S]trategy is easy, but tactics—the day-to-day and month-to-month decisions required to manage a business—are hard."[1] Some CEOs may be tempted to delegate this hard work to subordinates, but not Bill Gates, Andy Grove, and Steve Jobs. All three were intimately involved in day-to-day tactical decisions as well as longer-term strategy. Gates loved to go deep into the software code and challenge his engineers at the algorithm level, at least through the early 1990s. Grove liked to feel the weekly pulse of sales numbers and marketing campaigns as well as closely track the financial impact of manufacturing capacity decisions. And Jobs was famous for getting into the nitty-gritty of product design and marketing.

At the same time, all three were known for their "take-no-prisoners" style. Behind the facades of the geek, the engineer, and the aesthete, Gates, Grove, and Jobs were fierce competitors who sought to win at almost any cost. They showed little hesitation when it came to undercutting rivals, squeezing partners, or keeping errant customers in line. They led start-ups that grew into large, powerful companies, and they skillfully wielded their market power to stay on top. As a result, they were often tagged in the press—and sometimes by regulators—as bullies or worse.

But all three CEOs were more subtle tacticians than their public images suggest. While famous for maneuvers that relied on their companies' power and size—such as "buy or bury the competition," in Jack Welch's words[2]—they often employed tactics that put a premium on smarts, not strength. Throughout their tenures, Gates, Grove, and Jobs drew on an extensive repertoire of moves, picking and choosing depending on the situation they faced. Some of these choices may seem surprising, such as the "puppy dog ploy," which we describe below. Sometimes leaders of large, successful companies overlook such tactics or write them off as makeshift maneuvers they resorted to on their way up—and have now left behind. But Gates, Grove, and Jobs showed unusual flexibility in their approach to competition, freely adopting tactics more commonly associated with small, vulnerable start-ups as well as others that made full use of their strength.

In other words, all three proved to be masters of what we have previously called tactical judo and sumo.[3] Sumo tactics, as the name clearly suggests, rely fundamentally on a company's power and size. In this category belong such familiar moves as locking up suppliers, buying out competitors, and cutthroat price competition. Judo tactics, in contrast, require deftness, agility, and the ability to out-maneuver the competition. Judo competitors use leverage to maximize their impact. They also rely on stealth and speed to get into the game, move close to opponents to reduce their vulnerability to attack, and look for opportunities to neutralize or take advantage of their opponents' strengths.

Gates, Grove, and Jobs all employed a mix of judo and sumo tactics. In this chapter, we identify three judo-inspired principles and one sumo principle that figured prominently in their success.

RULE 4: EXPLOIT LEVERAGE *AND* POWER— PLAY JUDO *AND* SUMO

1. Stay under the radar.
2. Keep your enemies close.
3. Embrace and extend competitors' strengths.
4. Don't be afraid to throw your weight around.

Steve Jobs was no threat to the music industry . . . the labels were [not] afraid of him because Steve was just a guy with an idea.[4]
—JIMMY IOVINE [2013]

STAY UNDER THE RADAR

Being underestimated—in fact, encouraging underestimation—can give you a critical edge when entering a new market. This approach doesn't come naturally to many ambitious entrepreneurs or CEOs. Staying under the radar can go against the grain. Many leaders are self-confident extroverts who like to toot their own horns. But tactically, telling the world about your great ideas too early can be a terrible mistake. Staying out of the limelight and avoiding direct competition is often a better approach. We call this tactic the "puppy dog ploy," borrowing a term from two well-known economists, Drew Fudenberg and Jean Tirole, winner of the 2014 Nobel Prize in Economics.[5] The goal is to look as inoffensive as possible so that stronger players will either fail to notice you or choose to leave you alone. Or if looking inoffensive is impossible—and for successful companies it often is—try to keep competitors in the dark about your intentions or keep them guessing through feints and misdirection.

Play the Puppy Dog

While Steve Jobs was not known for ducking the limelight, in his own way he turned out to be one of the greatest adherents of the puppy dog ploy. A notable example was his approach to launching iTunes. When Jobs first decided that he needed a music store, he wanted to buy Universal Music, according to Apple senior executive Jon Rubinstein. But that plan was soon scrapped. As Rubinstein recalled, Apple CFO "Fred [Anderson] just about had a heart attack when he learned about the economics of the music business, so Fred wouldn't let Steve buy Universal. And, frankly, I think it was strategically right because if he had, the rest of the music labels would have been [our] enemies."[6] Instead, Jobs took advantage of the fact that the major labels saw Apple as a harmless outsider. Apple, unlike rival MP3 player manufacturer Sony, did not compete directly with the labels, and even within its primary market—PCs—its share was then a minuscule 2 percent. Rather than see this as a weakness, Jobs turned Apple's limited presence into an asset in his talks with music executives. As Rubinstein recalled, Jobs's pitch went something like: "What harm could it possibly do to license us the music on the Mac? Think of it as an experiment."[7]

The ploy worked. The music companies signed up for iTunes, believing that they would be the ones calling the shots. We get some perspective on this from Jimmy Iovine, cofounder and chairman of Interscope Geffen A&M Records as well as cofounder with Dr. Dre of Beats Electronics, the audio products and music streaming company that Apple purchased for $3 billion in March 2014. He claimed that everyone expected there to be "at least two or three competitors to iTunes, and the labels [thought they] had all the power because Jobs only got one- or two-year contracts for the music, and they could have pulled their licenses at any time. I don't think the labels were afraid of him because Steve was just a guy with an idea."[8] Ironically, this laid-back attitude helped Jobs in the tough negotiations over the terms of participation in iTunes: The labels wanted music sold as albums for a higher price; Jobs wanted to sell individual tracks at 99 cents each. If the music executives had taken Apple more seriously, they might have dug in their heels and prevailed—after all, Apple needed them more than they needed Apple. But in the end, being underestimated helped Steve Jobs get his way. Believing that there was little at stake made it easier for the labels to give in.

Leverage Stealth

Jobs did not try to look inoffensive as a general rule, but he did have a long-standing obsession with concealing Apple's plans as a way to stay under the radar. As early as 1981, when Jobs got word of an upcoming *InfoWorld* story on Apple's three new development projects, he called the reporter and chewed him out, saying that even revealing the projects' code names—Lisa, Macintosh, and Diana (later the Apple IIe)—would give a key advantage to his competitors. The story ran anyway. But Jobs had the last word. When an *Info-World* reporter was granted a "press tour" of the Macintosh building on Apple's campus in 1983, the tour consisted only of the building's lobby.[9] (*InfoWorld* got off lightly. In 2005, Jobs sued several websites that had revealed information about Apple and its products. In one case, Apple tried to force two websites to reveal their sources. Apple ultimately lost the case and had to pay $700,000 in legal fees.)

Inside Apple, Jobs was just as tough, creating a culture (some say a cult) of intense secrecy. One former employee recalled that, prior to meetings, Jobs reminded everyone that "anything disclosed from this meeting will result not just in termination but in prosecution to the fullest extent that our lawyers can."[10] Not surprisingly, Apple's organization was designed to maximize secrecy. When Jon Rubinstein headed up the team developing the iPod, no more than one hundred other people at Apple even knew the project existed.[11] As Rubinstein said in 2000, "We have cells, like a terrorist organization."[12]

This obsession with secrecy extended to Apple's supply chain. In the weeks leading up to a product launch, Jobs had electronic monitoring devices placed in boxes of parts to track their movement through factories. Reportedly, the company once shipped products in tomato boxes.[13] The purpose of this stealth was to protect Apple's trade secrets and intellectual property and make it harder for competitors to respond to the company's moves. It also prevented new releases from potentially harming sales of existing products, since customers were less likely to wait for the next version of a product if they didn't know when it would come out. Finally, and perhaps most important, tight secrecy was a prerequisite for the dramatic product launches for which Apple became famous. Jobs used secrecy like a lever to boost the drama and impact of Apple's marketing efforts and increase sales.

Use Misdirection

Jobs was not only intent on covering Apple's tracks. He also actively tried to lead Apple's competitors astray. Jobs may not have read Sun Tzu's *The Art of War*, but he took to heart the Chinese sage's advice: "All warfare is based on deception. Therefore, when capable, feign incapacity; when active, feign inactivity."[14] Gene Munster, an industry analyst who covered Apple for several years when Jobs was in charge, observed that Apple regularly "jams the frequencies" to prevent information about its product plans from becoming public. He recalled being told by a senior Apple executive that Apple had no plans to release an inexpensive iPod with no screen, only a short time before the company released the iPod Shuffle, which was exactly that. And Munster was only one of many analysts and reporters who found themselves on the receiving end of Apple misinformation.[15]

Walt Mossberg, the veteran technology reporter, interviewed Jobs in June 2003 for the *Wall Street Journal*'s first annual "All Things Digital" conference. The interview was a veritable cornucopia of misleading statements about Apple's vision for the future. Among the takeaways: Apple had no plans to make a phone or tablet and did not think that users would ever want to view photos or watch videos on an iPod (or any other portable device with a small screen). Describing the soul of the iPod, Jobs insisted, "It's the music, stupid, it's the music. It's about music." He told Mossberg he was "not convinced that people want to watch movies on a tiny little display they carry around" and dismissed photos and video on portable devices as a "speculative market." But just over a year later, Apple released an iPod with a color screen for viewing photos, and an iPod with video capability followed in 2005.

Similarly, when it came to tablets, which Bill Gates was promoting at the time (albeit with a stylus), Jobs told Mossberg, "people want keyboards," adding, "we look at the tablet and we think it's going to fail." Pressed about the tablet as a reading device, Jobs acknowledged that it would be superior to a laptop but insisted that the only market for it would be "a bunch of rich guys who can afford their third computer" (on top of a desktop and a laptop). That, he joked, was too much of a "niche market," even for Apple. In reality, however, tablets were a frequent topic of discussion within Apple.[16] According to Avie Tevanian, Apple had been experimenting with a touch keyboard and tablet as early as 2002,[17] and Jon Rubinstein confirmed that, by 2003, Apple was investing in multi-touch technology for tablets.[18] Since Apple filed a patent for a tablet device in March 2004, the company obviously had not written off the tablet as of the summer of 2003.[19]

Even after Apple released the iPad in 2010, Jobs continued to mislead the market about his plans for the device. For example, he mockingly dismissed competing products with smaller, seven-inch screens. (The original iPad had a ten-inch screen.) Jobs claimed:

> No tablet can compete with the mobility of a smartphone, its ease of fitting into your pocket or purse, its unobtrusiveness when used in a crowd. Given that all tablet users will already have a smartphone in their pockets, giving up precious display area to fit a tablet in our pockets is clearly the wrong tradeoff. The 7-inch tablets are "tweeners," too big to compete with a smartphone and too small to compete with an iPad.[20]

In fact, Apple executives were thinking about developing a "tweener" of their own. In a January 2011 email, iTunes head Eddy Cue wrote that he had expressed his favorable view of smaller tablets "to Steve several times since Thanksgiving and he seemed very receptive the last time."[21] This process eventually led to the release of a smaller tablet, the iPad Mini, in late 2012.

Until the very end of Jobs's tenure as CEO, his use of stealth paid handsome dividends. For example, as a result of Apple's success at staying under the radar, none of the incumbent players were remotely ready to compete with the iPhone. It was such a radical departure from existing products and technology that Nokia's management completely discounted the threat from the iPhone for several years. And Microsoft, which had almost 20 percent of the smartphone business before the iPhone's launch, dismissed it as a toy. Microsoft CEO Steve Ballmer famously proclaimed, "There's no chance that the iPhone is going to get any significant market share. No chance."[22] A few months after the iPhone's launch, Ballmer was still not convinced. He told an interviewer, "$500 . . . the most expensive phone in the world, and it doesn't appeal to business customers because it doesn't have a keyboard. . . . We are selling millions of phones a year, and Apple is selling zero."[23]

We have to let go of this notion that for Apple to win, Microsoft has to lose. . . . The era of setting this up as a competition between Apple and Microsoft is over, as far as I'm concerned.[24]

—STEVE JOBS [1997]

KEEP YOUR ENEMIES CLOSE

Cooperating with competitors—both current and potential—is another tactic that doesn't always sit well with some hard-driving executives. Competitive instincts usually drive the desire to "win." Many leaders are more interested in controlling their environments than in building partnerships or sharing their success. But by working with opponents, you can strengthen your position and limit their room to maneuver, while postponing, diverting, or even preempting efforts to attack you head-on. In judo, we call this *gripping* the opponent. Clever judo tacticians will find ways to engage in a cooperative relationship with key players while protecting their options. The goal of this maneuver is to get in close, control the relationship, and make it much harder for your opponent to knock you down.

Both Bill Gates and Steve Jobs became masters of "co-opetition," competing and cooperating with other companies at the same time.[25] (Intel, in contrast, generally competed directly with its rivals, in part due to concern about antitrust laws.) Early in Microsoft's history, Gates found ways to work with IBM while competing with the computer giant to define the future of the PC platform. Gates also cooperated closely with Jobs to build applications for the Macintosh; this helped him learn the nitty-gritty of developing GUIs, which he then leveraged for Windows development. For his part, Jobs scored a tactical coup when he made temporary peace with Bill Gates and Microsoft in 1997 and kept Microsoft developing applications on the Macintosh platform.

Co-opetition

Bill Gates was surprisingly good at co-opetition. We are accustomed to thinking of Microsoft as a dominant, powerful company, a software Goliath to everybody else's David—albeit a Goliath who usually triumphed in the end. Yet, as we discussed in Chapter 2, in the 1980s Microsoft was the junior partner in an uneasy relationship with IBM, the behemoth of the computer industry. For a decade, Gates kept a grip on the giant company, which he always viewed as a potential rival. His approach reminds us of the old adage "Keep your friends close and your enemies closer!"

Given IBM's size, resources, and power as the historical standard setter, it could have decided early in the industry's history to produce its own PC operating system, leaving Microsoft out in the cold. And during the mid-1980s, IBM tried to do just that. Company executives who were ready to say "the hell with Microsoft" pushed forward the development of a new operating system called CP-DOS.[26] IBM engineers were also working on a product called TopView, a potential competitor to Windows that Gates later described as "one of many attempts to design us out of business."[27] In response to these moves, Gates pitched IBM hard on Microsoft's plans for successive versions of DOS and Windows. IBM did not endorse Microsoft's road map, but Gates neutralized one threat when IBM decided to merge the CP-DOS project with Microsoft's work on DOS. The two companies also signed a joint development agreement to create a new operating system. In 1985, this project resulted in OS/2.

But even as Gates was pushing the joint development project, Microsoft went down a parallel path with Windows. Steve Ballmer had tried to convince Gates to abandon Windows and commit fully to OS/2, but Gates refused. Although Gates wanted to continue cooperating with IBM to avoid becoming head-to-head competitors, he also knew that the two companies had fundamental differences in culture and vision and the prospects for long-term cooperation were slim. At a Microsoft application retreat in 1986, Gates proclaimed: "IBM is f-ed and we all know that they're f-ed. What we're going to do for the next couple of years is play rats in a maze,"[28] trying one option after another as if they wanted to make the relationship work but knowing that they were all likely to be dead ends. In effect, Gates successfully collaborated with IBM for as long as possible to avoid a devastating attack, while preparing for an inevitable confrontation.

From Zero-Sum to Win-Win

Steve Jobs, like Bill Gates, was not known for his cooperative style. But Jobs, like Gates, could cooperate when it was in his interest. In August 1997, when Apple was struggling to stay alive, Jobs stunned the Apple faithful at the Macworld Expo in Boston by announcing that Apple had entered into a partnership agreement with

Microsoft, its longtime rival and chief nemesis. Under the terms of the deal, Microsoft would purchase $150 million in nonvoting Apple shares and hold them for at least three years. Microsoft also pledged to continue developing Macintosh versions of Microsoft Office and Internet Explorer for five years and to release new versions at least as often as it did for Windows. In addition, Microsoft agreed to pay Apple an undisclosed amount (rumored to be $100 million) to settle Apple's long-standing claim that Microsoft's Windows operating system infringed upon its patents. In return, Apple agreed to make Explorer the default Web browser for the Macintosh operating system.[29] Even though Apple had only a tiny slice of the computer market, Microsoft saw this agreement as an important part of its campaign to make IE the dominant Web browser.

Some in the crowd at Macworld—for whom Microsoft represented the evil empire—booed the announcement of the deal. Jobs responded with a mild rebuke:

> We have to let go of this notion that for Apple to win, Microsoft has to lose. . . . The era of setting this up as a competition between Apple and Microsoft is over, as far as I'm concerned. This is about getting Apple healthy, and this is about Apple being able to make incredibly great contributions to the industry, to get healthy and prosper again.[30]

As Jobs told *Wall Street Journal* reporter Walt Mossberg ten years later, "If the game was a zero sum game where for Apple to win, Microsoft had to lose, then Apple was going to lose."[31]

At the time, Apple was struggling to survive. The agreement with Microsoft was a shrewd tactical move. Apple's share of the desktop market had slipped to 2.8 percent, and the company had lost $1.6 billion over the previous eighteen months.[32] The deal not only provided Apple with a cash infusion and resolved a long-running legal dispute, but it was also a vote of confidence in Apple's future. Apple would have been "gone" without the Microsoft deal, in Jon Rubin-stein's words: "Who would have bought a Mac, without having Of-fice? We would have been dead, because you couldn't do anything without Office."[33] In fact, by signing the agreement, Gates may have made a colossal tactical error: if Gates had not bailed out Jobs, Apple might not have been around to harass Microsoft a decade later—and eventually to replace it as the most valuable company of all time.

Although Jobs said the era of competition between Apple and Microsoft was over, the rivalry between them remained fierce. In addition to resuming the battle over the desktop computing market, the two firms would compete in coming years over digital music players, smartphones, tablets, and cloud computing. In most of these markets, despite starting from a weaker position, Apple gained the upper hand. By gripping his opponent back in 1997, Jobs had man-aged not only to maintain his balance but also to move into a stron-ger position, which helped Apple defeat Microsoft on many fronts.

Let's embrace what's been done well [by our competitors] and go beyond that. . . .[34]
  —BILL GATES [1995]

EMBRACE AND EXTEND COMPETITORS' STRENGTHS

A third tactic that many senior executives reject out of hand is stoop-ing to copy the competition. Imitation is often viewed as a sign of weakness or a signal that the company is out of creative juice. It can also be an admission of failure: maybe the original strategy didn't pan out; maybe the direction was right, but the execution was poor. Whatever the cause, the company now finds itself following a competitor's lead. That's not an outcome many leaders actively pursue—or seek to prolong. However, Gates, Grove, and Jobs understood that one of the best ways to respond to a challenge is to embrace and extend an opponent's strengths and potentially turn them into weaknesses. By acting on this insight, even at the cost of their pride, they led their companies to greater success.

Even Steve Jobs, who was generally considered to be a great innovator, was not above imitation, as an internal email from 2010 shows. Addressing problems with the iPhone and Apple's approach to cloud computing, he minced no words in setting out what his company needed to do. His strategy for the iPhone operating system (iOS) was simple: "catch up to Android where we are behind (notifications, tethering, speech . . .) and leapfrog them (Siri . . .)."[35] And his prescription for MobileMe, the predecessor to iCloud, was no more complex: "Strategy: catch up to Google cloud services and leapfrog them (Photo Stream, cloud storage)."[36]

Similarly, Andy Grove followed the competition's lead in the early 1990s, when Intel faced a major threat in the form of RISC chips—high-performance microprocessors based on a competing technology. As we discussed in Chapter 3, at the time, RISC chips seemed destined to dominate the high end of computing, especially servers and workstations. Some observers also expected them to become standard in desktop computers and other devices, pushing Intel's CISC chips to the margins of the industry. David Yoffie, as a member of Intel's board, asked at the time: If RISC is really better, how do we win? If RISC is faster and cheaper, as the competition claims, is Intel doomed?

The answer turned out to be no. RISC had certain technical advantages, such as "superscalar pipelining," a kind of parallel processing on a single processor, but it was technically possible to add these features to Intel's CISC designs. Starting in the early 1990s, Intel began redesigning its chips to incorporate RISC features and deployed its manufacturing prowess to produce the new, higher-performance microprocessors at high volume. The performance of Intel chips increased, the company's costs fell, and Intel eventually grabbed between 80 and 90 percent of the workstation and server markets, which RISC machines had previously dominated.

Bill Gates used imitation to even greater effect. In the 1980s, for example, many software companies tried to eke out a business by selling utilities that could improve the performance of Microsoft DOS by freeing up disk space, protecting and managing data, creating networks of computers, or providing other services. In 1990, Novell released its own version of DOS that included many of these features and utilities. Microsoft responded by matching Novell and upping the ante. MS-DOS 5.0, released in 1991, introduced a long list of features that users had been clamoring for. These features ranged from simple utilities that stored lengthy commands to tools for recovering files the user had accidentally erased. Before DOS 5.0, other companies had offered those tools and features; after DOS 5.0, they had to scramble to find a new niche. As new vendors emerged to add value to DOS 5.0, Microsoft again incorporated the key ideas into its next release—DOS 6.0, shipped in 1993. One reviewer put it this way: "Add LapLink, Stacker, Take Charge, V-Buster, Norton Utilities and Battery Saver to MS-DOS 5.0 and you have something remarkably similar [to MS-DOS 6.0]. But MS-DOS 6.0 will sell for far less than all those programs put together."[37] For the developers of these programs, the outlook was bleak. For Microsoft and consumers, the proposition was win-win.

But Microsoft was about to face its greatest competitive challenge yet. In the fall of 1995, most of the world was proclaiming Microsoft to be a dinosaur, despite the enormous success of its new operating system, Windows 95. The Internet was taking off, and Netscape was leading the way with 90 percent of the market for

Web browsers. Microsoft, which had spent hundreds of millions of dollars on an old-fashioned, proprietary online service, seemed to have missed the Internet boat. But on Pearl Harbor Day that year, Gates announced a stunning plan of attack: rather than push back against the Web-based technologies Netscape had pioneered, Microsoft would "embrace and extend" them and ride the Internet's momentum. The company was prepared to abandon its homegrown technology and adopt or adapt "all the popular Internet protocols." Gates declared: "Anything that a significant number of publishers are using and taking advantage of, we will support. We will do some extensions to those things. This is exactly what Netscape does."[38]

Three months later, Microsoft also "embraced" and licensed Java, the self-proclaimed "write once, run everywhere" programming language developed by rival Sun Microsystems. Java initially came out as a platform that would run on top of different operating systems, such as Windows, UNIX, and the Mac OS. Rather than write separate versions of their software for each OS, developers would write a single downloadable version in Java that would run on multiple devices. If this vision materialized, customers would no longer be locked into an operating system by past investments in software. Not surprisingly, Microsoft's first instinct was to block Java wherever and however it could. But in March 1996, Gates switched gears and decided to adopt Java and extend it in ways that would cause the language to splinter into competing versions and defuse the "write once, run everywhere" threat.

"Embrace and extend" was a demonstration of pure leverage and great tactical prowess. Microsoft couldn't defeat the Web. By late 1995, it was too late to woo customers back to a vision defined by proprietary technologies and gated content communities like the original AOL. But by embracing Web technologies, including HTML and Java, Microsoft could match Netscape's Navigator feature-for-feature and win back the market by offering an equivalent browser for free. (Navigator cost $49.) In essence, Microsoft was using the power behind Netscape's attack—the momentum of the Internet—to bring about its defeat. As more and more people poured onto the Web, Microsoft would use Windows and Internet Explorer to scoop them up and eat away at Netscape's lead.

Moreover, Microsoft planned to go further and "extend" the browser by integrating it into Windows and Office, which would encourage even more users to pick IE over Navigator. Put simply, the plan was to turn the competitor's product into a commodity, catch up, and add differentiation over time. With Windows 98, for example, users could access Web content directly on the desktop and choose to have the desktop environment mimic the look and feel of the browser. It turned out that users had little interest in this feature. Nonetheless, Gates's determination to integrate Internet functionality into Windows and make Windows a robust platform for Internet-enabled applications preserved Microsoft's status as the dominant software development platform for personal computers and king of the desktop.

I can buy 20 percent of you or I can buy all of you or I can go into this business myself and bury you.[39]
—BILL GATES TO STEVE CASE, CEO OF AOL [1993]

DON'T BE AFRAID TO THROW YOUR WEIGHT AROUND

Judo tactics made up a significant and often unappreciated part of the portfolios of these three CEOs. But equally important, Gates,

HOW TO GET TO 30% SHARE IN 12 MONTHS

SUMMARY RECOMMENDATIONS

1. Get Internet Religion. Today Netscape is the Internet friendly company, and Microsoft is the company that doesn't understand the Internet. As a company, we need to have Internet religion. Each group at Microsoft needs to ask how they are making the Internet better for customers, and how they are providing new value to the Internet that other companies can benefit from. We need to be emotionally committed to Internet success just as we were to GUI and Windows. We need to get focused on a single PR campaign which articulates how we're making the Internet better for business, and how we are creating more opportunities, instead of how we are making it different.

2. Clone and Superset Netscape. PSD needs to get serious about cloning Netscape. We must have a plan to clone all the features they have today, plus new ones they will add between now and our next releases. We have to make this our only priority and put our top people on the job. In addition to our planned Win32/OLE work, we have to get serious about extending and owning HTML as a format, and in the process leverage our existing assets to get ahead. We need to ship the Forms³ runtime with the Internet Explorer, and make sure that the Forms³ runtime can handle HTML extended for 2D layout. We also have to take RTF, re-purpose it so it is a natural extension of HTML, and change our Word and other text editors to read and write this new format.

3. Get 80% of Top Web Sites to Target Our Client. Content drives browser adoption, and we need to go to the top five sites and ask them "What can we do to get you to adopt IE?" We should be prepared to write a check, buy sites, or add features — basically do whatever it takes to drive adoption. We need to refocus our existing ICP evangelism (MSN focused today) on this effort. We need to assign aggressive drivers to this problem, perhaps JonL/RSegal.

SOURCE: "How to Get to 30% Share in 12 Months," Microsoft internal memo, *United States v. Microsoft Corporation* (Civil Action No. 98-1232), Government Exhibit 684, accessed May 21, 2013, http://www.justice.gov/atr/cases/exhibits/684.pdf.

Grove, and Jobs were not afraid to throw their weight around. Gates did not rely solely on "embrace and extend" when he made it Microsoft's top priority to increase its share of the market for Internet technologies from virtually nothing to 30 percent in twelve months. More traditional tactics also played an important role: For example, one step in Microsoft's war plan was to "Get 80% of Top Web Sites to Target Our Client [Internet Explorer]." And in order to achieve this goal, Gates planned to draw directly on Microsoft's strength. In a famous memo, published by the Department of Justice, Microsoft's stated strategy was: "we need to go to the top five sites and ask them, 'What can we do to get you to adopt IE?' We should be prepared to write a check, buy sites, or add features—basically do whatever it takes."[40]

Gates, Grove, and Jobs never shied away from making the most of their reputation, resources, and market position in competitive situations. Once their companies became giants, they took full advantage of their strength when dealing not only with competitors, but with customers, partners, and suppliers as well. At times, all three overreached and became entangled in charges of illegal anticompetitive behavior. Nonetheless, Gates, Grove, and Jobs all kept their companies at the top of the heap for many years by skillfully manipulating public perceptions, minimizing their competitors' openings for attack, and taking a hard-nosed approach to negotiations.

Unnerve the Competition

In *The Art of War*, Sun Tzu advised the reader, "Those who win every battle are not really skillful; those who render others' armies helpless without fighting are the best of all."[41] Bill Gates seems to have taken this advice to heart. He was notorious for using Microsoft's market clout to spread "FUD" (fear, uncertainty, and doubt) across the industry by preannouncing new products or upgrades that were at best a long way from release. This was a technique pioneered by IBM during its heyday. The idea of such product announcements, dubbed "vaporware," was to freeze the market by discouraging consumers from buying a competing product while they waited to see what the market leader would produce.

Unnerving the competition with vaporware was especially potent in the software industry, which explains why Gates was an early devotee of this tactic. In 1982, for example, he used vaporware to head off a threat to DOS and Windows. That year at Comdex, a computer industry trade show, Microsoft competitor VisiCorp demonstrated its Visi On graphics-based windowing operating environment for an IBM PC. As soon as he saw the demo, Gates recognized that not only had VisiCorp beaten him to the punch on a GUI, but that Visi On could supplant DOS as the standard computing platform for applications development. Gates immediately began to tell computer manufacturers that Microsoft was developing its own GUI, which at that point was little more than an idea hastily dubbed "Interface Manager." He urged customers not to sign any deals with VisiCorp until they saw Microsoft's product. In January 1983, Gates hinted that Microsoft would ship its product before Visi On got to market, a prediction that turned out to be off by two years.[42] And in April, Microsoft presented "one of the most illusive demonstrations of all time," a mock-up of a screen with several overlapping windows running different programs, none of which did anything. Inside Microsoft, it was dubbed the "smoke and mirrors" demo.[43]

Nonetheless, the tactic worked. By late 1984, the *Financial Times* reported that Microsoft Windows had "attracted considerable industry support from applications software companies," even though it had not yet come to market a year after its announcement.[44] Windows remained just around the corner, always weeks away from shipment throughout 1984 and most of 1985, until it finally shipped in November. During this time, VisiCorp, Apple, IBM, Digital Research, and others all brought GUIs to market. But Gates's media campaign helped ensure that, other than Apple, they never gained much of a foothold in the market, leaving the way open for Windows to dominate the PC desktop.

Minimize Openings for Attack

A second tactic that relies on superior strength is plugging all the gaps in your product line in order to minimize openings for attack. When you dominate a rapidly growing industry, competitors typically look for holes in your product or service line that they can fill. If skillfully exploited, even small holes can create a tear in your universe by allowing competitors to build a beachhead, expand, and ultimately come after your core business. By filling all visible gaps, you can greatly reduce this threat.

Intel adopted this tactic in the early 1990s to head off competition from imitators or "clones," such as AMD, Cyrix, and Chips and Technologies, who also produced x86 chips. At the time, makers of Intel clones were gunning for a large share of industry sales. Jerry Rogers, the president of Cyrix, bragged that his company would "like to split the market with Intel," implying he wanted a 50 percent market share.[45] In response to these threats, Grove began with the obvious: he brought the imitators to court. Yet lawsuits often do little more than build speed bumps: by filing, you try to protect your intellectual property, raise your competitors' costs, and slow down their attack. But winning in the market demands more. In this case, "more" meant a full-scale effort to fill all the holes in Intel's product line. In 1991, Intel announced thirty new versions of its 386 and 486 microprocessors, with the goal of covering the vast majority of its customers' needs.[46] AMD had previously made successful inroads into Intel's market by introducing new products, such as higher-speed parts in plastic packages. Grove was determined not to repeat that mistake.

In addition to ensuring that Intel provided the variety of products the market demanded, Grove was determined to supply each product in sufficient volume to meet customers' needs. This meant making expensive investments in manufacturing capacity to ensure supply. As Grove told his leadership team in 1993, "Every processor we can't ship due to capacity (or no product) is one for [our competitors]. *They don't get in by themselves. We have to let them in.*"[47] "Mandate #1" for Intel's strategy at the time was "Don't Botch Up on Microprocessors." The company executed, and only AMD remained a viable competitor by the end of the Grove era.

MANDATE #1: DON'T BOTCH UP ON MICROPROCESSORS.

- Don't screw up and let them in (e.g., not enough mobile 4's).
- Every processor we can't ship due to capacity (or no product) is one for them.

They don't get in by themselves.
We have to let them in.

SOURCE: Re-created with permission from Andy Grove's SLRP presentation to Intel, 1993.

Even as he was fending off competition from makers of Intel clones, Grove also had to deal with the threat posed by manufacturers of RISC processors, such as IBM, Sun Microsystems, DEC, and MIPS. As we discussed earlier, "embracing and extending" RISC features was an important part of Intel's response. But Grove also attacked the RISC manufacturers head-on. These companies initially focused on the high-end computing market, which was not Intel's core business. But Grove understood that once RISC processors established a foothold at the top of the market, they could migrate down to desktop PCs. So Intel fought to minimize RISC's share of the high-end market by offering a viable alternative to workstation and server customers. If these customers wanted to run their business on a heavy-duty, UNIX-based operating system, Grove wanted them to run that operating system on a computer built around an Intel chip. This goal translated into a mandate to make Intel the "port of choice" for every operating system.

Intel invested significant resources in software that made it easier and cheaper for software companies to rewrite their operating systems to run on Intel CPUs. The effort quickly paid off. By 1993, virtually every major operating system could run on an Intel chip, and the threat from high-end RISC processors soon faded away. RISC chips, however, never went away. A decade after Grove retired, low-power RISC chips reemerged as the leading force in the smartphone and tablet markets.

A final example of Grove's commitment to minimizing strategic gaps was his plan to resist "gravity"—the downward pressure on the price of PCs and chips, which we described in Chapter 1. Grove had identified gravity as the greatest threat facing the company in 1997. His first step was to launch a fighting brand under a new name, called Celeron. The idea was to keep Pentium as the premium brand, while using Celeron to attack the low-priced competitors and appeal to value-conscious consumers. At the same time, "Andy was very conscientious about not allowing the race to the bottom," remembered Renée James, his technical assistant at the time. As a result, Grove segmented the market from top to bottom, creating clearly differentiated models for each segment. Third, and perhaps most important, he argued that Intel had to become a major player at the top of the market by focusing on the sale of chips for servers, as well as PCs. "Today's equation," he told the SLRP team in 1997, was to sell 100 million CPUs at $200 for a total of $20 billion in revenues. "Tomorrow's equation," he suggested, would combine 100 million CPUs at $100 for PCs and 10 million at $1,000 for servers and data centers. It turned out that Grove grossly underestimated the long-term demand for PCs and servers (fortunately for Intel), but he was directionally right on average selling prices. Success with this strategy was a key contributor to Intel retaining its leading position in CPUs for the next fifteen years.

In contrast to Grove, Steve Jobs chose to keep most of Apple's product lines limited. He focused on delivering "insanely great" products at the high end of the market while allowing competitors to grab share with less elegant, cheaper offerings. One exception to this philosophy was the iMac, introduced in 1999. Apple eventually sold as many as thirty-two variations (different colors, configurations, and prices) of this relatively expensive computer over the next four years.[48] With the iPod, Jobs took a page from Grove's playbook and went much further: he evolved the media player into a family of products with different features for different users and a wider range of price points. The iPod business, it turned out, was the only market in which Apple commanded a dominant share for many years.

When Apple introduced the iPod, it was not the first digital music player, but its sleek design and seamless integration with iTunes made it by far the best and dramatically redefined the category. Like most Apple products, it was priced accordingly: at $399, the iPod cost significantly more than existing digital music players. Apple justified the price by pointing to its superior design and ease of use as well as the unique combination of small size and large capacity, captured in the tagline "a thousand songs in your pocket." Some industry critics, unimpressed, declared that "iPod" stood for "Idiots Price Our Devices." But they were soon silenced when Apple broke with company tradition by releasing a range of models to cover different price points and user preferences, leaving no space for competitors to gain a foothold.

The original $399 iPod had 5GB of storage. Subsequent models delivered greater capacity at the same price. In addition, Apple began to add new members to the iPod family. In January 2004, it launched the iPod Mini, with less capacity (4GB) at a lower price ($249). One year later, Apple introduced the iPod Shuffle. Incredibly compact, with limited capacity and no display, it was aimed at the ultraportable market. Later that year Apple introduced the Nano to replace the Mini. By the end of 2005, customers could have an iPod at price points starting at $99 for the Shuffle, $199 for the Nano, and $299 for the original iPod. Having covered the low end of the market, Jobs added the iPod Touch—essentially an iPhone without phone capability—to the top end of the line in 2007. The strategy clearly worked: by early 2007, Apple had sold 100 million iPods (the total passed 200 million in 2009), and iPod's share of the digital music player market remained above 60 percent from 2005 through 2013.

Play Hardball

A final tactical skill Gates, Grove, and Jobs shared was the ability and willingness to play hardball with competitors, customers, partners, and suppliers alike. As George Stalk and Rob Lachenauer have noted, "When companies play hardball it means they use every legitimate resource and strategy available to them to gain advantage over their competitors."[49] This was an approach to which all three CEOs returned time and time again.

Bill Gates, for example, routinely played hardball with Apple. Apple was one of Microsoft's earliest customers, licensing its BASIC interpreter for the Apple II back in 1977. In 1985, the license was expiring. The Apple II was still the dominant source of revenue for Apple, and BASIC was essential software. Gates, sensing Apple's weak position, demanded that Apple cease work on the version of BASIC it was designing in-house for the Macintosh; otherwise, it would not renew the license. Apple agreed to kill off the product, called MacBASIC, and give the code to Microsoft. An Apple engineer later told the *Wall Street Journal* that Gates "insisted that Apple withdraw what was an exceptional product. He held a gun to our head."[50]

Later that year, Gates clashed with Apple again. In October, just weeks prior to the release of Windows 1.01, Apple lawyers told Gates that Windows infringed on Apple's intellectual property. Incensed, Gates called Apple CEO John Sculley to find out if Apple intended to sue. Sculley, though vague, insisted Apple would protect its technology. Gates responded by threatening to cut off work on Microsoft's Macintosh applications if Apple pushed the issue. At the time, Microsoft Word and Excel were among the most widely used applications on the Macintosh. According to Sculley, Gates told him, "If we're on a collision course, I want to know it because we'll stop all development on Mac products. I hope we can find a way to settle this thing. The Mac is important to us and to our sales."[51] The threat may have been a bluff—Macintosh applications were indeed a crucial business for Microsoft at that time, and Gates wanted to dominate that market—but it was enough to bring Sculley around.

In November 1985, Gates and Sculley reached an agreement that gave Microsoft broad leeway in employing Mac-like visual elements in its products. (How broad and for how long became matters of considerable debate that eventually landed the two companies in court.) In return, Gates agreed to continue developing Microsoft applications for the Mac and to delay the release of Excel for the PC for a year, to give the Macintosh version time to make its way into the business market. Most observers believed that Gates took Sculley to the cleaners: Apple gave Microsoft carte blanche to borrow its "look and feel" and got little in return. It was already in Microsoft's best interest to continue selling Word and Excel for the Mac, and the PC version of Excel was two years away from release.[52] By playing hardball, Gates had extracted a valuable concession from Apple in return for doing things Microsoft was going to do anyway.

In the summer of 1997, Gates used the same threat against Apple. Then in the thick of the browser war with Netscape, Gates was pushing Apple to adopt Internet Explorer as the default browser for the Mac. With negotiations stalled between Microsoft and Apple's then-CEO Gil Amelio, Gates told his team that he had called Amelio in June to ask "how we should announce the cancellation of Mac Office."[53] Without Office, the future of Apple was in jeopardy. Even the most die-hard Apple loyalists used Microsoft applications on the Macintosh. Without a word processor or spreadsheet that could communicate with the other 98 percent of the world's computers, Apple's future was bleak. No doubt Jobs had this threat in mind when he negotiated a détente with Microsoft that August.

Gates was equally hard-nosed in dealings with other CEOs, such as AOL's Steve Case. In one of their earliest conversations in 1993, when Microsoft was thinking about entering the online services business, Gates reportedly said, "I can buy 20 percent of you or I can buy all of you or I can go into this business myself and bury you."[54] Three years later, Gates had no hesitation about using Microsoft's considerable resources to court AOL. In a bid to get AOL to adopt Internet Explorer and throw out Netscape, Gates reportedly asked Case, "How much do we need to pay you to screw Netscape? ('this is your lucky day')."[55]

Gates was hardly unique in this regard. Steve Jobs was just as tough when he had the upper hand. Apple under Jobs, in the words of one longtime observer, "[ran] roughshod over its partners and competitors."[56] From the moment he returned to Apple in 1997, Jobs started playing the "heavy." According to Jon Rubinstein, in negotiations "Steve never left a nickel on the table. . . . It was never a win-win, not with him."[57]

The negotiations between Apple and book publishers in the run-up to the 2010 launch of Apple's iBookstore provided a showcase for Jobs's talent for hardball. At the time, Amazon had about 90 percent of the ebook market. It typically paid publishers a wholesale price of $12.50 or $13.00 (about the same as the wholesale price for a hardcover) for new releases and bestsellers, then turned around and sold them at $9.99. Amazon took a significant loss in order to secure dominance in the ebook market and drive sales of its Kindle readers. Publishers hated Amazon's $9.99 price, fearing that it was "destroying the value perceived by customers," in the words of Arnaud Nourry, CEO of the publishing giant Hachette Livre. However, if they wanted to sell ebooks, they had to accept Amazon's terms.

Apple's iBookstore, which sold digital books for the iPad, gave publishers a viable alternative for the first time. But they soon found that Jobs was just as tough a negotiator as Amazon's Jeff Bezos. Jobs was willing to let publishers price ebooks higher than Amazon. But he demanded a 30 percent cut of every sale, plus the right to match the lowest price set by any other distributor. Apple, in other words, was offering publishers even less for each ebook than Amazon. Internal emails reveal that publishers hated Apple's proposed terms. HarperCollins's head of digital books, Charlie Redmayne, wrote, "The terms they are offering would deliver long term damage to our business." He went on to say that it was "vital that we push back and get a deal that gives us a sustainable business. This is our moment to negotiate—there is no advantage to caving at this point."[58]

James Murdoch, an executive of News Corporation, HarperCollins's parent company, wrote Jobs to reiterate that HarperCollins could not go forward on Apple's terms. But Jobs would have none of it; he responded to Murdoch's requests by asserting Apple's market clout and HarperCollins's need for Apple. Jobs told Murdoch that Apple would sell far more iPads in the first few weeks after launch than all the Kindles Amazon had ever sold. In his final email, Jobs put a virtual gun to Murdoch's head:

> As I see it, [HarperCollins] has the following choices:
>
> 1. Throw in with Apple and see if we can all make a go of this to create a real mainstream ebooks market at $12.99 and $14.99.
> 2. Keep going with Amazon at $9.99. You will make a bit more money in the short term, but in the medium term Amazon will tell you they will be paying you 70% of $9.99. They have shareholders too.
> 3. Hold back your books from Amazon. Without a way for customers to buy your ebooks, they will steal them. This will be the start of piracy and once started there will be no stopping it. Trust me, I've seen this happen with my own eyes.
>
> Maybe I'm missing something, but I don't see any other alternatives. Do you?[59]

HarperCollins agreed to Apple's terms a few days later. As Brian Murray, CEO of HarperCollins Publishers, told Murdoch after the deal was signed, "The economics [*sic*] for publisher and author are terrible compared to hardcover economics or current Kindle economics. All value accrues to Apple and the consumer. But the strategic value of an Apple bookstore is very high."[60] In a memo outlining the deal for other HarperCollins executives, Murray admitted, "We fought the pricing caps and the commission to the bitter end and lost."[61]

Losing was also a common experience for negotiators who faced off against Andy Grove. While Grove showed more respect for antitrust regulations than Gates and Jobs, he still found plenty of opportunities to throw Intel's weight around. For example, when Intel brought out a new chip, production capacity was usually limited. This gave Grove an opportunity to ration supplies as he saw fit. Intel's customers—companies like Compaq, Dell, and Hewlett-Packard—had to queue up to get their chips. If they annoyed Grove, he sometimes put them into his own personal "penalty box." Once there, customers might experience delays in receiving their allocations of scarce parts until they once again toed the line.

Grove's punitive side was also on display in Intel's 1997 dispute with DEC. DEC was a customer, selling Intel-based PCs, but the company was also trying to promote its own Alpha microprocessor. After DEC brought a lawsuit claiming that Intel's Pentium chip infringed upon Digital's patents and seeking an injunction and billions of dollars in damages, Grove reached out to DEC CEO Robert Palmer, who refused to take Grove's call. Even DEC's general counsel wouldn't respond. So Grove called David Yoffie, reasoning that since he worked twenty miles from DEC's Massachusetts headquarters, he would be most likely to know someone on DEC's board. As it turned out, David did know a DEC director—Kate Feldstein, an economist married to Harvard professor Martin Feldstein. After some reluctance, two directors from each company met for dinner. Before the meeting, Yoffie asked Grove what, if anything, Intel would do in response to the lawsuit. Grove replied that Intel would demand the return of confidential technical information that was critical for designing and building computers around Intel's future microprocessor technology.

The DEC board members were shocked that Grove would take such a step, and, in the following weeks, DEC refused to comply. Intel countersued and implied it would cut off DEC's supply of Pentium chips once the existing purchase agreement expired in two months. Behind the scenes, though, the dinner among directors had served to open up a dialogue, which Intel COO Craig Barrett quickly took over. Within months, Barrett negotiated a settlement that provided for DEC to drop its lawsuit and for Intel to purchase DEC's Massachusetts semiconductor manufacturing plant and a few semiconductor product lines.[62] Grove's hard line had paid off.

But Grove's heavy-handed approach attracted government scrutiny. In June 1998, the U.S. Federal Trade Commission filed suit against Intel for antitrust violations, alleging that the company had abused its position by threatening to withhold crucial information from customers. When the case was settled in 1999, the FTC banned Intel from "impeding, altering, suspending, withdrawing, withholding or refusing to provide access" to its intellectual property for any customer. However, the FTC would only enforce such a ban if "that customer agrees in writing not to seek an injunction" and is not "seeking or has sought compensation, damages or any other legal or equitable remedies."[63] In effect, the FTC banned Intel from using Grove's approach—unless a customer did the same thing as DEC. Put another way, the FTC said they didn't like it, but, when under attack, Grove was within his rights to use tough measures to solve the problem.

Respect the Rules

This case reminds us that a critical caveat applies to playing hardball: don't assume that anything goes. Laws and regulations, particularly in the area of antitrust policy, define the boundaries of what's legitimate. Once a firm becomes dominant, senior executives must assume that it will be constantly under a microscope and act accordingly. In this area, two of our three CEOs fell short.

Andy Grove was as paranoid about antitrust regulators as he was about the competition.[64] But the same was not true of Gates or Jobs. For most of his career as CEO, Gates showed little fear of antitrust authorities. Even though Microsoft had signed a consent decree with the U.S. Department of Justice (DOJ) in 1994, company executives did not believe that it placed significant limits on their freedom of action, arguing that the "objectives of that agreement were limited," in the words of Microsoft's associate general counsel.[65] When we interviewed Steve Ballmer in 1998, the year he became Microsoft's president, we urged him to consider antitrust training, but he balked, saying that it would take the edge off the sales force.[66] Senior management, including Gates, did not get religion on antitrust policy until it was almost too late: when the DOJ went after Microsoft again in 1998, it nearly broke up the company.

Jobs may have been even worse than Gates. He could be high-handed to the point of irresponsibility when it came to bullying competitors, customers, and even employees. Winning was everything; antitrust rules be damned. Initially, Jobs's bravado seemed to pay off, but eventually it backfired. In 2010, the Department of Justice charged Apple and five other high-tech companies with conspiring to prevent employees from jumping ship. A class-action lawsuit targeting a similar set of firms was filed the following year. Jobs, it turned out, had threatened Palm executives with patent lawsuits if they did not stop recruiting Apple employees, and, according to an email by Google's Sergey Brin, Jobs called him and screamed, "If you hire a single one of these people that means war."[67] The DOJ case was settled in 2012. Apple also lost an even more important case—a lawsuit brought by the DOJ charging that Apple had colluded with five major publishers—Hachette, HarperCollins, Macmillan,

Penguin, and Simon & Schuster—to raise ebook prices. Jobs, who died in October 2011, was no longer around when the courts handed down these decisions, but they were certainly not the legacy he had wanted to leave behind.

LESSONS FROM THE MASTERS

Master strategists understand that day-to-day tactical decisions are just as important as big competitive moves. Strategy creates the playing field; tactics define how you play the game—and ultimately whether you win or survive to play another day. If Bill Gates had not figured out in 1995 how to embrace and extend the Internet, Microsoft could have lost the browser war and seen its core franchise weaken as use of the Internet increased exponentially. If Andy Grove had not aggressively invested in engineering and manufacturing in the early 1990s to fill the holes in his microprocessor line, Intel never would have retained its 80 percent worldwide market share, which was key to the company's short- and long-term revenues and profits. And if Steve Jobs had not figured out the importance of looking unthreatening when he approached music executives in 2003 about selling through iTunes, then the online store, the iPod, and Apple's fortunes might never have taken off. For that matter, if Jobs had not made peace with Bill Gates in 1997, Apple might have died right then and there.

Knowing when to stay under the radar, when to work with your rivals, when to embrace and extend competitors' strengths, and when to throw your weight around can make the difference between success and failure. A few CEOs have some of these skills, but not all. Others rely on a subset of their repertoire at different points in time—using judo tactics when their companies are relatively small and turning to sumo tactics when they have bulked up in size and market position. Gates, Grove, and Jobs were unusual in their willingness and ability to deploy all four approaches throughout their tenures, depending on the challenge at hand.

Combining judo and sumo tactics is not easy because they reflect different mind-sets. Tactical judo requires mental flexibility, the ability to compromise, and the discipline necessary to put aside corporate pride and follow a competitor's lead. Tactical sumo, on the other hand, requires toughness above all. It is only a slight exaggeration to say that sumo players measure their success by the fear they inspire. Witness the observation Andy Grove put forward in a 1990 SLRP presentation: "Influence—Everybody is afraid of us—we must have a lot."[68]

Creating, managing, and exerting influence was a central task for Gates, Grove, and Jobs. The tactical choices they made were fundamental to their success. But their ability to lead organizations that were able to execute around these choices was just as critical. In the following chapter, we examine how all three CEOs used their individual knowledge bases and skills to shape companies that would become known for effective execution.

CHAPTER 5

Shape the Organization around Your Personal Anchor

Strategy without execution is as worthless as execution without strategy. Getting both right is a challenging task, but one that Bill Gates, Andy Grove, and Steve Jobs all accomplished to an impressive degree. All three had weaknesses as leaders, and they all benefited greatly from the help and support of their executive teams and other employees. Nonetheless, we cannot deny the strength of their track records at Microsoft, Intel, and Apple. Their success leads us to ask: What did these three CEOs do to drive performance and organizational effectiveness? Why were they able to deliver more powerful results than their rivals and successors, despite their well-known flaws?

The answer may sound surprising: none of the three was the type of well-rounded general manager that top business schools (including our own) try to produce. Gates, Grove, and Jobs had no formal business training, and it often showed. All three exhibited behavior that experts on leadership would call "imperfect" and sometimes seriously counterproductive.[1] Although willing to be proved wrong, each CEO typically saw himself as the smartest person in the room. They could be harsh, even unfair, toward subordinates, and they built cultures that encouraged independent thought as well as fierce debate and sometimes personal confrontation.

However, they also had unique strengths that profoundly affected the companies they led. Gates brought to Microsoft a deep understanding of software as a technology and as a business; Grove brought to Intel an intense commitment to instill "engineering-like" discipline in management and operations; and Jobs brought to Apple a unique sense of product design, with an intuitive understanding of how to make complex technology accessible to the nontechnical person. These strengths provided each CEO with a "personal anchor" that grounded his contributions to the company and shaped the way their organizations evolved. The anchors drove their day-to-day focus as CEOs and guided strategic thinking as well as helped them make decisions ranging from who to recruit to how to delegate authority. The values and priorities they embodied became elevated into organizational routines and competencies that remain in place even today at Microsoft, Intel, and Apple.

Such strong identification with a CEO's strengths—or more generally, with a visionary founder or transformational leader—can have a downside as well. In particular, overdependence on a single person can constrain an organization's ability to act and adapt to change. Like a ship's anchor, a CEO's personal anchor both prevents drift and limits movement in new directions—whether that means new markets and technologies or new strategies and business models. Microsoft, Intel, and Apple all confronted this dilemma in varying degrees. For the most part, though, Gates, Grove, and Jobs were relatively good at identifying their own weaknesses while they were in charge, and finding partners and colleagues to fill those gaps.

Many CEOs try to do too much on their own. Gates, Grove, and Jobs were guilty of this failing early in their careers. Over time, however, they learned to focus on a few key areas and management levers and built high-powered teams to run big chunks of their companies. They paid extraordinary attention to key details of critical products and operations but delegated in other areas with which they were less familiar. They got into the trenches with their employees in the areas where they believed they could add the most value, but always remained focused on the big picture—their higher-level strategic goals or product ambitions. In order to keep the best minds in their companies trained on the biggest problems, they dug deep into their organizations to find the most knowledgeable individuals, regardless of status or seniority. In other words, they didn't just "follow the money." They followed the knowledge. And they also made sure to combine people with ideas, as Bill Gates explained:

> . . . the rules for running a strong business and creating value haven't changed. For one thing, there's an essential human factor in every business endeavor. It doesn't matter if you have a perfect product, production plan and marketing pitch; you'll still need the right people to lead and implement those plans. That is a lesson you learn quickly in business. . . .[2]

Gates, Grove, and Jobs relied on their personal anchors in similar ways as they tackled the challenges of strategy execution and organization building. Each was an imperfect but ultimately effective leader, and all three demonstrated the value of the following four principles—in differing degrees and with varying approaches:

RULE 5: SHAPE THE ORGANIZATION AROUND YOUR PERSONAL ANCHOR

1. Know thyself—warts and all.
2. Pay extraordinary attention to detail—selectively.

3. Never lose sight of the big picture.
4. Give power to people with "the knowledge."

Getting fired from Apple was the best thing that could have ever happened to me. The heaviness of being successful was replaced by the lightness of being a beginner again, less sure about everything. It freed me to enter one of the most creative periods of my life.[3]

—STEVE JOBS, STANFORD UNIVERSITY COMMENCEMENT ADDRESS [2005]

KNOW THYSELF—WARTS AND ALL

To turn ideas and values into action, CEOs and entrepreneurs need passion, self-confidence, and focus. They also need a solid base of knowledge and competence that they can draw on to shape the business and the organization as well as put together a management team. Together, these assets make up a personal anchor that defines the distinctive value that any leader brings to an organization.

The first step in identifying a personal anchor is to "Know Thyself," as the ancient Greeks advised. This process requires a frank evaluation of both your strengths and weaknesses.[4] Gates, Grove, and Jobs did not possess this high level of self-awareness when they first became CEOs. They acquired it over time, sometimes through painful trial and error. But, once they understood what they could do and where they needed to rely on others, they became increasingly effective as company leaders.

A Passion for Technology

For Bill Gates, his personal anchor was a rare knowledge of how to program the early personal computers, combined with a passionate belief that computer *software*—not hardware—would change the world. He also believed that technology provided the foundation for a pioneering and potentially lucrative business model: selling *software products*.[5] In the late 1960s, when Gates discovered computers as a middle school student, most companies in the industry made their money either by selling hardware systems or by selling software services—writing programs from scratch to solve the problems of each customer one by one. But Gates soon realized that he could write a piece of software once and then sell it many times as a product, at little or no additional cost. A few companies had taken this approach to software for mainframe computers, but no one had tried it for the mass market.[6]

Microsoft launched in 1975 as the first company selling software products for the personal computer. Gates believed, rightly, that there would someday be a mass market for personal computers that would drive demand for consumer software. In the short term, the niche nature of the market and Gates's own interests led Microsoft to focus on creating tools (mostly programming languages) that helped other developers write their own software. As Gates told Michael Cusumano and Richard Selby in 1993, he believed that this focus gave Microsoft a critical advantage when it entered the market: "Why could we write software for the Macintosh and nobody else could? We wrote our own tools. . . . Why does the company exist in the first place? We wrote our own tools. There were no tools nearly as good. It was a massive competitive edge."[7] This technical focus—a key part of Gates's personal anchor—would become both an organizational strength and a limitation for Microsoft. This orientation toward the technology rather than the consumer side of the business helps explain why

Microsoft has often been slow and awkward when moving too far beyond its original technical focus.

Gates may not have fully anticipated the limitations that his technical bent would create for Microsoft in the future, but he was relatively quick to understand that his personal limitations restricted Microsoft's potential to grow. For this reason, in 1980 he asked his college classmate, Steve Ballmer, who had worked at Procter & Gamble, to drop out of Stanford Business School to help fill Microsoft's gaps in marketing and sales. Over the next few years, Gates then hired seasoned executives such as Jon Shirley from Radio Shack and Mike Maples from IBM to handle day-to-day operations as the business expanded. In addition, he recruited talented software engineers and product managers from Apple, Xerox PARC, and other companies when Microsoft began to move into the consumer market in the early 1980s to provide applications for the Macintosh as well as DOS PCs. Together, this top-flight executive team compensated for Gates's deficiencies in day-to-day management and helped him build Microsoft into a broad-based enterprise and consumer software products company.

A Passion for Discipline

Andy Grove's personal anchor was not based on a specific skill like software coding; rather, his greatest asset was the "engineering-like" discipline of a highly educated scientist who was equally at home at a university or a Fortune 500 company. According to Les Vadasz, one of Grove's oldest friends and most trusted managers, "discipline . . . in anything he does, whether he's thinking about strategy, thinking it through, or whether it's operational," was at the heart of Grove's approach to leadership at Intel.[8]

We noted earlier that Grove began his career as a chemical engineer, graduating from City College in New York and then completing a Ph.D. at Berkeley. As a student, Grove was trained to pursue "truth"—or at least to get close to the best answer possible—in whatever endeavor he tackled. He admitted to us that he never had the "entrepreneurial drive" that Gates and Jobs displayed, which is why he did not himself establish a company.[9] However, he had little fear of risk, as he showed by venturing alone from Hungary to America at the age of twenty and leaving Fairchild Semiconductor with Robert Noyce and Gordon Moore in 1968 to become Intel's first employee.

At Intel, Grove quickly found himself tasked with figuring out how to manage a complex manufacturing company in the new but enormously important semiconductor industry. No one had yet truly mastered the mass production of semiconductor memory products. In fact, Grove had joined Intel believing that Fairchild never reached its potential because it was not a sufficiently "disciplined organization."[10] He made it his mission to make sure this would not happen at Intel.

Grove set out to create systematic processes for the often messy activities of engineering and manufacturing at the technology frontier. In the process, as Vadasz pointed out, he paid a lot of attention to creating a strong culture in Intel around disciplined thinking and action, precisely because he knew a complex organization would be difficult to control. As Vadasz recalled, Grove often said, "You can't write down everything in systems and procedures. You have to depend on people." Vadasz added, "That is one of his biggest legacies and probably the most valuable one. At the end of the day, big organizations succeed or fail by their culture. No one man can keep track of everything."[11]

Although Grove recognized the need to rely on other people to manage all the areas that affected a company like Intel, he worked hard to fill his personal gaps in knowledge. He relied on internal experts to educate him on advances in semiconductor technology. He became a serious student of new domains critical to driving company performance, such as RISC technology and the Internet, and never stopped studying. He also tried to clarify his thinking by writing down his thoughts, especially in books. In 1967, to bolster his knowledge of semiconductor technology, Grove published a textbook, *Physics and Technology of Semiconductors*, now considered a classic in the field. As his management responsibilities increased, Grove read widely about business and in 1983 published *High Output Management*. This second book provides a rare window into Grove's mind as he grappled with the challenge of being president of Intel.

High Output Management argues that an organization can perform at an optimal level only if managers draw out "peak performance" from their employees.[12] Accordingly, Grove devoted increasing attention to evaluating and motivating people as well as empowering them to contribute ideas and feedback. Grove also thought carefully about how to use his own time and improve his managerial "leverage." He emphasized the importance of clear priorities: "We must realize—and act on the realization—that if we try to focus on everything we focus on nothing. A few extremely well-chosen objectives impart a clear message about what we say 'yes' to and what we say 'no' to."[13] This form of discipline became central to his management style.

A Passion for Design

Steve Jobs's personal anchor was impeccable taste in product design combined with a vision of what technology, made simple and elegant, could do for the average person. With the help of cofounder Steve Wozniak and other Apple engineers and managers, he translated this aesthetic sense into radical new product designs and user interfaces, first for personal computers and then for other products and services like the iPod, iPhone, and iPad, as well as iTunes, the App Store, and iCloud. In many ways, Jobs was someone who could have been an artist but who happened to become a technology entrepreneur. [14]

Jobs's background strongly shaped his approach to technology and business. He had minimal technical training in high school and college, so he wanted to build products that were simple enough for most people to use. Yet Jobs grew up in Silicon Valley, surrounded by master craftsmen and engineers. In particular, his father loved tinkering with cars and carpentry, and many neighbors worked at respected engineering companies like Hewlett-Packard.[15] At an early age, Jobs began to think about what technology could do for people, if only it were more accessible. This emphasis on usability led him to create in Apple a unique company that would set new standards for simplicity, usability, and design elegance for the entire industry. Jobs even had an enormous impact on archrival Bill Gates, whose R&D agenda at Microsoft for many years was largely to copy the "look and feel" of the Macintosh operating system.

When it came to the design of Apple's products, Jobs tried to control every detail. In Apple's early days, he even insisted on having a say in how printed circuit boards looked inside the computer. However, Jobs had little interest or knowledge in many of the areas involved in running a company, such as operations and finance. Initially cocky, he eventually came to appreciate the need to surround himself with experts in these fields. This was particularly true after he rejoined Apple in 1997: a top-notch executive team saved Jobs more than once when his instincts led him astray. For example, the iPod might have languished in the marketplace if CFO Fred Anderson had not stopped him from buying Universal Music in the early 2000s, or if his team had not browbeat him to make the iPod compatible with Windows in 2003. However, Jobs never let his "domain experts" run totally free. Having been fired once from Apple in 1985, Jobs always remained on guard. He frequently pitted one manager against another and compartmentalized information into functional "silos" so that he remained in control. Ron Johnson, Apple's former head of retail, observed that Jobs, after returning to Apple, never again left himself vulnerable to ouster: "Steve is always getting input, but he doesn't want to lose control."[16]

■

EXECUTION IS GOD![17]
—Andy Grove [1996]

PAY EXTRAORDINARY ATTENTION TO DETAIL—SELECTIVELY

A leader's personal anchor provides focus and direction not only for the organization's strategy, but for its evolution as well. For example, it helps determine where CEOs focus their attention and how they choose to lead. A leader without a clear sense of direction can easily become obsessed with minutiae that turn out to be irrelevant to the customer and the business. Gates, Grove, and Jobs generally avoided this trap. They learned to trust their instincts in order to cut through the clutter of information and to identify what truly mattered to the business. They paid extraordinary attention to detail—but selectively—and, in the process, they instilled the same discipline throughout their organizations.

Identify a Few Key Leverage Points

One technique that Gates, Grove, and Jobs used to sort through conflicting data and increasingly complex operations was to identify and then manage around a few key leverage points. Grove focused on marketing and sales, but also—and this is somewhat surprising given his engineering background—the corporate culture, which emphasized disciplined thinking. As he told us in an interview for this book, "There are so many freaking knobs to turn. So I turned the ones that meant something to me. . . . Marketing was definitely one. Sales was another. Design wasn't. *Culture* was."[18] Ultimately, Grove argued, "exquisite marketing and exquisite fabs defined Intel"[19]—by which he meant that Intel under his leadership tried to give equal weight to both marketing and manufacturing.

Gates shaped Microsoft's organization and culture by identifying a different set of leverage points. Since software expertise was his anchor, early on he sought to master every feature in every Microsoft product. At first, he recalled, "I wouldn't let anybody write any code. I went in and took every statement that anybody else had written in BASIC and rewrote it myself, just because I didn't like the way they coded."[20] Well into the 1990s, Gates continued to astonish company engineers with his grasp of programming details. The test manager for Windows 95 described Gates as "a maniac" and claimed, "Bill knows more about the product than any of us. You go into meetings and you come out just sweating because, if there is any flaw, he will land on it immediately and pick it to bits."[21] This unrelenting attention to technical details during the 1980s and through at least the mid-1990s kept Microsoft's developers and executives constantly "on their toes."

It was possible for Gates to take this approach because, for much of his tenure as CEO, he had the skills to understand Microsoft's products at the lowest levels—the code and algorithms.[22] Although the technology had outstripped Gates's personal programming experience by the mid-1990s, he still knew what questions to ask and learned new things easily. But is probing the code what the CEO of a software company should do? Yes, when the firm is new and the CEO best understands the technology and the customer; probably not, as the firm's product portfolio expands and the technology moves forward. Gates realized this fairly quickly, and, by the early

1990s, he had decided to focus his attention on Microsoft's most important products. He then used project reviews and reports to keep track of what was going on elsewhere in the company.

As Gates told Cusumano and Selby in 1993, "The products that comprise 80 percent of our revenues I choose to understand very, very deeply."[23] He continued to work directly with these product teams, helping to define new versions and features as best he could, especially when they faced new challenges, such as networking and the Internet. In addition, Gates maintained tight control over investment decisions for new product development: "I have not delegated the general idea of products to develop. . . . That is a good decision for a CEO of a software company to keep in his hands."[24]

For less critical products, rather than exercise direct oversight, Gates relied on the major program reviews and planning sessions held in April and October each year. Microsoft supplemented these sessions with biweekly and then monthly project status reports sent via email. Gates explained, "I get all the status reports . . . [and] I read every one of those things. . . . The thing that jumps out right away is are they changing the date this time? . . . It's easy then just to shoot off a piece of mail and say, 'Come on, I thought I asked to get drag-and-drop into this thing, and I don't see it in the status report.'"[25]

This oversight system worked well for several years, but its success required Gates's full attention, expertise, and force of will. After he became increasingly involved with Microsoft's antitrust legal battles in the late 1990s, and then retired as CEO, the company's execution began to falter. The Windows group grew increasingly large and disorganized, leading to such fiascos as the five-year delay in releasing Windows Vista, which involved as many as seven thousand engineers and finally shipped in 2007.[26] In addition, Microsoft badly misjudged the market opportunities in mobile devices and online services opened up by Apple's iPhone and iPad. When the company finally responded by releasing Windows 8 and the Surface tablet in 2012, its products failed to gain much of a market following.

Gates remained at Microsoft during these difficult years as chief software architect until 2006 and as chairman of the board until 2014. But his role in influencing key projects and setting new strategic directions essentially ended when Steve Ballmer replaced him as CEO in 2000. Gates may well have more influence in the future. In 2014, Microsoft's newly appointed CEO, Satya Nadella, asked Gates to return to a more active role in the company, serving as a mentor and advisor for product strategy.[27]

Instill Discipline with Attention to Detail

Steve Jobs's focus on design was just as intense as Gates's focus on software. Like architect Ludwig Mies van der Rohe, whom he admired, Jobs believed that "God is in the details"—particularly when it came to the design of Apple's products.[28] Jobs cared deeply about anything that impacted the customer experience, beginning with the look of a product and ending with packaging and advertisements. No detail was too small because he believed customers would notice, just as he noticed. Jobs saw it as his special responsibility to make sure everything at Apple reflected his taste. This is what gave all of Apple's products, online services, packaging, and marketing that consistent "look and feel." Jobs saw this type of consistency as the best route to the customer.

The impact of Jobs's extraordinary but selective attention to detail first became evident with the Apple II, which debuted in 1977, and then the Macintosh, which followed in 1984. Positive customer reactions to both products reinforced his hands-on approach to design in later years. For example, after returning to Apple in 1997, Jobs immediately got involved in the user interface for the new operating system, OS X, meeting weekly with the design team. Cordell Ratzlaff, the project lead, remembered that Jobs "would scrutinize everything, down to the pixel level." Jobs even wanted the scroll bars on the windows to look a certain way, forcing the team to present multiple versions in a process that took almost six months.[29]

During this process, and continuing through the 2000s, Jobs worked hand in hand with lead designer Jonathan (Jony) Ive and his team. Jobs spoke with Ive at least once a day, and they often had lunch together. Jobs also visited the design studio frequently to examine prototypes and models under development. During those interactions, he made suggestions for changes in a highly iterative design process. These informal conversations influenced Apple's approach to product development as much as the company's formal product presentations and reviews. In addition, Jobs's frequent visits and consultations ensured that new product designs never wandered too far from what he had in mind.[30]

Nearly fanatical attention to detail not only led to better products, it also influenced Apple's culture and organizational competencies. If Jobs paid attention even to seemingly trivial design decisions, then everyone else at Apple had to pay attention as well—and understand why. As a former Apple product manager observed, "Jobs stayed involved from beginning to end to make sure everything matched his vision. He'd check off on the smallest things. That's how you get discipline."[31] As a result, according to one member of Apple's elite Industrial Design Team, it was common in Apple to "obsess over every detail."[32]

Beyond design, marketing was Jobs's other great passion and here again he showed extraordinary attention to detail. For the iPod campaign, Jobs worked directly with Apple's advertising executives on everything from the images used for billboards to the songs played in television ads. He did the same for the iPad in 2010, shooting down multiple suggestions before Apple's ad agency let him personally articulate the tone, style, and voice that would guide the advertising campaign.[33] Jobs also oversaw the layout of Apple's retail stores, from their high-level design down to the materials used in their construction.

Test the Logic, and Follow Up, Follow Up, Follow Up

While Gates and Jobs were passionate about software and product design, Grove was passionate about disciplined thinking. He dove deep into areas such as marketing and sales, capacity planning, and the technology road maps that laid out how new Intel products would stack up compared to the competition. To keep on top of current operations and make the best decisions possible, Grove wanted access to as much data as possible. He also became convinced that mastering the most important details himself—and requiring follow-up from everyone involved, regardless of rank—was the best way to ensure discipline and effective execution.

Most weeks, on Tuesday, Wednesday, and Thursday, Intel held business reviews, group reviews, and strategic reviews. During these sessions, Grove posed difficult, penetrating questions. The answers he received were often less important than the thought process they revealed. If Grove sensed sloppy thinking, then "all hell would break loose." If Grove believed his managers were on top of their subjects, he would give them a pass. One of Grove's protégés, Pat Gelsinger, gave a particularly apt description of how Grove worked: "[Grove] would challenge people's thinking; he'd probe and he'd prod; he'd prick. . . . He would probe all the way through a strategy and force people to really justify it. And if he could get all the way down to the bottom and if it still was coherent and solid, then the strategy was probably okay."[34]

Grove also became famous within Intel for issuing "ARs" ("Action Required") at the end of each meeting. He expected follow-up, and his staff tracked the ARs—even those that Grove "issued" to his bosses, Intel cofounders Bob Noyce and Gordon Moore. No one wanted to come to a meeting unprepared, and no one wanted to come to a meeting without having completed his or her AR assignment. This was execution at its best.

◼

Senior management needed to step in and make some very tough moves. . . . I became very directive in prescribing the strategic direction from the top down.[35]
—ANDY GROVE [1996]

NEVER LOSE SIGHT OF THE BIG PICTURE

The inclination to dive deeply into the details of products and operations that Gates, Grove, and Jobs shared is all the more remarkable because they rarely took their eyes off the big picture. Their high-level goals—create the dominant software and semiconductor companies, or wow customers with simple but elegant product designs—determined which details mattered to them and which did not. Yet the ability to balance the big picture with attention to even the smallest details did not come naturally or easily to any of them. It is another skill they learned, or at least learned to do better.

Provide Direction from the Top

Grove struggled the most with finding the right balance between details and big-picture ideas, and with the related challenge of balancing top-down direction against lower-level autonomy. From the late 1960s through the mid-1980s, Grove led a strategic planning process that he intended to be "resolutely bottom-up." He firmly believed that middle managers—not senior executives like him—were in the best position to make resource-allocation decisions. Consequently, Intel's early planning process called for middle managers to prepare their own strategic plans and then show them to Grove and other senior executives, who then asked the hard questions about goals, resources, and competition, but without mandating a higher-level direction for managers to follow.

The value of this approach became clear in the mid-1980s, when middle managers led a historic shift in Intel's business. Until then, the company's goal had been simple: to "produce bigger and better semiconductor memories ahead of the competition," in Grove's words.[36] But, by the mid-1980s, the industry had changed and microprocessors, not memories, were capturing most of the value. Middle managers "in the trenches" saw these changes before Grove and other executives because they were "following the money," so to speak. PC manufacturers were suddenly willing to pay a lot more for microprocessors compared to memory products. In response, Intel's production planners and finance specialists gradually allocated production capacity away from the money-losing memory business and into more profitable microprocessors. "Simply by doing their daily work, these middle managers were adjusting Intel's strategic posture," Grove later observed.[37] By the time Grove and Moore decided to exit the memory business formally, only one of Intel's eight silicon fabrication plants was producing memory chips. The decisions of middle managers made Intel's strategic shift to microprocessors far less drastic and painful than it might have been.

This episode also made it clear to Grove that bottom-up planning was inadequate to help Intel change as fast or faster than the industry. Intel needed its senior leadership—the "generals standing on top of the hill"—to use their vantage point to reshape the company. While middle managers could shift resources among existing lines of business, only top executives had the authority to close old factories, establish new ones, and channel bigger chunks of R&D or marketing resources in new directions. As Grove recalled:

> Senior management needed to step in and make some very tough moves. . . . [W]e also realized then that there must be a better way

to formulate strategy. What we needed was a balanced interaction between the middle managers, with their deep knowledge but narrow focus, and senior management, whose larger perspective could set a context.[38]

Grove's solution, after becoming CEO in 1987, was to turn the SLRP (Strategic Long-Range Planning) process that we discussed in Chapter 1 on its head. From this point on, once or twice a year, he and a technical assistant would spend weeks, and sometimes more than a month, studying and then preparing presentations, some of which ran to two hundred slides. They put considerable debate and research into these presentations, which provided a road map for the entire management team. Then, in the broader management meetings, rather than hear first from line managers, Grove would begin with his assessment of the environment, followed by his statement of the company's strategy and four or so high-level strategic mandates that he expected everyone to adopt, after discussion and refinement. Intel managers then plastered those mandates on virtually every wall of the company, worldwide. Grove explained: "I became very directive in prescribing the strategic direction from the top down. This defined the strategy for all of the groups, and it provided a strategic framework for different groups at different levels of management."[39]

However, Grove did not abandon his earlier belief that middle managers should have the authority to make key decisions on their own. The new corporate-level SLRP session became the foundation for group-level strategic planning. Business managers worked out strategies and tactics for their individual units that would push Grove's corporate objectives forward. Each group developed detailed plans for its product lines, based on corporate strategic objectives, and presented them to Grove and other members of the executive team.

Throughout this process, Grove continued to act on the conviction that good strategic thinking requires different points of view and clarifying those different points of view requires intensive, ongoing debate involving the executive team and domain experts inside and outside the company. The phrase used inside Intel to characterize the atmosphere Grove encouraged was "constructive confrontation." As Grove described his own role, "[I] fenced; I challenged. I also studied hard. I never went into meetings unprepared."[40] He wanted strategy debates to be "like the process through which a photographer sharpens the contrast when developing a print. The clearer images that result permit management to make a more informed—and more likely correct—call."[41]

Intel documents from the early 1990s suggest that Intel's planning process became similar to how coaches manage sports teams. The corporate SLRP resembled instructions sent from the bench to the players. The product group planning document was analogous to the signals the players sent back to the coach, either acknowledging and accepting the instruction or suggesting other ways to achieve the same goals. This directed back-and-forth process solicited input from the players and allowed for dialogue in setting and executing Intel's corporate strategy. At the same time, it was clear that the coach set the strategic direction.

Dedicate Time for Thinking and Learning

In addition to encouraging intensive debates over strategy, Gates, Grove, and Jobs also provided fuel for these discussions by dedicating time to think and to learn new things. As students of the game, not just players, they actively sought out information that would help them understand how technology, customers, and competitors were changing. In addition, they were conscientious about filling basic gaps in their own knowledge.

Steve Jobs, for example, got much of his education in business from Mike Markkula, an early investor in Apple who served as CEO from 1981 to 1983 and as chairman of the board from 1985 to 1997. Markkula taught Jobs about business plans, marketing, and the need to focus on doing one thing really well for the customer.[42] Jobs also learned a great deal at Pixar about making movies and graphics; and once he returned to Apple, he often consulted Jimmy Iovine about the ins and outs of the music business. Within Apple, Ron Johnson tutored Jobs in retail management. Other key lieutenants, including Jony Ive, Tim Cook, Jon Rubinstein, and Avie Tevanian, taught him about such essential topics as industrial design, supply-chain management, manufacturing, and software architecture.

Andy Grove made learning one of his highest priorities while at Intel. Initially the consummate operations-oriented manager, he dedicated himself to learning about strategy after becoming CEO in 1987. In addition to reading extensively, he attended and eventually taught business school classes, first at Harvard and later at Stanford. Similarly, when he recognized in the late 1980s that Intel was no longer a broad-line semiconductor company, Grove threw himself into understanding computers, sales, and consumer marketing, rely-ing heavily on Intel managers such as Les Vadasz and Dennis Carter, as well as outside experts and board members. More than twenty years later, Grove still remembered learning that "a brand is a prom-ise" from David Aakers, a marketing professor at Berkeley's Haas School of Business whom Carter had brought in to give a talk.[43]

But it is Bill Gates who became best known for dedicating time for thinking and learning. Twice a year he went on "Think Weeks"—seven days in seclusion to study new subjects and ponder the implications for Microsoft. In one such week, for example, Gates tackled the evolution of natural language interfaces and reportedly read 112 articles and technical papers on topics ranging from the theory of language and cutting-edge computer science to trends in education.[44]

Gates also routinely wrote four or five major memos each year, often during his Think Weeks. Sometimes they analyzed tactical issues, such as improving customer support, which became a major challenge in the early 1990s as the number of Windows customers surged from tens of thousands to tens of millions.[45] Most of the time, though, he offered high-level strategic commentary on the biggest challenges facing Microsoft.

The "Internet Tidal Wave," written in May 1995, is Gates's most famous Think Week memo. After years of internal debate over the best strategy for creating a ubiquitous online network, Gates used these days of study and reflection to crystallize his thinking. He saw a revolution in the works and used his memo as a call to arms for everyone in the company. Russ Siegelman, who ran the MSN group in the early 1990s, gave us this account of how Gates thought at the time:

> He combined [his] knowledge of how markets work and why people buy stuff, and how you beat the competition, with this insight into technology that was really unique. The Internet memo, if you read it carefully, is not something about technology. It's about, "Look, these people are going to disintermediate all the things we know of today. It's going to get fragmented. Everybody's going to be able to be their own newsstand." He got there before other people did. . . . That was consistently what he did and that's what his memos were all about. "I see the future. It's a combination of business model and technology. We have to get there."[46]

Gates's memo, like other conclusions he reached during his Think Weeks, may not have spelled out every aspect of Microsoft's strategy. It also came after a lot of research and analysis by other senior leaders in the company. But this one document established the main themes of Microsoft's agenda for years to come. Ultimately, deciding on these themes is a job that only the CEO can do effectively.

Product Plans Become the Strategic Plan

In contrast to Gates and Grove, Steve Jobs did not rely on traditional strategic planning or detailed memos and competitor analyses to set direction. Instead, he created a less formal process centered on conversations and debates about products among the executive team and selected outsiders. These discussions did take place, however, within a big-picture context. Jon Rubinstein explained: "We talked about overall strategy—digital hub strategy, the cloud strategy, the apps. We did talk about the big picture." Yet the focus, he says, was always on the current product plan rather than some grand corporate vision. This approach reflected what Rubinstein called Jobs's "serial" personality: "Steve could not focus on two things. So he didn't start thinking about the next thing until he finished the last one."[47] Typically, Jobs concentrated on one product at a time, such as the new Macintosh, or the iPod, or the iPhone, before going on to his "next big thing." Once he had moved on, Jobs knew he could rely on the team behind him to finish the current product and join him afterward. Rubinstein summarized: "We didn't do strategic planning. We planned on what's the next product. There was always, 'Okay, we're at the fork in the road, which one do we take?' "[48]

In other words, Apple's corporate strategy emerged from Jobs's vision and product plans, implemented one at a time, rather than from an Intel-like technology road map or a Microsoft-style three-year plan. And Apple's product plans, in turn, came from Jobs's sense of what customers wanted. As he explained at Apple's 1997 Worldwide Developers Conference: "One of the things I've always found is that you've got to start with the customer experience and work backwards to the technology. You can't start with the technology and try to figure out where you're going to try to sell it. And I've made this mistake probably more than anybody else in this room."[49]

To reinforce this focus on one product at a time, Jobs reorganized Apple. He replaced its product-divisional structure, which he felt was overly complex, with a simple functional structure. Ironically, Jobs had years before introduced the divisional structure to separate the Lisa and Macintosh divisions from the Apple II.[50] Now he wanted to use organizational structure to change behavior in a different way. Separate profit and loss (P&L) statements for each division gave way to a single statement for the entire company. This simpler organization made it easier for Jobs to translate his ideas for new products into the key activities of the entire company—product development, supply-chain management, manufacturing, marketing, and sales—without having to go through divisional executives. He only had to work with functional managers. The one P&L also encouraged the entire senior leadership team to pay close attention to how the company overall, rather than a particular product division, was going to make money.[51]

Jobs also presided over weekly meetings of the executive team, which kept the organization on track and tightly coordinated, albeit highly dependent on his ability to keep people in sync. Ron Johnson, who ran retail under Jobs, recalled: "The executives would meet weekly and work well together, but there was very little interaction outside of those meetings between executive team members. Steve was kind of the one who knitted it all together. . . . That's why [the product lineup] looks so perfect in many ways, as close to perfect as a brand can be from every touch point."[52]

It was very unusual in a multibillion-dollar company for a CEO to eliminate product divisions and to maintain direct oversight of nearly everything that touched the customer. The result was that Apple's management systems relied heavily on Jobs's personal involvement. On the one hand, he would encourage functional rivalries and personal confrontations; but on the other hand, his leadership style could produce stunning product innovations such as the iPod, iPhone, iTunes, and iPad.

After he fell ill and then stepped down from the CEO position in 2011, it was clear that no one person could replace Steve Jobs. Jony Ive remained in charge of design, but the company rotated the coordination role in product development across different functional managers. There were also reports that CEO Tim Cook was trying hard to break down the functional silos and introduce more formal coordination through process and organizational changes. As we write these words, it is too early to say what results these new measures will produce. Apple is still in a transition period as Cook, Ives, and other members of Apple's senior leadership team seek to retain the best of what Jobs had brought to the company—his passion for design elegance and attention to detail, and his ability to champion category-defining innovations—while making Apple the company less dependent on any one individual. If they succeed in this extraordinarily difficult task, Apple is much more likely to do well in the future.

From our inception on, we at Intel have worked very hard to break down the walls between those who possess knowledge power and those who possess organization power.[53]
—ANDY GROVE [1996]

GIVE POWER TO PEOPLE WITH "THE KNOWLEDGE"

To this point, we have focused on the key traits that made Gates, Grove, and Jobs effective leaders—their self-awareness, attention to detail, and grasp of the big picture. But no CEO, no matter how talented, can lead a company like Intel, Microsoft, or Apple without help. All leaders have gaps in their knowledge, skills, and interests that other executives and employees need to fill. Gates, Grove, and Jobs successfully addressed this problem in two ways: First, they recruited highly talented "brain trusts" composed of top-level executives and empowered them to act. Second, they looked deep within their organizations to find domain experts, regardless of age and rank, who best understood how technology and markets were changing, and gave them influence and resources.

Find a Partner (or Two or Three)

Gates, Grove, and Jobs all formed close partnerships with key executives who complemented their skills. Steve Ballmer, for example, the high-energy salesman and corporate "cheerleader," was the perfect complement to Bill Gates, the reflective, often sarcastic software "nerd."[54] In Paul Maritz's words, Bill Gates was all about strategy and "the platform," whereas Steve Ballmer was all about competition—beating the other guy: "The soul of Steve is competition. He's the greatest competitor in the world. His modus operandi is you lock your teeth onto somebody's ankle and then you just keep moving up."[55] Whatever Ballmer's shortcomings as a technology visionary, it is hard to imagine Microsoft achieving the same success without both Gates and Ballmer at the helm for two decades.

Andy Grove also sought help from his brain trust, especially in areas that required deep technical knowledge of computer architecture, semiconductor design, and manufacturing. Within a decade of Intel's launch, the science of advanced semiconductors had moved well beyond his expertise. He relied on Intel's Ph.D.s in physics, chemistry, and materials science, as well as electrical engineers and computer scientists, to keep Intel on the path defined by Moore's Law. In addition, after becoming CEO in 1987, he appointed other executives to handle tasks for which he had no particular affinity.[56] For example, Grove recalled in 2013 that Craig Barrett, his COO and ultimate successor, took charge of manufacturing, traveling to out-of-the-way places and "doing a lot of the things I hated."[57]

But of the three, Steve Jobs was probably the most dependent on his executive team and other company experts. Jobs's skills were formidable but limited in scope. As he told his biographer, "What I'm best at doing is finding a group of talented people and making things with them."[58] Fred Anderson, Apple's CFO under Jobs, noted, "Steve wanted to control whatever touched the customer, whether it was the GUI of the operating system, the fit and finish of applications that Apple did, the industrial design, the packaging of the products, the advertising. . . . That's where his passion was and that's where he spent his time." He had little interest in other activities that were critical to the company, including finance. Anderson recalled: "I couldn't get him to talk to Wall Street or the financial community, even major shareholders. . . . I got him toward the end to agree with a once-a-year meeting. . . . It's not his interest. He didn't want to spend time on it."[59]

One of Jobs's biggest weaknesses was operations. He had no interest in operational issues and lacked the skills to manage them effectively. But over time, he came to recognize their importance to Apple's performance and the need to put a strong executive in charge. Donna Dubinsky, who worked for Jobs in the 1980s, told us that during his first stint at Apple, "he absolutely disdained operations. Any logistical issues were simply uninteresting and unimportant. But when he returned to Apple, he realized it was critical to bring in world-class talent. . . . He totally changed the level of respect and resources that he gave to the operations function."[60]

In fact, one of Jobs's first hires in his second go-around was Tim Cook, who joined Apple in 1998 after stints at IBM and Compaq. Cook's job was to clean up the company's manufacturing, distribution, and supply-chain systems. Jobs later said, "I realized that he and I saw things exactly the same way. . . . [Tim] had the same strategic vision I did, and we could interact at a high strategic level, and I could just forget about a lot of things unless he came and pinged me."[61] Cook took over sales and customer support in 2000 and the Macintosh hardware division in 2004. When Jobs named him COO in 2005, Cook was involved in more aspects of Apple's business than any other executive. In 2011, he became Apple's CEO, succeeding Jobs, who was fighting a losing battle with pancreatic cancer.

Other important hires at Apple included Jon Rubinstein, who headed manufacturing at Apple after running engineering at NeXT. Rubinstein had previously worked at Hewlett-Packard and was able to introduce disciplined yet flexible engineering processes both to NeXT and Apple. (He left Apple in 2006 and became CEO of Palm and then a board member at Amazon and Qualcomm.) Avie Tevanian, a Ph.D. in computer science from Carnegie Mellon, also worked for Jobs at NeXT, before joining Apple in 1997. He brought deep technical knowledge in software architecture and design.[62] On the marketing side, Jobs hired Ron Johnson in 2000, a Harvard MBA from Target, to set up Apple's new retail business. Jobs told Johnson, "What's going to happen here is you're going to have to teach me retail and I'm going to have to teach you consumer electronics. Let's go walk the mall." The day after Macworld 2000, they spent four hours strolling through the Stanford Shopping Center.[63]

Along with Cook, Jobs's most important partner was Jony Ive, who headed industrial design. Hired by Apple in 1992, Ive worked for many years under Rubinstein, with whom he had a tense relationship as design goals often clashed with manufacturing realities.[64] But Ive came to share a special sense of kinship with Jobs. As Jobs said, "If I had a spiritual partner at Apple, it's Jony. Jony and I think up most of the products together and then pull others in and say, 'Hey, what do you think about this?' "[65] In 2005, Jobs promoted Ive to senior vice president of industrial design, reporting directly to the CEO and at the same level as Rubinstein. According to Jobs, from this time on, Ive had "more operational power than anyone else at Apple except me. There's no one who can tell him what to do, or to butt out. That's the way I set it up."[66]

The ability to attract and retain so many talented executives reflected both the intangible and material benefits that Jobs offered the members of his team. He had a well-known penchant for treating subordinates harshly. But Jobs could also be extremely charming and charismatic, especially with colleagues who met his demanding standards. According to Ron Johnson, "Steve was the best delegator I've ever met, if he trusted you."[67] In addition, Jobs offered key employees the opportunity to make an extraordinary amount of money. Jon Rubinstein received one million stock options merely to sign up.[68] Johnson got 600,000 shares, worth about one hundred times what he would make in a good year at his previous employer, Target.[69] For most of the executives Jobs courted, joining him at Apple and then staying for a while was not a hard decision, especially in the boom years when the iPod and iTunes were followed by the iPhone and the iPad and Apple became the most valuable company in the world.

Connect Knowledge Power to Organization Power

In addition to recruiting top-flight executives, Gates, Grove, and Jobs sought to hire only the best and the brightest for jobs at all levels. As Gates told us more than twenty years ago, he searched for employees with high IQs. If you could get really smart people, he believed, Microsoft could teach them about software. The key was to get smart people, and they would provide new ideas. Similarly, Steve Jobs liked to say that A players hire A players, and B's hire C's— which leads eventually to a "Bozo explosion."[70] The solution to this problem was to hire only A players—a task that became increasingly difficult as Microsoft and Apple grew.

Andy Grove was just as dedicated to hiring talent as Gates and Jobs. But what distinguished him from his peers was his focus on reaching deep into the organization to identify standout performers and put them in positions where Intel could get the full benefit of their expertise. He was well-known for going outside the formal management hierarchy to find the most knowledgeable employee in the company on the topic of importance to him at the time. For

Grove, this was a matter of "leveling the playing field." Who got to influence him depended on what you knew, not who you were.

Part of Grove's determination to give equal weight to employees, regardless of rank, stemmed from his realization that Intel had a relatively closed culture. Most executives came from within the company and had similar backgrounds in science or engineering. Only a handful of senior managers under Grove had formal management training or extensive outside experience. Given the rapid changes affecting Intel during the 1980s and 1990s, Grove increasingly felt a need to go beyond the executive team for information and ideas, and occasionally for new leadership.

In 1986, for example, Grove put Pat Gelsinger, a twenty-seven-year-old engineer, in charge of the critical 486 microprocessor business. Five years later, Gelsinger became the youngest group VP in the history of the company, and in 2012, he became CEO of VMware. As software became more important to the business, Grove tapped Renée James, then in her late twenties, to be his technical assistant. She went on to head the Software and Services Group and become Intel's president in 2013.[71] These appointments reflected Grove's awareness that, while he had great "organization power," he did not have the "knowledge power" that others possessed. In 1996, he described this dilemma in *Only the Paranoid Survive*:

> From our inception on, we at Intel have worked very hard to break down the walls between those who possess knowledge power and those who possess organization power. The salesperson who knows his territory, the computer architect and engineer who are steeped in the latest technology possess knowledge power. The people who marshal or shuffle resources, set budgets, assign staff and remove them from projects possess organizational power. One is not better than the other in managing strategic change. Both of them need to give their best to guide the corporation to good strategic results. Ideally, each will respect the other for what he or

she brings to the party and will not be intimidated by the other's knowledge or position.[72]

Listening only to senior executives, no matter how capable they are, can leave a CEO dangerously isolated from what is really going on inside the company as well as outside in the marketplace. Grove always feared this would happen to him and blamed this kind of isolation for his slow response to the Pentium crisis in 1994.[73] As a countermeasure, Grove brought new, younger people into his inner circle (including David Yoffie, then only thirty-four years old, whom he invited to join Intel's board). In addition, he often sought the counsel of employees at the "distant periphery" of the business. Grove called the latter "helpful Cassandras" and expected them to bring him new perspectives and news, especially bad news, from outside his usual information sources.[74]

Cast a Wide Net for Information

Bill Gates similarly looked for diverse sources of information as well as negative reports, once writing, "Sometimes I think my most important job as a CEO is to listen for bad news."[75] But he cast a wider net than Grove, frequently going outside Microsoft to find technical experts who could fill the gaps in his skills and experience. In the 1980s and 1990s, these hires included, as just a small sample, Charles Simonyi from Xerox PARC, a Stanford Ph.D. in computer science who studied applications design as well as programming methods; Nathan Myhrvold, a Princeton physics Ph.D. who had studied with Nobel Prize winner Stephen Hawking; Brad Silverberg, a software engineer who had worked at Apple and Borland before heading the Windows 95 project and then founding a new Internet Platforms and Tools division; and Paul Maritz, a software engineer who had previously worked at Intel and would go on to lead the Windows division. Gates even sought out executives such as

Craig Mundie, who had cofounded a supercomputer company (Alliant Computer Systems) that went bankrupt in 1992. Gates felt he had never failed at anything important and wanted people around him who could sense the signs of corporate failure before it occurred to Microsoft.[76]

Gates also encouraged information to flow freely among Microsoft employees by creating an open culture, based mainly on email. (His email address *billg@microsoft.com* was widely known throughout the company and the industry.) Paul Maritz, who headed the Windows division in the 1990s, confirmed that anyone could contact Gates, and some people even succeeded in changing his mind: "You could get through to him. . . . If you sent him a thoughtful piece of email, you would get a thoughtful email back."[77]

Gates's awakening to the Internet provides a striking example of how Microsoft's culture worked. In early 1994, a young Microsoft engineer named J Allard began emailing Gates about this new thing called the World Wide Web.[78] At the time, Gates and other executives were preoccupied with rolling out Windows NT and Windows 95, as well as a proprietary online network (MSN) to compete with AOL. They had little attention to spare for the growing Web. To his credit, Steve Ballmer had learned from customers that the Internet might become important, and later in 1994 he asked Allard to add TCP/IP connectivity—the plumbing of the Internet—to Windows 95. Otherwise, company executives spent almost no time discussing the Internet, as Michael Cusumano found during his frequent interactions with company employees in 1993–95.[79] Gradually, though, the pressure from below began to grow. Two other young managers began to email Gates urging action on the Internet: Ben Slivka, who was heading the last of the DOS development projects (and would later lead the first three Internet Explorer projects), and Steven Sinofsky, who had been Gates's technical assistant and was moving to the Office group (and would later become president of the Windows division).

Despite the many other demands on his time, Gates paid attention. In the summer of 1994, he gave the go-ahead to a young engineer, Thomas Reardon, to start building a browser for Windows 95, based on technology licensed from Spyglass. In early 1995, Gates also asked Sinofsky, who had seen students using the Internet during a recruiting trip to Cornell, to organize a major off-site for the senior management team. Gates then devoted a Think Week to the Internet. After better understanding what he was up against, he issued the "Internet Tidal Wave" memo in May 1995. Russ Siegelman summarized the process that led up to that point:

> Bill figured out, usually through emails and memos, the smart people that had something interesting to say. The best example was this guy [J Allard] who was a junior developer or in program management in the MSN group, who basically ended up not only driving but eventually managing a lot of the Internet-related software for the company. . . . Bill figured out this guy was really smart. He understood that guy was with the Internet in the early days before other people were, and he said, "Look, we're gonna listen to this guy. He knows what's going on."[80]

In his 1999 book, *Business @ the Speed of Thought*, Gates acknowledged the importance of this lower-level input: "The impetus for Microsoft's response to the Internet didn't come from me or from our other senior executives. It came from a small number of dedicated employees who saw events unfolding. Through our electronic [mail] systems they were able to rally everybody to their cause." Gates ended his comments with words that mirror Grove's point about giving organization power to people with knowledge power: "Their story exemplifies our policy, from Day One, that smart people anywhere in the company should have the power to drive an initiative."[81]

LESSONS FROM THE MASTERS

Figuring out a strategy is one thing; executing effectively can be quite another. Gates, Grove, and Jobs largely succeeded at both tasks, although none looked from the outside like a model CEO. Relying on their personal anchors, they created distinctive strategic positions, organizational competencies, and corporate cultures that served Microsoft, Intel, and Apple well for decades. Not even the Internet was able to destroy the business foundations of these companies. Microsoft and Intel successfully navigated the transition from PCs to the new Web era, although they have yet to recover the full measure of influence they enjoyed in the 1990s. Meanwhile, Apple survived and then thrived in the new environment while also experiencing explosive growth by selling novel products and services.

Gates, Grove, and Jobs contributed directly to the success of their companies not only by setting strategy but also by raising the execution bar—for everyone. No one at Microsoft, Intel, or Apple believed he or she could "get away" with mediocre work or half-baked thinking in areas of interest to the CEO. Yet none of the three allowed himself to get distracted by trivia. All three CEOs kept a steady focus on what was most important to customers and the business, and they confidently directed high-level strategy from the top of the organization.

To aid them in their roles, the three CEOs found and developed a small number of key partners, backed by a larger brain trust. These "teams of teams," in Grove's words,[82] compensated for their weaknesses and gaps in knowledge or interest. Gates's key partner was Steve Ballmer, but he also worked closely with many other managers and engineers; Grove relied heavily on Craig Barrett, as well as other key executives; and Jobs had a long list of partners, including the current CEO, Tim Cook, and head of design Jony Ive. These executive team partners proved to be essential complements to the

CEO: Gates, Grove, and Jobs could not have delivered so much and so consistently without their assistance.

But Gates, Grove, and Jobs did not rely solely on their brain trusts for insight and information. All three leaders were willing to set aside traditional hierarchies in order to get fresh perspectives and new ideas, drive accountability, and gather information about changes in technology, customers, or the competition. Gates and Grove would not have survived the Internet challenge without the insights of several young engineers. And most of Apple's products percolated up from lower levels of the company, with Jobs serving principally as a curator and "orchestra leader," drawing heavily on his ability to identify and synthesize great ideas.

In short, Gates, Grove, and Jobs were very different people and very different leaders, but they approached key aspects of execution in similar ways and were all remarkably effective. Their individual passions and distinctive personal anchors became ingrained in their companies and served as a source of strength while they were CEOs and for many years afterward. Each organization lost an invaluable leader when the moment came for them to step aside.

At the same time, we can trace many of the limitations that Microsoft, Intel, and Apple have displayed in recent years to the decisions that Gates, Grove, and Jobs made as well as to the cultures and business models they established. Today, Microsoft is still mostly a software products company, highly dependent on the Windows and Office platforms for most of its revenue and profits. Intel is still aggressively pursuing Moore's Law and making most of its profits selling microprocessors for personal computers and servers. And Apple still derives most of its sales from a small number of breakthrough consumer products designed while Jobs was CEO. The enormous influence that Gates, Grove, and Jobs wielded over their companies was a potent asset, but it also became a significant limitation, as we discuss in the concluding chapter.

Lessons for the Next Generation

What makes a great strategist? What makes some CEOs and entrepreneurs stand out so far above the rest of their contemporaries? Our goal in this book has been to tackle these questions and create a guide to best practices. After decades of studying Bill Gates, Andy Grove, Steve Jobs, and their companies, we have extracted a set of rules that capture the key principles they used to lead their organizations. We have also identified critical ways in which they fell short or failed. These lessons, both positive and negative, are particularly valuable for managers in fast-paced, platform-driven industries. However, their relevance is not limited to the high-tech world. Anyone can become a more effective strategic thinker and organization leader by learning from Gates, Grove, and Jobs.

If this task seems daunting, remember that our three CEOs were not always the "titans of industry" who inspired this book. Yes, they were all gifted with unusual intelligence, intensity, and passion. But the art of company leadership was something they learned over time. Through continuous effort and perseverance, as well as trial and error, they made themselves into masters of strategy and figured out how to shape their organizations to promote better, sharper execution. Our goal has been to point you in the same direction.

THE FIVE RULES

The table on page 201 summarizes the five rules we distilled from the collective track record of Gates, Grove, and Jobs. We have devoted one chapter to each rule and broken down each rule into four principles.

The first rule demands that CEOs and entrepreneurs look beyond the immediate problems of today. When we teach strategy to senior executives, we frequently ask, "What will you do differently tomorrow?" After reading this book, ask yourself the same question. What do you want your *company* to look like in three to five years? What do you want the *world* to look like? What might the next killer *product* look like? Or more precisely, what do you think *customers* will want in the future? What are your *competitors* likely to do? And what *changes* lie in wait, not just for your firm, but for your industry or the economy at large? Not everyone can be a great visionary—a quality we often associate with luminaries such as Gates, Grove, and Jobs. But any CEO or strategist can learn to ask better questions and become a disciplined curator of ideas, choosing the most powerful insights about the future, whether they originate within the company or come from the outside.

Looking forward is essential, but it is just the beginning. Gates, Grove, and Jobs took the next critical step of reasoning back to connect their long-term perspectives to immediate actions. All three knew that, in order to make that five-year vision a reality, you must have a plan for today, the next six months, and the six months after that. This means setting priorities so you don't get thrown off track; ensuring that you cultivate the capabilities required to satisfy customers' needs; taking steps, such as building barriers to entry, to thwart competitors' moves; and most critically, moving early and decisively to build a competitive edge on those rare occasions when you glimpse a 10X change in the offing.

The second rule that Gates, Grove, and Jobs embraced was to make bold bets, but without betting the company. All three under-

Strategy Rules

Look Forward, Reason Back (Chapter 1)	Make Big Bets, Without Betting the Company (Chapter 2)	Build Platforms *and* Ecosystems—Not Just Products (Chapter 3)	Exploit Leverage *and* Power—Play Judo *and* Sumo (Chapter 4)	Shape the Organization around Your Personal Anchor (Chapter 5)
Create or curate a vision; set priorities	Bet big to change the game	Think platforms, not just products	Stay under the radar	Know thyself—warts and all
Anticipate customer needs; match to capabilities	Don't bet the company	Think ecosystems, not just platforms	Keep your enemies close	Pay extraordinary attention to detail—selectively
Anticipate competitors' moves; build entry barriers	Cannibalize your own business	Create some of your own complements	Embrace and extend competitors' strengths	Never lose sight of the big picture
Anticipate strategic inflection points; commit to change	Cut your losses	Evolve and invent new platforms to avoid obsolescence	Don't be afraid to throw your weight around	Give power to people with "the knowledge"

stood that you can't win big by betting small. Rather than go for easy wins, they chose to swing for the fences—whether that meant competing directly with an industry leader, overturning industry norms, or creating a brand-new product category. Yet they avoided putting their companies in too much jeopardy. All-or-nothing bets are reckless behavior; no master of strategy risks it all on a "roll of the dice." While some entrepreneurs are happy making "all-or-nothing" bets, that never would have satisfied Gates, Grove, or Jobs (at least during his second stint at Apple). They wanted more, and not for the sake of money. Gates, Grove, and Jobs wanted to build products and companies that would have a lasting impact on their customers and the world. In order to have such impact, they needed big ideas, big dreams, and large-scale, bold actions—but they also needed to ensure that their companies survived.

Third, Gates, Grove, and Jobs all looked beyond the boundaries of their firms. They focused not just on building products, but on creating and controlling platforms for third-party innovation and supporting ecosystems of complementary products and services. However, there were important differences in how each CEO embraced platform concepts. Their diverse approaches to managing ecosystem partners and facilitating industry-wide innovations illustrate some of the key challenges and trade-offs between a platform strategy and a product focus.

The fourth rule concentrates on commonalities at the tactical level. Gates, Grove, and Jobs were all masters in the use of both leverage and power. Not surprisingly, as heads of some of the world's largest companies, they were not shy about making full use of their strengths and resources, which ranged from legal action to locking up distribution and exploiting deep pockets. We call moves that rely on this kind of power sumo tactics. But all three CEOs were also adept at judo tactics, which leverage cleverness and speed more than strength, such as staying under the radar and working with competitors until the moment is ripe for an attack. Their ability to draw on both sets of skills made them especially fearsome competitors.

Finally, Gates, Grove, and Jobs shaped their companies—and their companies' ability to execute—in similar ways. Each had unique passions and strengths that helped determine his company's strategic direction, distinctive competencies, and organizational culture. None of the three tried to be a perfect leader or a prototypical general manager. Instead, while always keeping the bigger picture in mind, they dove deeply into the details they cared passionately about and relied on trusted managers in areas of secondary concern. By their example, they taught others in the organization what to focus on and why. In addition, they constantly sought out new sources of expertise, especially in areas where they were weak, often searching widely throughout their companies for the people who had the greatest knowledge, regardless of seniority or rank.

THE NEXT GENERATION

Gates, Grove, and Jobs led the first generation of rock stars in the modern technology world. Other well-known CEOs, inside and outside technology, built great franchises by applying many of these same rules. Even more relevant, there is a new generation of "rock stars" in the twenty-first century, such as Larry Page of Google, Mark Zuckerberg of Facebook, Jeff Bezos of Amazon, and Huateng "Pony" Ma of China's Tencent. In examining this group's performance to date, we find striking parallels between their approach to strategy and leadership and the practices we associate with Gates, Grove, and Jobs. These similarities reinforce our belief that these five rules constitute an effective guide to best practices in strategy, execution, and entrepreneurship in the current world.

Larry Page:
Look Forward, Make Big Bets, Build Platforms

Google CEO Larry Page, like Andy Grove, started down the path of a Ph.D. in the sciences. Caught up in the dot-com boom, he dropped out of Stanford's doctoral program in computer science to cofound Google with Sergey Brin in 1998. From the very beginning, he and Brin looked forward and aimed high. Their initial ambition for Google was nothing less than to organize the world's information, beginning with a better search engine. Eventually, as it became clear that the computing world was undergoing a radical shift into what we now call "the cloud," this goal coalesced into a vision of

Google as a universal provider of Internet-based products and services, all funded by advertising.

In order to realize this vision, the Google team was prepared to make big bets and build large-scale platforms for search and other Internet services. The 2004 founders' letter, written for Google's IPO, states, "We will not hesitate to place major bets on promising new opportunities. We will not shy away from high-risk, high-reward projects because of short term earnings pressure."[1] True to their word, Google repeatedly made bold moves to secure the capabilities required to meet customers' needs. In the early 2000s, Google began buying up fiber optic cable networks, constructing its own servers, and making large capital investments to build enormous data centers in anticipation of future growth and infrastructure needs. Similarly, as video came to play a central role in the online experience, Google spent $1.6 billion on YouTube in 2006 and stuck with it, losing money for years.

But it may be one of Google's smaller bets during this period that turns out to have the biggest return. In 2005, Google spent $50 million to acquire a tiny firm with a mobile operating system called Android. Page, Brin, and then-CEO Eric Schmidt, who joined Google in 2001, decided to give Android away for free. Their goal was to create the dominant mobile platform and use it to generate revenue through ads on smartphones and then tablets.[2] The strategy quickly paid off. In 2014, Android market share hit 80 percent—more than five times the share of Apple's iOS—and Google's market value climbed close to $400 billion.[3]

Mark Zuckerberg: Platform Thinking in the Finest Tradition

Mark Zuckerberg followed a path that was remarkably similar to that of Bill Gates. Even Gates noted, "We're both Harvard dropouts, we both had strong, stubborn views of what software could do. . . . I'm more of a coder. . . . But you know, that's not that major a difference."[4] Gates might also have added that both men became billionaires in their twenties and early thirties by creating industry platforms that experienced exponential growth. Zuckerberg launched Facebook as a social networking site for Harvard students in 2004. He then expanded to more colleges, then to high school students, and eventually to the broader population. A milestone came in May 2007, when Zuckerberg announced the Facebook Platform. This is a set of software tools that enables outside developers to create applications that make use of Facebook data, such as apps that let users share photos and play games. Zuckerberg's ambitions for the platform were bold from the start: at the time, he told an interviewer, "We want to make Facebook into something of an operating system, so you can run full applications."[5]

This move transformed Facebook from a niche phenomenon into a global franchise, with a rapidly growing user base and ecosystem of partners, advertisers, and application developers. The platform strategy separated Facebook from slightly older rivals, such as MySpace and Friendster. When the Facebook Platform launched in 2007, MySpace users outnumbered those on Facebook by 4 to 1: 100 million to 25 million. Within a couple of years, Facebook was the unquestioned winner. While MySpace counted 50 million users in 2014, Facebook had grown to more than 1.3 billion, with at least 20 million applications installed on Facebook accounts every day and 7 million applications and websites integrated into the platform.[6] Zuckerberg also made bold, but controversially expensive moves to expand the Facebook Platform. In 2012, he paid $1 billion for the photo-sharing Instagram platform, which then had 30 million users and no revenues ($33 per user). In October 2014, he acquired the smartphone messaging company WhatsApp and its 600 million users and modest revenues (roughly $20 million) for the extraordinary price of approximately $22 billion in cash and stock ($37 per user). That year he also bought Oculus, a small company that developed virtual reality technology, for $2 billion in stock and cash. Despite paying these very high prices, Facebook remained one of the most valuable companies in the world, with a value of around $200 billion in late 2014.

Jeff Bezos:
Extraordinary Attention to Detail, Users, and Platforms

If Zuckerberg appears to be following in Gates's footsteps, Jeff Bezos seems akin in many ways to Steve Jobs: He has been incredibly focused on delivering a great consumer experience; he has shown the ability to drive one innovation after another into the market, including the Kindle and Amazon Web Services; and he enjoys crushing the competition. Bezos has excelled as a visionary, founding Amazon in 1994 and grasping the Internet's potential before many of his contemporaries. He has also skirted the border between bold and reckless behavior. Like Jobs at Apple in the 1980s, Bezos often seemed to be betting the company, as he incurred huge losses in Amazon's early days. Even in 2014, Amazon continued to generate operating losses as Bezos invested aggressively in growth and new ventures.

Where Bezos parts company with Jobs is in his focus on platform thinking. Making Amazon a platform and not just a store has been central to his strategy. Amazon not only allowed competitors to sell through its site, but it handled fulfillment and delivery for them. In addition, Amazon Web Services evolved into a platform for hosting Web-based applications. As Amazon's power as a multifaceted platform has grown, Bezos has used its size and influence to push around suppliers, notably book publishers who were helpless to stop him from driving down prices. Bezos also has used ruthless price competition, backed by the willingness to lose money, to attack competitors, such as shoe retailer Zappos.com. Faced with eroding margins, some competitors have had little choice but to accept Amazon's acquisition bids.[7]

In implementing his strategy, Bezos has used selective attention to detail as an important management tool. Not surprisingly, he sees pricing as a key management lever. As he explained in 2007, "I need to be sure that we are in fact competitive and focused on offering our customers the lowest possible prices. That's one of the things I think is so highly leveraged that I am involved from heading level one all the way to heading level five."[8] More broadly, and very similar to Steve Jobs, Bezos focused his attention on anything that directly affected the customer experience.[9] One former colleague recalled, "The good and the bad of Jeff is that he wanted to be involved with every new Web change, even if it was just to change the colors of a tab."[10] An Amazon engineer put it more colorfully, saying that Bezos "makes ordinary control freaks look like stoned hippies."[11] This approach seems to have paid off. In Amazon's early years, many observers wondered if the company would survive, but in late 2014, it was one of the most feared retailers in the world with a market value of around $150 billion.

Pony Ma:
Multiple Platforms and Network Effects

All the CEOs we have profiled to this point have been American citizens and their companies have been based in the United States. But great strategy knows no borders. Entrepreneurs around the world have created successful businesses following the same rules. Huateng "Pony" Ma is a notable example. Ma received a degree in computer science from Shenzhen University and worked on Internet paging systems at a telecommunications company before founding Tencent, China's largest Internet company, in 1998.[12] He and his four cofounders "looked forward" by studying Internet services in more advanced economies and "reasoned back" to introduce the free QQ instant messaging service in 1999. Based closely on ICQ, which had been developed by an Israeli company and acquired by AOL in 1998, QQ quickly became extremely popular in China.

Ma built on this success to expand into related markets, embracing the innovations introduced by companies like AOL and Yahoo and extending them to better fit the Chinese market. Backed by overseas venture capital and the proceeds of a 2004 IPO in Hong Kong, Tencent invested in multiple, interconnected Web platforms, with common interfaces and a "freemium" business model, giving away basic services and charging for enhanced options. The company's offerings include microblogs, multiplayer gaming, social media, avatars, electronic payments, online commerce, and, more recently, the mobile phone WeChat platform, an extension of the QQ service available both inside and outside China. Like Intel with its strategy of filling any gaps in its product line, Tencent's full range of services has made it extremely difficult for competitors to find an opening for attack. In addition, Ma's strategy demonstrates a deep understanding of technology and platform thinking. Tencent generates strong cross-platform network effects by offering complementary services to a single user base, and it has created a broad ecosystem mostly within but increasingly outside China to provide everything from games to digital content and e-commerce delivery services. The company has also moved deftly to offer its products and services on mobile devices, which play a much larger role in providing connectivity outside the United States.

The diversification strategy has given Tencent an unusually broad revenue base. Ads account for less than 10 percent of its revenues, compared with 80 to 90 percent or more at Yahoo and Google. Value-added services on PCs and mobile devices, including games and other third-party content and applications, made up the bulk of sales. In 2014, Tencent had more than 800 million users and a market value topping $150 billion.[13] The company's success made Pony Ma, who remains the largest shareholder, with a 10.5 percent stake, one of China's richest entrepreneurs.

BEYOND THE FIVE RULES

This brief look at some of the brightest stars of the current generation of CEOs and entrepreneurs shows how much they have in common with Gates, Grove, and Jobs. Whether they have consciously studied their predecessors' tenures at Microsoft, Intel, and Apple, subconsciously absorbed the lessons of those companies, or independently settled on similar approaches, they seem to rely to a significant extent on the five rules we identify in this book. If our analysis is correct, this augurs well for their companies' futures.

However, they would be wrong—as would any manager—to stick too closely to the path first trod by Gates, Grove, and Jobs. All three were imperfect as individuals and as organization leaders, as we have noted throughout this book. In earlier chapters, we highlighted their ability to recognize their own weaknesses and take steps to compensate for those flaws. A strength they shared was the willingness to hire executives who had skills they lacked and to study and learn from experts in new fields. Nonetheless, despite this heightened self-awareness, Gates, Grove, and Jobs all fell short in some measure when it came to anticipating what type of leadership their companies might need in the future—a future when they would no longer be in charge. So the final lessons we can learn from these masters of strategy are really two notes of caution: "personal anchors" can ground you but also hold you back; and executives who are "complements" may be essential to your success, but they may not be "substitutes" for your leadership.

Anchors Can Hold You Back

Gates, Grove, and Jobs all had distinctive interests and strengths, which we have summed up as a passion for software in Gates, a passion for discipline in Grove, and a passion for design in Jobs. These passions anchored not just their contributions to Microsoft, Intel, and Apple, but also their companies' culture, competencies, and strategic direction. In an era of economic and business uncertainty, their personal anchors provided focus and prevented organizational drift. Yet anchors can also play a less positive role. Think about the metaphor's origins: an anchor prevents a ship from moving in new directions; when the tide rises, an anchored boat may be swamped; a fleet at anchor is more vulnerable to attack.

Something similar happened to all three companies. This should not be surprising. The recipe for success in the past will not always work in the future. Technology and markets change. New competitors appear. Core competencies can easily become blind spots or "core rigidities," in our colleague Dorothy Leonard's words.[14] Microsoft in 2014, for example, still seemed too closely tied to the business model that powered its rise—selling software products with backward and forward compatibility with DOS and Windows. Even in the 1990s, Gates recognized the importance of investing in new devices and Internet-based approaches to computing, but he and his executive team were slow to move beyond their traditional and enormously lucrative base in PC software. Similarly, Grove and his successors at Intel found it extremely difficult to move beyond what had long been "Job 1," selling x86 microprocessors, mostly for PCs and servers. And at Apple, Jobs and his successors have proved largely unable to move beyond their reliance on a small number of "hit" consumer products that Apple tightly controlled. The resulting weakness of Apple's platform strategy has ceded a growing share of the smartphone and tablet markets to competitors such as Google and its Android partners.

To some extent, it was the strength of each company's original business model that made it so hard to move on. What software products could Microsoft possibly develop that would deliver better margins than Windows and Office, even today? None! But the days of extraordinary profit margins for packaged software seem to be over for most firms and will eventually end for Microsoft as well.

Microsoft is gradually diversifying its sources of profits, but the new leadership team will have to learn how to make money with lower-priced (or free) software as well as new models of pricing and delivery, such as software as a service and cloud computing.

What semiconductor product would deliver higher margins than an Intel x86 microprocessor? None! Yet future growth in Intel's core PC business is limited as well. The explosion of smartphones and tablets along with the emerging "Internet of Things" has created a higher volume market for CPUs embedded in nearly every device imaginable. Eventually, there will be microprocessors in tens of billions of products. Intel's new management is aggressively attacking these new segments, but they will have to discover how to compete profitably with new competitors, such as Britain's ARM Holdings, which designs the vast majority of low-priced, low-power microprocessors used in smartphones and other programmable devices.

And what phone or tablet could deliver higher margins than the traditional iPhone and iPad? None! But, as Apple continues to charge premium prices for new versions of its devices with relatively minor improvements, its market share remains low. In the meantime, Android vendors ranging from Korea's Samsung to China's Xiaomi pick up the pace, and Google's mobile ad revenues increase. Products such as the iWatch may well prove to be another major source of growth for Apple but, once more, we do not see Apple opening up its new platform to the majority of smartphone users, which rely on software from Google.

It was more than the prospect of lower revenue that made it difficult for Microsoft, Intel, and Apple to move deftly to new markets and business models. The very identity of the business became a brake on innovation. At Microsoft, Paul Maritz admitted to us, "The company wasn't blind to those [new mobile] devices. It's just that we always believed that our role was going to be to make things that contributed to the greater glory of the PC."[15] This was the attitude that led Microsoft to use the same operating system—the widely panned but technically novel Windows 8—for PCs as well as smartphones and tablets. As Maritz explained:

> None of us had a consumer bone in our bodies. It was just not what really at the end of the day motivated us. We were system software guys. . . . We got excited about internal architecture, how things worked internally. In spite of protestations to the contrary, we didn't really care much about the user interface. It's just not who we were. And certainly because of our technology bent, we reached too far. We tried to cram too much into something that really couldn't be delivered at that time. So, you know, you either produce things that are not a compelling experience or were too expensive or both.[16]

Similarly, Intel's focus on the core microprocessor business for Windows computers made it difficult to transition to new growth areas. As Les Vadasz pointed out, due to Grove's decision to "narrow the company's focus on a very narrow part of the PC business, the company continuously found itself void of technology depth in neighboring technologies that it increasingly needed."[17] Grove talked at strategy meetings in the company and to the outside world about diversifying beyond the x86 architecture, but he never committed the same level of personal time, focus, attention, and, most important, corporate resources, to win in those new businesses.

In the last few years of Grove's tenure as CEO, David Yoffie had several conversations with him about his tendency to be too risk-averse. David observed several strategy meetings where Grove shot down one proposal after another to make aggressive moves in communications and related businesses. Frank Gill, who ran those businesses, had argued vehemently that Intel should enter networking—before Cisco had become an Internet powerhouse. Gill recalled believing that "networking would be totally complementary to Intel. . . . I thought all PCs are going to get connected one day." Grove, however, wanted to stay focused, to a fault. Gill continued: "We had a failing systems business, which I wanted to redirect to become a networking products company. To do so would require buying companies and technologies to build market position, recognition, and needed competencies." From Gill's perspective, Intel was missing a huge opportunity. Yet Grove, Gill said, "was not open to any significant acquisitions that could have catapulted us into a serious player in networking. He limited us to organic growth plus a few very small purchases. Increasingly, his sole focus was on the microprocessor business and building the Intel Inside brand." Carl Everett, who ran Intel sales after Gill, also commented that Grove could be very difficult to convince to move in a new direction. "He was not immovable," noted Everett, "but he could be so hard to move to a new position that many people would give up, even if they were right. . . . If I look at Intel in 2013 from the outside . . . [i]t's the same model from the 1990s. That inflexibility has Grove's fingerprint on it."[18]

In contrast, Jobs did a far better job of pushing Apple to invent new products and move into new markets. His gift, and perhaps his curse, was that he never looked back. Jobs got bored very quickly with the last success, and this led him to focus all his energy and attention on the next great opportunity. Ironically, this gift for envisioning great products partially blinded him to the power of platform competition and ecosystem partnerships. Jobs had a front-row seat when Microsoft and Intel relegated the Macintosh, despite its superior design, to a tiny sliver of the computer industry. Yet he resisted developing more open platforms that might have made it harder for Google and Android to do the same thing to the iPhone and iPad.

Of course, the verdict is still out. Apple's great brand, loyal installed base, and large ecosystem of applications developers and service providers left the company in a powerful position. Apple's historical strategy has also delivered spectacular returns over the past decade. But if Jobs's successors do not find a better balance between platform strategy and product strategy, competition from Android could pose a serious long-term threat to Apple's future. Imagine, for example, how different the future might look if Apple designed the iWatch or Apple Pay to be compatible with all smartphones, and not just iPhones?

Complements Are Not Substitutes

And so we come to the final challenge—preparing an organization for succession. As CEOs, Gates, Grove, and Jobs each recruited partners with different personalities and skills to complement themselves and help run their companies. Each CEO then chose a key partner to succeed him. What they seemed not to recognize at the time, but which is apparent in retrospect, is that *complements are not substitutes*. Gates, Grove, and Jobs all chose loyalty over other qualities. They did not seem to apply the same fierce logic and detachment to choosing successors as they did to choosing their competitive strategies and business partners.

This last observation is critical for powerful leaders—and their boards of directors—to think about when anointing successors. Steve Ballmer was the perfect complement to Bill Gates. He focused on people and customers, while Gates focused on technology and strategy. Craig Barrett was the perfect complement to Andy Grove. He managed manufacturing and operations, while Grove drove strategy, marketing, and sales. Tim Cook was the perfect complement to Steve Jobs. He took care of the supply chain, operations, and sales, while Jobs oversaw products and marketing.

Ballmer, Barrett, and Cook were absolutely essential to the success that Gates, Grove, and Jobs enjoyed. Yet Ballmer, Barrett, and Cook struggled to replace our three CEOs. While Gates, Grove, and Jobs focused on organic growth and innovation to drive performance, Ballmer and Barrett desperately tried to put their distinctive stamps on the companies they inherited, often turning to expensive acquisitions that rarely worked. Early in his tenure, for example, Craig Barrett went on a $12 billion buying spree in the dot-com boom, which proved to be a total write-off; and Steve Ballmer spent more than $20 billion on acquisitions, including the $7 billion "Hail Mary" acquisition of Nokia to save the Windows smartphone business. Even Tim Cook tried to carve a new path by making the most expensive acquisition in Apple's history with the $3 billion purchase of headset maker Beats in 2014.

Perhaps no one could replace leaders with the stature of our three CEOs. But Gates, Grove, and Jobs did not have to anoint loyal lieutenants to succeed them. They could have looked for new leaders more attuned to the next generation of technology, customers, and competitors, or encouraged a more competitive succession process. In any case, choice of successors should *not* be about loyalty to the team or to past ways of doing things. It should be about grooming or choosing successors who demonstrate the ability to learn new things, break with the past when necessary, and champion the products, services, and platforms we have yet to imagine.

Reginald Jones and Walter Wriston, for example, were legendary CEOs at General Electric and Citibank in the 1970s and 1980s who avoided this trap. Their solution for the succession problem was to run visible "horse races," giving a number of senior managers the opportunity to demonstrate that they could be the next great leader.[19] Rather than loyalty driving the eventual decision, two dark horses, Jack Welch and John Reed, emerged from the competitions. Sometimes companies can go one step further: In 2013, the boards at Microsoft and Intel ran internal and external searches, without the active involvement of the CEOs. In both cases, the board of directors—not the sitting CEO—made the ultimate choice.

To be fair, though, it is extraordinarily difficult for a board of directors to control the succession process when replacing a legendary

CEO. Leaders with the global acclaim and historic accomplishments of our three CEOs usually get their way.

Bill Gates, Andy Grove, and Steve Jobs paved an extraordinary path as the first generation of high-tech superstar CEOs. There is much we can learn from them. They set strategic directions and built deep organizational capabilities that, as we have seen, continue to produce impressive returns for Microsoft, Intel, and Apple, long after their departures as CEO. Times change, though, and at some point successors need to become inspired strategists in their own right. The new leaders of Microsoft, Intel, and Apple must discover their own paths forward. They will need to reshape these powerful organizations around *their* personal anchors and lead *their* companies into yet another uncertain future—through new generations of technologies, customers, and business models. Creating a new set of rules and outdoing the original masters of strategy are perhaps the greatest challenges that Gates, Grove, and Jobs have left for the next generation.

NOTES

Preface

1. Bill Gates quote at http://www.strategicbusinessteam.com/famous
-small-business-quotes/famous-bill-gates-quotes-some-famous-business-
quotes-from-one-of-the-worlds-richest-billionaires-part-1/, accessed July
27, 2014.

Introduction: The Making of a Master Strategist

1. See Robert A. Burgelman and Andrew S. Grove, *Strategic Dynamics:
Concepts and Cases* (Boston: McGraw-Hill, 2006), 58.
2. Tom Mainelli, "Worldwide and U.S. Media Tablet 2012–2016 Fore-
cast," IDC Research, April 2012, 1–2, accessed November 10, 2013,
http://www.idc.com.
3. David B. Yoffie and Penelope Rossano, "Apple Inc. in 2012," Harvard
Business School Case No. 712-490, May, 2012, 8, 23. (Revised August
2012.) Original source was Gabriel Madway, "Windows 7 Release May
Test Apple's Winning Streak," Reuters, October 14, 2009, via Factiva.
4. See Charles H. Fine, *Clockspeed: Winning Industry Control in the Age
of Temporary Advantage* (Reading, MA: Perseus, 1998).
5. As one measure of Intel's growing brand awareness, the number of
hits on "Intel" in a Lexis-Nexis search increases from 161 for 1986 to
3,923 for 1998.
6. Stephen Manes and Paul Andrews, *Gates: How Microsoft's Mogul Reinvented an Industry—and Made Himself the Richest Man in America*
(New York: Doubleday, 1993), 174.
7. Ibid., 306–7; James Wallace and Jim Erickson, *Hard Drive: Bill Gates
and the Making of the Microsoft Empire* (New York: John Wiley &
Sons, 1992), 330.
8. Manes and Andrews, *Gates*, 347.

9. Michael A. Cusumano, "The Legacy of Bill Gates," *Communications of the ACM* 52, no. 1 (January 2009): 25–26.

10. Walter Isaacson, *Steve Jobs* (New York: Simon & Schuster, 2011), 6, 16–17.

11. Ibid., 474.

12. Ibid., 498.

13. Richard S. Tedlow, *Andy Grove: The Life and Times of an American* (New York: Portfolio/Penguin, 2006), 136–37.

14. Isaacson, *Steve Jobs*, 373–74.

15. Steve Jobs frequently criticized the quality and lack of "taste" in Microsoft's products. See, for example, his statements in the documentary *The Triumph of the Nerds: The Rise of Accidental Empires*, PBS, June 1996.

16. Paul Allen, *Idea Man: A Memoir by the Cofounder of Microsoft* (New York: Portfolio/Penguin, 2012), 114.

17. Michael A. Cusumano and Richard W. Selby, *Microsoft Secrets: How the World's Most Powerful Software Company Creates Technology, Shapes Markets, and Manages People* (New York: Free Press/Simon & Schuster, 1995), 10.

18. Quoted in Claudine Beaumont, "Bill Gates's Dream: A Computer in Every Home," *Telegraph* (online), June 27, 2008, accessed January 2, 2013, http://www.telegraph.co.uk/technology/3357701/Bill-Gatess-dream-A-computer-in-every-home.html.

19. Isaacson, *Steve Jobs*, 94.

20. "Intel Corporation History," FundingUniverse, accessed March 9, 2014, http://www.fundinguniverse.com/company-histories/intel-corporation-history.

21. Jeff Goodell, "Bill Gates: The Rolling Stone Interview," *Rolling Stone*, March 13, 2014, 76.

22. Andrew S. Grove, *Only the Paranoid Survive: How to Exploit the Crisis Points That Challenge Every Company and Career* (New York: Currency Doubleday, 1996), 162.

23. Joanna Hoffman, quoted in Isaacson, *Steve Jobs*, 121.

24. Renée James, interview with the authors, October 9, 2013.

25. Steve Jobs, "The Lost Interview," Amazon, accessed November 2, 2013, http://www.amazon.com/Steve-Jobs-The-Lost-Interview/dp/B008GJVAW4.

26. Bill Gates, *Business @ the Speed of Thought: Using a Digital Nervous System* (New York: Warner Books, 1999), 182.

Chapter 1: Look Forward, Reason Back

1. Intel documents, Intel Strategic Long Range Plan, June 1991 (with permission).
2. Steve Jobs, "Apple's One-Dollar-a-Year Man," *Fortune*, January 24, 2000, accessed May 27, 2014, http://money.cnn.com/magazines/fortune/fortune_archive/2000/01/24/272277/index.htm.
3. "Playboy Interview: Bill Gates," *Playboy*, July 1994, 63.
4. See Edgar H. Schein, *DEC Is Dead, Long Live DEC: The Lasting Legacy of Digital Equipment Corporation* (San Francisco: Berrett-Koehler, 2003), 38.
5. Paul Maritz, interview with the authors, October 7, 2013.
6. Russell Siegelman, interview with the authors, October 9, 2013.
7. "Steve Jobs Introduces the 'Digital Hub Strategy' at Macworld 2001," January 9, 2001, accessed August 8, 2013, https://www.youtube.com/watch?v=9046oXrm7f8.
8. Jon Rubinstein, interview with the authors, October 11, 2013.
9. Ron Johnson, interview with the authors, October 10, 2013.
10. Andy Grove, SLRP presentation, March 30, 1990.
11. Ibid.
12. "In Focus: Lou Gerstner," CNN.com, July 2, 2004, accessed September 20, 2013, http://edition.cnn.com/2004/BUSINESS/07/02/gerstner.interview.
13. Andy Grove, SLRP presentation, March 30, 1990.
14. Andy Grove, SLRP presentation, 1991.
15. Quoted in Jay Greene, "Microsoft's Big Bet," *BusinessWeek*, October 30, 2000, 152.
16. Quoted in Adam Lashinsky, "How Apple Works: Inside the World's Biggest Startup," *CNNMoney*, August 25, 2011, accessed January 24, 2013, http://tech.fortune.cnn.com/2011/08/25/how-apple-works-inside-the-worlds-biggest-startup.
17. Peter Burrows and Ronald Grover, "Steve Jobs' Magic Kingdom," *Bloomberg Businessweek*, February 5, 2006, accessed January 22, 2013, http://www.businessweek.com/stories/2006-02-05/steve-jobs-magic-kingdom.
18. Fred Anderson, interview with the authors, October 9, 2013, and Avie Tevanian, interview with the authors, October 9, 2013; Jon Rubinstein, interview with the authors, October 11, 2013.
19. Fred Anderson, interview with the authors, October 9, 2013.

20. Quoted in Burrows and Grover, "Steve Jobs' Magic Kingdom."
21. Leander Kahney, *Inside Steve's Brain* (New York: Portfolio, 2008), 31.
22. Quoted in Burrows and Grover, "Steve Jobs' Magic Kingdom."
23. Bo Burlingham and George Gendron, "The Entrepreneur of the Decade: An Interview with Steve Jobs," *Inc.*, April 1, 1989, accessed October 9, 2013, http://www.inc.com/magazine/19890401/5602.html/5.
24. Michael A. Cusumano and Richard W. Selby, *Microsoft Secrets: How the World's Most Powerful Software Company Creates Technology, Shapes Markets, and Manages People* (New York: Free Press/Simon & Schuster, 1995), 130–45.
25. Walter Isaacson, *Steve Jobs* (New York: Simon & Shuster, 2011), 567.
26. Fred Anderson, interview with the authors, October 9, 2013.
27. Isaacson, *Steve Jobs*, 97ff.
28. Quoted in Kahney, *Inside Steve's Brain*, 64.
29. Ibid., 65.
30. Fred Anderson, interview with the authors, October 9, 2013.
31. Dennis Carter, interview with the authors, November 11, 2013.
32. For a history of Windows versions, see Microsoft, "A History of Windows," accessed May 20, 2014, http://windows.microsoft.com/en-us/windows/history#T1=era0.
33. Ron Johnson, interview with the authors, October 10, 2013.
34. Ron Johnson, email correspondence with the authors, March 3, 2014.
35. On ProShare see Richard S. Tedlow, *Andy Grove: The Life and Times of an American* (New York: Portfolio, 2006), 357–64.
36. Pat Gelsinger, interview with the authors, October 7, 2013.
37. Avie Tevanian, interview with the authors, October 8, 2013.
38. Ibid.
39. Jon Rubinstein, interview with the authors, October 11, 2013.
40. Les Vadasz, interview with the authors, October 7, 2013.
41. Bill Gates, quoted at the Computer History Museum, October 1, 2004, accessed May 27, 2014, http://www.infoworld.com/t/platforms/gates-undaunted-linux-769.
42. Andrew S. Grove, *Only the Paranoid Survive: How to Exploit the Crisis Points That Challenge Every Company and Career* (New York: Currency Doubleday, 1996), 3.
43. Andrew S. Grove, *High Output Management* (New York: Random House, 1983), 109.
44. Andy Grove, SLRP presentation, 1991.
45. Kahney, *Inside Steve's Brain*, 55.

46. Tarun Khanna, David B. Yoffie and Israel Yellen Ganot, "Microsoft, 1995," Harvard Business School Case No. 795-147, April 1995, 14.

47. Bill Gates, "Netscape," Microsoft internal memo, May 19, 1996, *United States v. Microsoft Corporation* (Civil Action No. 98-1232), Government Exhibit 41, accessed April 9, 2013, http://www.justice.gov/atr/cases/exhibits/41.pdf.

48. Bill Gates, "As Promised: OEM Pricing Thoughts," Microsoft internal memo, December 17, 1997, *United States v. Microsoft Corporation* (Civil Action No. 98-1232), Government Exhibit 61, accessed March 20, 2013, http://www.justice.gov/atr/cases/exhibits/61.pdf.

49. Bruce D. Henderson, *Henderson on Corporate Strategy* (Cambridge, MA: Abt Books, 1979), 10–11.

50. Andy Grove's SLRP presentation, 1993.

51. "Playboy Interview: Bill Gates," *Playboy*, July 1994, 64.

52. Cusumano and Selby, *Microsoft Secrets*, 164–65.

53. Our thanks to Jeremy Bulow of Stanford Business School for this example.

54. Isaacson, *Steve Jobs*, 409.

55. Grove, *Only the Paranoid Survive*, 30.

56. Ibid., 35.

57. Andy Grove, SLRP presentation, 1997.

58. Bill Gates, "Internet Tidal Wave," Microsoft internal memo, May 26, 1995, *United States v. Microsoft Corporation* (Civil Action No. 98-1232), Government Exhibit 20, accessed April 4, 2013, http://www.justice.gov/atr/cases/exhibits/20.pdf.

59. Grove, *Only the Paranoid Survive*, 113–14.

60. Russell Siegelman, interview with the authors, October 9, 2013.

61. For the browser competition, see Michael A. Cusumano and David B. Yoffie, *Competing on Internet Time: Lessons from Netscape and Its Battle with Microsoft* (New York: Free Press/Simon & Schuster, 1998).

62. Jon Shirley, interview with David Yoffie, January 29, 1991.

63. Walter Mossberg, "Apple's Mobile Me Is Far Too Flawed to Be Reliable," *Wall Street Journal*, July 24, 2008.

Chapter 2: Make Big Bets, Without Betting the Company

1. Merriam-Webster dictionary online, accessed March 25, 2013, http://www.merriam-webster.com/dictionary/bold.

2. Quoted in Robert A. Burgelman, *Strategy Is Destiny: How Strategy-*

Making Shapes a Company's Future (New York: Free Press/Simon & Schuster, 2002), 137.

3. Quoted in Alan Deutschman, *The Second Coming of Steve Jobs* (New York: Broadway Books, 2000), 298.

4. Owen W. Linzmayer, *Apple Confidential 2.0: The Definitive History of the World's Most Colorful Company* (San Francisco: No Start Press, 2004), 75.

5. Walter Isaacson, *Steve Jobs* (New York: Simon & Schuster, 2011), 97.

6. Jeffrey S. Young and William L. Simon, *iCon: Steve Jobs, the Greatest Second Act in the History of Business* (Hoboken, NJ: John Wiley & Sons), 62.

7. David B. Yoffie, "Apple Computer 1997," Harvard Business School Case No. 9-797-098 (Boston: Harvard Business School Publishing, 1997), 4.

8. Wintel was the common acronym for computers with a Windows operating system and an Intel chip.

9. David B. Yoffie and Michael Slind, "Apple Computer, 2006," HBS Case No. 706-496 (Boston: Harvard Business School Publishing, 2007), 16.

10. Phillip Michaels, "Survey: Intel Transition May Cool Mac Sales," *Macworld*, June 21, 2005, accessed April 3, 2014, http://www .macworld.com/article/1045413/readersurvey.html.

11. Peter Burrows, "Apple Hits the Intel Switch," *Bloomberg Businessweek*, June 6, 2005, accessed February 4, 2013, http://www.businessweek .com/stories/2005-06-06/apple-hits-the-intel-switch.

12. Stephen Shankland, "Apple to Ditch IBM, Switch to Intel Chips," *CNET News*, June 3, 2005, accessed April 3, 2014, http://news. cnet.com/Apple-to-ditch-IBM,-switch-to-Intel-chips/2100-1006_3-5731398.html.

13. Fred Anderson, interview with the authors, October 8, 2013.

14. "Macbook," *Wikipedia,* accessed April 12, 2014, http://en.wikipedia .org/wiki/MacBook.

15. David B. Yoffie and Penelope Rosanno, "Apple Inc, 2012," HBS Case No. 712-490 (Boston: Harvard Business School Publishing, 2012), 19.

16. Ron Johnson, interview with the authors, October 9, 2013.

17. Jon Rubinstein, interview with the authors, October 11, 2013.

18. Paul Maritz, interview with the authors, October 7, 2013.

19. Interview with Bill Gates, "Gates & Grove: Mr. Software and Mr. Hardware Brainstorm Computing's Future," *Fortune*, July 8, 1996.

20. Ibid.

21. Paul Maritz, interview with the authors, October 7, 2013.

22. Russ Siegelman, email correspondence with the authors, March 25, 2014.

23. Ibid.

24. Stephen Manes and Paul Andrews, *Gates: How Microsoft's Mogul Reinvented an Industry—and Made Himself the Richest Man in America* (New York: Doubleday, 1993), 406, 418.

25. Paul Maritz, interview with the authors, October 7, 2013.

26. Ramon Casadesus-Masanell, David Yoffie, and Sasha Mattu, "Intel Corporation: 1968–2003," HBS Case No. 703-427 (Boston: Harvard Business School Publishing, 2002), 5.

27. Ibid., 6.

28. Tom Dunlap, email correspondence with the authors, December 19, 2013.

29. Ibid.

30. Andrew S. Grove, *Only the Paranoid Survive: How to Exploit the Crisis Points That Challenge Every Company and Career* (New York: Currency Doubleday, 1996), 70.

31. Casadesus-Masanell, Yoffie, and Mattu, "Intel Corporation: 1968–2003," 6.

32. Quoted in Kathleen Wiegner, "The Empire Strikes Back," *Upside*, June 1992, 34.

33. Senior IBM executive, interview with David Yoffie, 1990.

34. Andy Grove, telephone interview with the authors, March 25, 2014.

35. Frank Gill, interview with the authors, October 15, 2013.

36. "The Intel 80386 Case," video, the Computer Museum, accessed October 18, 2013, https://www.youtube.com/watch?v=XFgFWdxHILc.

37. "Andy Grove Quotes," Thinkexist.com, accessed March 27, 2013, http://thinkexist.com/quotes/andy_grove/.

38. CNNMoney/Fortune, November 9, 1998, quoted in "The Top 20 Most Inspiring Steve Jobs Quotes," TNW, accessed July 2, 2014, http://thenextweb.com/apple/2011/09/20/the-top-20-most-inspiring -steve-jobs-quotes/.

39. Jon Rubinstein, interview with the authors, October 11, 2013.

40. Andy Hertzfeld, *Revolution in the Valley: The Insanely Great Story of How the Mac Was Made* (Sebastopol, CA: O'Reilly Media, 2005), 19–20. Also recounted in Isaacson, *Steve Jobs*, 114.

41. Michael S. Malone, *Infinite Loop: How the World's Most Insanely Great Computer Company Went Insane* (New York: Doubleday, 1999), 250.

42. Owen W. Linzmayer, *Apple Confidential 2.0: The Definitive History of the World's Most Colorful Company* (San Francisco: No Starch Press, 2004), 17, 23.

43. Jim Carlton, *Apple: The Inside Story of Intrigue, Egomania, and Business Blunders* (New York: Random House, 1997), 13–14.

44. Linzmayer, *Apple Confidential*, 98.

45. Ibid, 31.

46. Jon Rubinstein, interview with the authors, October 11, 2013.

47. Steven Levy, *The Perfect Thing* (New York: Simon & Schuster, 2006), 220–21.

48. Owen Thomas, "Why Apple Chose Intel," CNNMoney.com, July 22, 2005, accessed February 4, 2013, http://money.cnn.com/2005/07/22/technology/techinvestor/tech_biz/.

49. Laurie J. Flynn and Vikas Bajaj, "Apple Moves Quickly to Use Intel Chips," *New York Times*, January 10, 2006.

50. David B. Yoffie and Michael Slind, "Apple Inc., 2008," HBS Case No. 708-480 (Boston: Harvard Business School Publishing, 2008), 17.

51. Jon Shirley, former president of Microsoft, interview with David Yoffie, January 29, 1991.

52. Bill Gates talk for the Boston Computer Society, October 18, 1993, quoted in Michael Cusumano and Richard W. Selby, *Microsoft Secrets: How the World's Most Powerful Software Company Creates Technology, Shapes Markets, and Manages People* (New York: Free Press/Simon & Schuster, 1995), 142.

53. Jon Shirley, interview with David Yoffie, January 29, 1991.

54. Data on Intel CPU sales can be found in Dan Steere and Robert Burgelman, "Intel Corporation (D): Microprocessors at the Crossroads," Graduate School of Business, Stanford University, BP-256D, 30–31.

55. Stephen Elop, "Burning Platform," memo, accessed June 5, 2014, http://blogs.wsj.com/tech-europe/2011/02/09/full-text-nokia-ceo-stephen-elops-burning-platform-memo/.

56. Isaacson, *Steve Jobs*, 408.

57. Cusumano and Selby, *Microsoft Secrets*, 146.

58. Donna Dubinsky, personal communication with the authors, October 21, 2013. Dubinsky played a variety of roles at Apple, including running distribution, in the early 1980s and later became CEO of Palm and one of the founders of Handspring.

59. Jon Rubinstein, interview with the authors, October 11, 2013.

60. Ibid.

61. See Isaacson, *Steve Jobs*, 465.

62. Adam Lashinsky, *Inside Apple: How America's Most Admired—and Secretive—Company Really Works* (New York: Business Plus, 2012), 3–4.

63. Steve Jobs "Keynote Address," *Macworld*, January 9, 2007, accessed March 15, 2013, http://www.youtube.com/watch?v=s72uTrA5EDY.

64. See Owen Thomas, "Why Apple Cannibalized the iPod," *Business Insider,* October 27, 2012, accessed March 8, 2013, http://www.business insider.com/apple-ipod-cannibalization-2012-10.

65. Isaacson, *Steve Jobs*, 498.

66. Erick Schonfeld, "Apple's Tim Cook: The iPad Is Cannibalizing Some Mac Sales, There Are 'A Lot More Windows PCs to Cannibalize than Macs,'" *TechCrunch*, July 19, 2011, accessed March 5, 2013, http://techcrunch.com/2011/07/19/ipad-cannibalizing-pc.

67. Ibid.

68. Paul Otellini, interview with David Yoffie, January 13, 2000.

69. Grove, *Only the Paranoid Survive*, 18–19.

70. Andy Grove, discussion on September 6, 2013.

71. Conversation between Harold Hughes, Intel CFO, and David Yoffie.

72. "Compaq to Drop Intel Inside Logo from Its PC Range," *PC User*, September 21, 1994.

73. Grove, *Only the Paranoid Survive*, 93.

74. These were the words used by Russell Siegelman to describe Bill Gates, in an interview with the authors, October 9, 2013. Renée James, Andy Grove's technical assistant in the mid-1990s, used the same words in an interview with the authors, October 9, 2013.

75. Grove, *Only the Paranoid Survive*, 14.

76. See, for example, *New York Times*, December 21, 1994, B8.

77. David B. Yoffie, "Microsoft Goes Online: MSN 1996," HBS Case No. 9-798-019 (Boston: Harvard Business School Publishing, 1997), 1.

78. Ibid., 10.

79. Ibid., 1.

80. Russell Siegelman, interview with the authors, October 9, 2013.

81. "Usage Share of Browsers," *Wikipedia*, accessed February 10, 2014, http://en.wikipedia.org/wiki/Usage_share_of_web_browsers#Web SideStory_.28USA.2C_1999-02_to_2006.E2.80.9306.29.

82. Steven Levy, "Apple Computer Is Dead; Long Live Apple," *Newsweek*, January 9, 2007, accessed June 21, 2013, http://www.newsweek.com/steven-levy-apple-computer-dead-long-live-apple-98429.

83. Michael Arrington, "iPhone App Store Has Launched," *Tech-Crunch*, July 10, 2008, accessed November 8, 2013, http://techcrunch.com/2008/07/10/app-store-launches-upgrade-itunes-now/; "App Store (iOS)," *Wikipedia*, accessed November 8, 2013, http://en.wikipedia.org/wiki/App_Store_(iOS).

84. Renée James, interview with the authors, October 9, 2013.

85. Avie Tevanian, interview with the authors, October 8, 2013.

Chapter 3: Build Platforms and Ecosystems—Not Just Products

1. See Annabelle Gawer and Michael A. Cusumano, *Platform Leadership: How Intel, Microsoft, and Cisco Drive Industry Innovation* (Boston: Harvard Business School Press, 2002); and Michael A. Cusumano and Annabelle Gawer, "The Elements of Platform Leadership," *MIT Sloan Management Review* 43, no. 3 (Spring 2002): 51–58.

2. Thomas Eisenmann, Geoffrey Parker, and Marshall W. Van Alstyne, "Strategies for Two-Sided Markets," *Harvard Business Review* 84, no. 10 (2006): 92–101; and Michael A. Cusumano, *Staying Power: Six Enduring Principles for Managing Strategy and Innovation in a Changing World* (Oxford: Oxford University Press, 2010), 54–55.

3. John Donne, "Meditation XVII," accessed September 3, 2013, http://www.poemhunter.com/poem/no-man-is-an-island/.

4. Interview with Bill Gates, 1994, cited in Tarun Khanna and David Yoffie, "Microsoft, 1995," Harvard Business School Case No. 795-147 (Boston: Harvard Business School Publishing, 1995), 1.

5. Michael J. Miller, "The Rise of DOS: How Microsoft Got the IBM PC OS Contract," PCMag.com, August 10, 2011, accessed September 10, 2013, http://forwardthinking.pcmag.com/software/286148-the-rise-of-dos-how-microsoft-got-the-ibm-pc-os-contract.

6. Stephen Manes and Paul Andrews, *Gates: How Microsoft's Mogul Reinvented an Industry—and Made Himself the Richest Man in America* (New York: Doubleday, 1993), 162–63.

7. Manes and Andrews, *Gates*, pp. 203–4.

8. Moore quoted in Robert A. Burgelman, *Strategy Is Destiny: How Strategy-Making Shapes a Company's Future* (New York: Free Press, 2002), 108.

9. Quoted in Richard S. Tedlow, *Andy Grove: The Life and Times of an American* (New York: Portfolio, 2006), 269.

10. Ibid.

11. Pat Gelsinger, interview with the authors, October 7, 2013.

12. Frank Gill, interview with the authors, October 15, 2013.

13. Andrew S. Grove, *Only the Paranoid Survive: How to Exploit the Crisis Points That Challenge Every Company and Career* (New York: Currency Doubleday, 1996), 106.

14. Walter Isaacson, *Steve Jobs* (New York: Simon & Schuster, 2011), 381.

15. Ibid, 568.

16. Our thanks to Intuit founder Scott Cook for pointing out Jobs's early dependence on platforms.

17. Isaacson, *Steve Jobs*, 404.

18. "iPod Sales Chart," *Wikipedia,* accessed March 30, 2014, http://en.wikipedia.org/wiki/File:Ipod_sales_per_quarter.svg; data comes from Apple press releases.

19. Fred Anderson, interview with the authors, October 8, 2013.

20. Isaacson, *Steve Jobs*, 405.

21. Jon Rubinstein, interview with the authors, October 11, 2013.

22. Quoted in Isaacson, *Steve Jobs*, 406.

23. Leander Kahney, *Inside Steve's Brain* (New York: Portfolio, 2008), 200.

24. For iPod sales to 2007 see David Carr, "Steve Jobs: iCame, iSaw, iCaved," *New York Times*, September 10, 2007, C1. Bank of America Securities estimated the Mac installed base at 22 million in March 2007; see Slash Lane, "Mac Install Base Estimated at 22 Million pre-Leopard," *Apple Insider*, March 2, 2007, accessed March 1, 2013, http://appleinsider.com/article/?id=2541.

25. See Annabelle Gawer and Michael A. Cusumano, "How Companies Become Platform Leaders," *MIT Sloan Management Review* 49, no. 2 (2008): 28–35; and also Cusumano, *Staying Power*, 22–68.

26. Isaacson, *Steve Jobs,* 502.

27. Bill Gates presentation in Burden Hall, Harvard Business School, November 19, 1991, video, accessed July 25, 2014, http://video.hbs.edu/videotools/play?clip=billgate.

28. David Johnson, quoted in Cusumano and Gawer, "The Elements of Platform Leadership," 51.

29. Jobs Keynote Address, Macworld Boston, August 1997, accessed June 12, 2013, http://www.youtube.com/watch?v=WxOp5mBY9IY.

30. Andy Grove, interview with David Yoffie, Spring 2003.

31. Gawer and Cusumano, *Platform Leadership*, 22.

32. Ibid., 23.

33. Grove, quoted in ibid., 32.

34. Ibid., 33.
35. Ibid., 41–42.
36. Renée James, interview with the authors, October 9, 2013.
37. Gawer and Cusumano, *Platform Leadership*, 149–51.
38. Jim Manzi, interview with David Yoffie, 1990.
39. D. Clark, "Microsoft Will Keep Making Products for Apple's Macintosh, Gates Pledges," *Wall Street Journal*, March 22, 1995, B6.
40. For the settlement, see *United States v. Microsoft* (Civil Action No. 98-1232), Modified Final Judgment, September 7, 2006, accessed August 4, 2013, http://www.justice.gov/atr/cases/f218300/218339.htm. For examples of earlier complaints about unfair advantages for Microsoft applications development, see Michael A. Cusumano and Richard W. Selby, *Microsoft Secrets: How the World's Most Powerful Software Company Creates Technology, Shapes Markets, and Manages People* (New York: Free Press/Simon & Schuster, 1995), 168–69, and Manes and Andrews, *Gates*, 349–50.
41. Grove, interview with the author, quoted in Gawer and Cusumano, *Platform Leadership*, 120.
42. Frank Gill, interview with the authors, October 15, 2013.
43. Ibid.
44. Manes and Andrews, *Gates*, 433.
45. Daniel Ichbiah and Susan L. Knepper, *The Making of Microsoft* (Rocklin, CA: Prima, 1991), 101–3, 108–18.
46. Calculated from Microsoft 10K report, 2013.
47. Bill Gates, "Internet Tidal Wave," Microsoft internal memo, May 26, 1995, *United States v. Microsoft Corporation* (Civil Action No. 98-1232), Government Exhibit 20, accessed April 4, 2013, http://www.justice.gov/atr/cases/exhibits/20.pdf.
48. See Michael A. Cusumano, "The Platform Leader's Dilemma," *Communications of the ACM* 54, no. 10 (2011): 21–24. This dilemma is similar to that described for product strategy in Clayton Christensen, *The Innovator's Dilemma: When New Technologies Cause Great Firms to Fail* (Boston: Harvard Business School Press, 1996).
49. Jobs quoted in Isaacson, *Steve Jobs*, 349.
50. David B. Yoffie, "Wintel (B): From NSP to MMX," HBS Case No. 704-420 (Boston: Harvard Business School Publishing, 2003), 1–2.
51. Pat Gelsinger, interview with the authors, October 7, 2013.
52. John C. Dvorak, "How the Itanium Killed the Computer Industry," *PC*, January 26, 2009, accessed June 23, 2014, http://www.pcmag.com/article.aspx/curl/2339629.

53. Quoted in Tedlow, *Andy Grove,* 315.

54. Robert A. Burgelman, *Strategy Is Destiny* (New York: Free Press/ Simon & Schuster, 2002), 236.

55. Bill Gates, *Business @ the Speed of Thought: Using a Digital Nervous System* (New York: Warner Books, 1999), 174.

56. Bill Gates, "As Promised: OEM Pricing Thoughts," Microsoft internal memo, December 17, 1997, *United States v. Microsoft Corporation* (Civil Action No. 98-1232), Government Exhibit 61, accessed April 10, 2013, http://www.justice.gov/atr/cases/exhibits/61.pdf.

57. Paul Maritz, interview with the authors, October 7, 2013.

58. Avie Tevanian, interview with the authors, October 8, 2013.

59. Scott Mace, "Emulator Lets Apple II Programs Run on a Mac," *InfoWorld,* July 14, 1986, 13, accessed July 12, 2013, http://www. landsnail.com/ii-in-a-mac.htm.

60. Jon Rubinstein, interview with the authors, October 11, 2013 and Avie Tevanian, interview with the authors, October 8, 2013.

61. Jon Rubinstein, interview with the authors, October 11, 2013.

Chapter 4: Exploit Leverage and Power—Play Judo and Sumo

1. Arthur Rock, "Strategy vs. Tactics from a Venture Capitalist," *Harvard Business Review,* November–December 1987, 2.

2. Quoted in Michael Hogan, "Jack Welch Gives 'Em Hell at VF/ Bloomberg Panel," *Vanity Fair Online,* May 29, 2009, accessed September 10, 2013, http://www.vanityfair.com/online/daily/2009/05/ jack-welch-gives-em-hell-at-vfbloomberg-panel.

3. David B. Yoffie and Michael A. Cusumano, "Judo Strategy: The Competitive Dynamics of Internet Time," *Harvard Business Review,* January–February 1999, 71–81; and David B. Yoffie and Mary Kwak, *Judo Strategy: How to Turn Your Competitors' Strengths to Your Advantage* (Boston: Harvard Business School Press, 2001).

4. Jimmy Iovine, interview with the authors, October 23, 2013.

5. Drew Fudenberg and Jean Tirole, "The Fat-Cat Effect, the Puppy -Dog Ploy and the Lean and Hungry Look," *American Economic Review* 74, no. 2 (May 1984): 361–66.

6. Jon Rubinstein, interview with the authors, October 11, 2013.

7. Ibid.

8. Jimmy Iovine, interview with the authors, October 23, 2013.

9. Paul Freiberger and John Markoff, "Macintosh May Be for the

Masses," *Infoworld* 5, no. 29 (July 18, 1983): 35; John Markoff, "To Cut Online Chatter, Apple Goes to Court," *New York Times*, March 21, 2005, C1.

10. Quoted in Adam Lashinsky, *Inside Apple: How America's Most Admired—and Secretive—Company Really Works* (New York: Business Plus, 2012), 39.

11. Leander Kahney, *Inside Steve's Brain* (New York: Portfolio, 2008), 229.

12. Lashinsky, *Inside Apple*, 42.

13. Adam Satariano and Peter Burrows, "Apple's Supply-Chain Secret? Hoard Lasers," *Bloomberg Businessweek,* November 3, 2011, accessed November 9, 2012, http://www.businessweek.com/magazine/apples -suppplychain-secret-hoard-lasers-11032011. html.

14. Sun Tzu, *The Art of War,* translated by Samuel B. Griffith (Oxford: Oxford University Press, 1963), 66.

15. Brad Stone and Ashlee Vance, "Apple Obsessed with Secrecy on Products and Top Executives," *New York Times*, June 23, 2009.

16. See Walter Isaacson, *Steve Jobs* (New York: Simon & Schuster, 2011), 491.

17. Avie Tevanian, interview with the authors, October 8, 2013.

18. Jon Rubinstein, interview with the authors, October 11, 2013.

19. The patent, dated March 17, 2004, can be found at http://www. google . com/patents?id=6BsWAAAAEBAJ&printsec=abstract&zoom=4&d q=steve+jobs+tablet&source=gbs_summary_r&cad=0_0#v=one page&q=stevepercent20jobspercent20tablet&f=false. See also Brian X. Chen, "Steve Jobs' 6 Sneakiest Statements," Wired.com, February 16, 2010, accessed April 30, 2013, http://www.wired.com/gadgetlab/ 2010/02/steve-jobs/.

20. Quoted in Kim Yoo-chul, "Samsung-Apple Tablet War to Define Industry Standard," *Korea Times*, October 21, 2010.

21. Tim Bradshaw, "Jobs Emails Show Apple Eyed Seven-Inch Tablet," *Financial Times*, August 4, 2012.

22. "CEO Forum: Microsoft's Ballmer Having a 'Great Time,'" *USA Today*, April 30, 2007, accessed June 27, 2014, http://usatoday30 .usatoday.com/money/companies/management/2007-04-29- ballmer-ceo-forum-usat_N.htm.

23. Interview with Steve Ballmer, September 18, 2007, accessed June 27, 2014, https://www.youtube.com/watch?v=eywi0h_Y5_U.

24. Steve Jobs, "Keynote Address," Macworld Boston, August 6, 1997, accessed March 8, 2013, http://www.youtube.com/watch?v=4pAhay 9tYaE.

25. See Adam M. Brandenberger and Barry J. Nalebuff, *Co-opetition* (New York: Doubleday, 1996).

26. Stephen Manes and Paul Andrews, *Gates: How Microsoft's Mogul Reinvented an Industry—and Made Himself the Richest Man in America* (New York: Doubleday, 1993), 282.

27. Ibid., 266.

28. Ibid., 323.

29. Apple also agreed to collaborate with Microsoft to make sure the version of Java shipped with the Mac OS was compatible with Microsoft's implementation of Java. For contemporary accounts of the announcement, see John Markoff, "Computing's New Alliance: The Partnership," *New York Times*, August 7, 1997, A1; Eric Evarts, "Bitten by Reality, Apple Saves Its Skin," *Christian Science Monitor*, August 8, 1997, 1; Steven Levy, "A Big Brother?" *Newsweek*, August 18, 1997, 22ff. See also Walter Isaacson, *Steve Jobs* (New York: Simon & Schuster, 2011), 321–26.

30. Steve Jobs, "Keynote Address," Macworld Boston, August 6, 1997, accessed July 9, 2014, http://www.youtube.com/watch?v=4pAhay9tYaE.

31. Interview with Steve Jobs at the All Things Digital Conference, 2007, accessed June 21, 2013, http://www.youtube.com/watch?v=_5Z7 eal4uXI&list=PL024C995E1DDCAFB0.

32. Evarts, "Bitten by Reality."

33. Jon Rubinstein, interview with the authors, October 11, 2013.

34. Dan Farber, "Mix '06: Gates Ready to Embrace and Extend," ZDNet, March 20, 2006, accessed June 27, 2014, http://www.zdnet.com/ blog/btl/mix-06-gates-ready-to-embrace-and-extend/2740.

35. Steve Jobs email, October 25, 2010, accessed May 8, 2014, http:// cdn2.vox-cdn.com/assets/4244355/DX489_Rev_03-07-14.pdf.

36. Ibid.

37. Gareth Powell, "Dazzling Power of New Version of MS-DOS," *Age* (Melbourne), February 16, 1993; see also Peter Jackson, "Computer (Workspace): What a DOS," *Guardian*, February 7, 1991; Peter H. Lewis, "Personal Computers: DOS Goes on a Streamlined Diet," *New York Times*, June 11, 1991; Cairn MacGregor, "Help Is Too Little, Too Late in the Latest Version of MS-DOS Operating Program," *Gazette*

(Montreal), July 17, 1991; Richard Morochove, "Here Comes Microsoft's Software Winner for '93," *Toronto Star*, February 15, 1993.

38. Transcript of Bill Gates's remarks at Microsoft's December 7, 1995, Internet strategy briefing.

39. David Banks, *Breaking Windows: How Bill Gates Fumbled the Future of Microsoft* (New York: Free Press/Simon & Schuster, 2001), 105.

40. "How to Get to 30% Share in 12 Months," Microsoft internal memo, *United States v. Microsoft Corporation* (Civil Action No. 98-1232), Government Exhibit 684, accessed May 21, 2013, http://www.justice.gov/atr/cases/exhibits/684.pdf.

41. Sun Tse [Sun Tzu], *The Art of War: Complete Texts and Commentaries*, trans. Thomas Cleary (Boston: Shambhala, 2000), 68.

42. James Wallace and Jim Erickson, *Hard Drive: Bill Gates and the Making of the Microsoft Empire* (New York: John Wiley & Sons, 1992), 251.

43. Manes and Andrews, *Gates*, 221.

44. Louise Kehoe, "Brave Faces After the Software 'Quake," *Financial Times*, October 9, 1984, 18.

45. Kathleen Wiegner, "The Empire Strikes Back," *Upside*, June 1992, 32.

46. Ibid., 38.

47. Slide 108, Andy Grove SLRP 1993.

48. Leander Kahney, *Jony Ive: The Genius Behind Apple's Greatest Products* (New York: Portfolio/Penguin, 2013), 139–41.

49. George Stalk and Rob Lachenauer, *Hardball: Are You Playing to Play or Playing to Win?* (Boston: Harvard Business School Press, 2004), 1.

50. See Owen W. Linzmayer, *Apple Confidential: The Definitive History of the World's Most Colorful Company* (San Francisco: No Starch Press, 2004), 170; Manes and Andrews, *Gates*, 278–80; Brenton R. Schlender, "Software Hardball: Microsoft's Gates Uses Products and Pressure to Gain Power in PCs," *Wall Street Journal*, September 25, 1987.

51. John Sculley, *Odyssey: Pepsi to Apple . . . A Journey of Adventure, Ideas, and the Future* (New York: Harper & Row, 1987), 344.

52. Linzmayer, *Apple Confidential*, 171–72; Manes and Andrews, *Gates*, 288–93; Jim Carlton, *Apple: The Inside Story of Intrigue, Egomania, and Business Blunders* (New York: Times Books, 1997), 53–56.

53. See Banks, *Breaking Windows*, 157.

54. Ibid, 105. Russ Siegelman, who attended the meeting, confirmed the conversation in an interview with the authors, October 9, 2013.

55. Navisoft, "GatesWorld," AOL internal memo, January 21, 1996,

United States v. Microsoft Corporation (Civil Action No. 98-1232), Government Exhibit 38, accessed January 22, 2013, http://www.usdoj.gov/atr/cases/exhibits/38.pdf.

56. Lashinsky, *Inside Apple*, 149.

57. Jon Rubinstein, interview with the authors, October 11, 2013.

58. Charlie Redmayne email to Jonathan Miller et al., January 22, 2010; Plaintiff's Exhibit PX-0308; *US v. Apple*, (12-cv-02826), accessed June 13, 2013, http://www.justice.gov/atr/cases/apple/exhibits/px-0308.pdf.

59. The exchange between Jobs and Murdoch, which took place between January 22 and January 24, 2010, is available at https://www.documentcloud.org/documents/702951-email-exchange-between-steve-jobs-and-james.html, accessed March 5, 2013.

60. *United States v. Apple, Inc.* (12-cv-02826), Plaintiff's Proposed Finding of Fact, 60, accessed June 13, 2013, http://www.justice.gov/atr/cases/f296700/296796.pdf.

61. Brian Murray, "Apple Cheet [*sic*] Sheet," HarperCollins internal memo, January 27, 2010, *United States v. Apple, Inc.* (12-CV-02826), Plaintiff's Exhibit PX-0637, accessed June 11, 2013, http://www.justice.gov/atr/cases/apple/exhibits/px-0637.pdf.

62. Laurence Zukerman, "Intel and Digital Settle Lawsuit and Make Deal," *New York Times*, October 28, 1997, D1.

63. Federal Trade Commission, In the Matter of Intel Corporation, Docket No. 9288, Decision and Order II.A, August 6, 1999, accessed June 4, 2013, http://www.ftc.gov/os/1999/08/intel.do.htm.

64. David B. Yoffie and Mary Kwak, "Playing by the Rules: How Intel Avoids Antitrust Litigation," *Harvard Business Review* 79, no. 6 (June 2001): 119–22.

65. "Microsoft's 1994 Consent Decree: Boon or Bust?," interview with Brad Smith, Microsoft General Counsel, *CNET News*, July 9, 2004, accessed July 9, 2013, http://news.cnet.com/Microsofts-1994-consent-decree-Boon-or-bust/2100-1016_3-5262600.html.

66. Steve Ballmer, interview with David Yoffie and Michael Cusumano, March 23, 1998.

67. Yoni Heisler, "Emails Revealed That Steve Jobs Angrily Called Sergey Brin over Google's Recruitment of Apple's Safari Team," TUAW.com, accessed May 4, 2014, http://www.tuaw.com/2014/03/24/emails-reveal-that-steve-jobs-angrily-called-sergey-brin-over-go/.

68. Andy Grove, SLRP presentation, 1990, 45.

Chapter 5: Shape the Organization around Your Personal Anchor

1. See, for a recent example, Deborah Ancona et al., "In Praise of the Incomplete Leader," *Harvard Business Review*, February 2007.

2. Bill Gates, "Bill Gates' Favorite Business Book," *Wall Street Journal Online*, July 11, 2014, accessed July 12, 2014, http://online.wsj.com/ articles/bill-gatess-favorite-business-book-1405088228?mod=WSJ _hp_EditorsPicks.

3. "'You've Got to Find What You Love,' Jobs Says," *Stanford News*, accessed June 27, 2014, http://news.stanford.edu/news/2005/june15/ jobs-061505.html.

4. Our thanks to Mel Horwitch for pointing out that aspects of our view of leadership in this chapter—the ability to communicate passion as well as to recognize one's own strengths and weaknesses—corresponds closely to the ideas of the late Warren Bennis. See, in particular, Warren Bennis, *On Becoming a Leader*, 4th ed. (New York: Basic Books, 2009).

5. See Michael A. Cusumano, "The Legacy of Bill Gates," *Communications of the ACM* 52, no. 1 (January 2009): 25–26.

6. For a history of the software products business, see Michael A. Cusumano, *The Business of Software* (New York: Free Press, 2004), 86–127.

7. Interview with Bill Gates, August 1993, cited in Michael A. Cusumano and Richard W. Selby, *Microsoft Secrets: How the World's Most Powerful Software Company Creates Technology, Shapes Markets, and Manages People* (New York: Free Press/Simon & Schuster, 1995), 290.

8. Les Vadasz, interview with the authors, October 7, 2013.

9. Andy Grove, interview with authors, October 9, 2013.

10. Richard S. Tedlow, *Andy Grove: The Life and Times of an American* (New York: Portfolio, 2006), 129.

11. Les Vadasz, interview with the authors, October 7, 2013.

12. Andrew S. Grove, *High Output Management* (New York: Random House, 1983), 172.

13. Ibid., 111.

14. See Michael A. Cusumano, "The Legacy of Steve Jobs," *Communications of the ACM* 54, no. 12 (December 2011): 26–28.

15. Walter Isaacson, *Steve Jobs* (New York: Simon & Schuster, 2011), 5–12.

16. Ron Johnson, interview with the authors, October 9, 2013.

17. Andy Grove, presentation in the 1996 Intel SLRP document.

18. Andy Grove, interview with authors, October 9, 2013.

19. Ibid.

20. Gates interview, August 1993, quoted in Cusumano and Selby, *Microsoft Secrets*, 33.
21. Ibid, 25.
22. Ibid., 27.
23. Ibid., 28.
24. Ibid., 33.
25. Ibid., 28–29.
26. See Michael A. Cusumano, "What Road Ahead for Microsoft and Windows," *Communications of the ACM* 49, no. 7 (July 2006): 23–26.
27. Shira Ovide, Joann Lublin, and Monica Langley, "Microsoft Prescription: More Bill Gates," *Wall Street Journal*, February 5, 2014.
28. Isaacson, *Steve Jobs*, 126.
29. Leander Kahney, *Inside Steve's Brain* (New York: Portfolio, 2008), 51–54; the quotation from Ratzlaff appears on 51.
30. Isaacson, *Steve Jobs*, 345–46; and Adam Lashinsky, *Inside Apple: How America's Most Admired—and Secretive—Company Really Works* (New York: Business Plus, 2012), 54–55. See also a more detailed discussion of Apple's product development process and the interactions between Ive and Jobs in Leander Kahney, *Jony Ive: The Genius Behind Apple's Greatest Products* (New York: Penguin, 2013).
31. Michael Hailey, quoted in Lashinsky, *Inside Apple*, 22.
32. Christopher Stringer testimony in *Apple Inc. v. Samsung Electronic Co.,* transcripts of the proceedings, July 31, 2012, 530, accessed May 20, 2013, http://www.groklaw.net/pdf4/ApplevSamsung-1547.pdf.
33. See Isaacson, *Steve Jobs*, 391–92; 499–500.
34. Pat Gelsinger, interview with the authors, October 7, 2013.
35. Andrew S. Grove, *Only the Paranoid Survive: How to Exploit the Crisis Points That Challenge Every Company and Career* (New York: Currency Doubleday, 1996), 161–62; Robert A. Burgelman, Dennis L. Carter, and Raymond S. Bamford, "Intel Corporation: The Evolution of an Adaptive Organization," Stanford Graduate School of Business Case SM-65 (Stanford: Trustees of Leland Stanford University, 1999), 12–13.
36. Grove, *Only the Paranoid Survive,* 161–62.
37. Ibid., 96–97.
38. Ibid., 161–62.
39. See Burgelman, Carter, and Bamford, "Intel Corporation: The Evolution of an Adaptive Organization," 12–13.
40. Andy Grove, interview with the authors, September 23, 2013.
41. Grove, *Only the Paranoid Survive*, 114.
42. Isaacson, *Steve Jobs*, 75–78.

43. Andy Grove, interview with the authors, October 9, 2013.

44. "In Secret Hideaway, Bill Gates Ponders Microsoft's Future," *Wall Street Journal*, March 28, 2005, accessed October 3, 2013, http://online.wsj .com/article/0,,SB111196625830690477,00.html.

45. See Cusumano and Selby, *Microsoft Secrets*, 362–65.

46. Russ Siegelman, interview with the authors, October 9, 2013.

47. Jon Rubinstein, interview with the authors, October 11, 2013.

48. Ibid.

49. Steve Jobs, quote from the 1997 Apple Worldwide Developer Conference, video, accessed February 26, 2014, http://www.youtube.com/ watch?v=GnO7D5UaDig. Our thanks to Karim Lakhani of Harvard Business School for pointing us to this video.

50. Email comments on the manuscript from Donna Dubinsky to authors, May 7, 2014.

51. Jobs's discussion of how he changed the organizational structure can be found in his comments at the 1997 Apple Worldwide Developer Conference, accessed February 26, 2014, http://www.youtube.com/ watch?v=GnO7D5UaDig.

52. Ron Johnson, interview with the authors, October 9, 2013.

53. Grove, *Only the Paranoid Survive*, 120.

54. See Michael A. Cusumano, "The Legacy of Steve Ballmer," *Communications of the ACM* 57, no. 1 (January 2014): 30–32.

55. Paul Maritz, interview with the authors, October 7, 2013.

56. Andy Grove, interview with the authors, September 6, 2013.

57. Ibid.

58. Jobs, quoted in Isaacson, *Steve Jobs*, 218.

59. Fred Anderson, interview with the authors, October 8, 2013.

60. Donna Dubinsky, written comments on the manuscript, May 7, 2014.

61. Isaacson, *Steve Jobs*, 360.

62. Avie Tevanian, interview with authors, October 8, 2013.

63. Ron Johnson, interview with the authors, October 10, 2013.

64. See Kahney, *Jony Ive*, 199 and elsewhere for more on the relationship between Ive and Rubinstein.

65. Isaacson, *Steve Jobs*, 342.

66. Ibid., 342.

67. Ron Johnson, interview with authors, October 10, 2013.

68. Apple Computer, Inc., 1999 Form DEF 14A (filed February 9, 1999), from Securities and Exchange Commission website, accessed January 20, 2014, http://www.sec.gov/Archives/edgar/data/320193/0001047469 -99-003858.txt.

69. Ron Johnson, interview with the authors, November 18, 2013.

70. http://blog.brightmesh.com/2011/10/24/jobs-a-players-work-with-a-players/.

71. Grove, interview with the authors, October 9, 2013.

72. Grove, *Only the Paranoid Survive*, 120.

73. Tedlow, *Andy Grove*, 226.

74. Grove, *Only the Paranoid Survive*, 110.

75. Bill Gates, *Business @ the Speed of Thought: Using a Digital Nervous System* (New York: Warner Books, 1999), 182

76. Cusumano and Selby, *Microsoft Secrets*, 59–61, 144–45.

77. Paul Maritz, interview with the authors, October 7, 2013.

78. Russ Siegelman, interview with the authors, October 9, 2013; also see Kathy Rebello, "Inside Microsoft: The Untold Story of How the Internet Forced Bill Gates to Reverse Course," *BusinessWeek*, July 15, 1996, 56–70.

79. While researching *Microsoft Secrets*, Cusumano and Selby interviewed dozens of Microsoft executives and engineers and heard almost nothing about their interest in the Internet until later in 1995, though they often talked about the emerging "Information Highway." See Cusumano and Selby, *Microsoft Secrets*, 180–85.

80. Russ Siegelman, interview with the authors, October 9, 2013.

81. Gates, *Business @ the Speed of Thought*, 166.

82. Grove, *High Output Management*, 120.

Conclusion: Lessons for the Next Generation

1. "An Owner's Manual for Google Shareholders," accessed October 31, 2013, http://investor.google.com/corporate/2004/ipo-founders-letter.html.

2. Steven Levy, *In the Plex: How Google Thinks, Works, and Shapes Our Lives* (New York: Simon & Schuster, 2011), 215–17.

3. Jim Edwards, "Proof That Android Is Really for the Poor," *Business Insider*, June 27, 2014, accessed June 28, 2014, http://www.businessinsider.com/android-v-apple-ios-market-share-revenue-income-2014-6.

4. Jeff Goodell, "Bill Gates: The Rolling Stone Interview," *Rolling Stone*, March 13, 2014, 50.

5. David Kirkpatrick, *The Facebook Effect: The Inside Story of the Company That Is Connecting the World* (New York: Simon & Schuster, 2010), 217.

6. See "Number of Monthly Active Facebook Users Worldwide from 3rd Quarter 2008 to 2nd Quarter 2014 (in Millions)," Statista,

accessed May 22, 2014, http://www.statista.com/statistics/264810/
number-of-monthly-active-facebook-users-worldwide/ and "Facebook Statistics," Statistic Brain, accessed May 22, 2014, http://www
.statisticbrain.com/facebook-statistics/.

7. See Brad Stone, *The Everything Store: Jeff Bezos and the Age of Amazon*
(New York: Little, Brown, 2013), 269–273, 295–99.

8. "The Institutional Yes: An Interview with Jeff Bezos." *Harvard Business Review,* October 2007.

9. David Streitfeld and Christine Haughney, "Expecting the Unexpected
from Jeff Bezos," *New York Times*, October 21, 2013.

10. Gary Rivlin, "A Retail Revolution Turns 10," *New York Times*, July
10, 2005.

11. Matt Rosoff, "Jeff Bezos 'Makes Ordinary Control Freaks Look Like
Stoned Hippies,' Says Former Engineer," *Business Insider*, October
12, 2011, accessed October 30, 2013, http://www.businessinsider
.com/jeff-bezos-makes-ordinary-control-freaks-look-like-stoned
-hippies-says-former-engineer-2011-10#ixzz2kM7zwabS.

12. See A. Farhoomand, "Tencent's Business Model," Asia Case Research
Center, University of Hong Kong, Case #1003 (HBS Publishing),
2013; Iian Alon and Wenxian Zhang, *Biographical Dictionary of New
Chinese Entrepreneurs and Business Leaders* (Cheltenham, England,
and Northampton, MA: Edward Elgar, 2009), 111; company annual
reports and website, http://www.tencent.com/en-us/index.shtml.

13. Paul Mozur, "Tencent's Market Cap Rises Above $150 Billion," *Wall
Street Journal Blogs*, March 11, 2014, accessed July 5, 2014, http://
blogs.wsj.com/digits/2014/03/11/tencents-market-cap-rises-above
-150-billion/.

14. Dorothy Leonard-Barton, "Core Capabilities and Core Rigidities: A
Paradox in Managing New Product Development," *Strategic Management Journal* 13 (1992): 111–25.

15. Paul Maritz, interview with the authors, October 7, 2013.

16. Ibid.

17. Les Vadasz, interview with the authors, October 7, 2013.

18. Carl Everett, interview with the authors, October 10, 2013.

19. John Reed, interview with the authors, May 14, 2014.

INDEX

ABOUT THE AUTHORS

DAVID B. YOFFIE is the Max and Doris Starr Professor of International Business Administration at Harvard Business School. He first met Andy Grove in 1987 and joined the Intel board of directors in 1989. He remains the longest-serving member of the Intel board. Yoffie has also written forty Harvard Business School cases on Intel, Microsoft, and Apple, which are the most widely used cases on these companies. He is an author or editor of nine books, including the bestselling *Competing on Internet Time* with Cusumano. He has also written extensively for the *New York Times*, the *Wall Street Journal*, and the *Harvard Business Review*.

MICHAEL A. CUSUMANO is the Sloan Management Review Distinguished Professor of Management at the Massachusetts Institute of Technology's Sloan School of Management, with a joint appointment in the MIT Engineering Systems Division. He began studying the software business in 1985. He is an author or editor of twelve books, including a classic bestseller on the company, *Microsoft Secrets*, as well as *Platform Leadership*, *The Business of Software*, *Staying Power*, and *Competing on Internet Time* with Yoffie. His last book, *Staying Power: Six Enduring Principles for Managing Strategy & Innovation in an Uncertain World*, was named one of the top business books of 2011 by *Strategy + Business* magazine.